THE THESAURUS FOR KIDS

By Evelyn Pesiri
Illustrated by Linda Bild

LOWELL HOUSE JUVENILE
LOS ANGELES
NTC/Contemporary Publishing Group

To Elizabeth Ross, friend indeed
—E. P.

Library of Congress Cataloging-in-Publication Data

Pesiri, Evelyn.
   The thesaurus for kids / by Evelyn Pesiri ; illustrated by Linda Bild.
      p.   cm.
   Summary: An illustrated thesaurus containing synonyms, antonyms, and idioms for more than 2,000 words.
   ISBN 1-56565-693-8 (hardcover : alk. paper). — ISBN 1-56565-694-6 (pbk. : alk. paper)
   1. English language—Synonyms and antonyms—Juvenile literature. [1. English language—Synonyms and antonyms.]   I. Title.
[PE159.P49 1998]
423'.1—dc21   98-20848
                                                                                                      CIP
                                                                                                      AC

This edition published 1998 by Lowell House
A division of NTC/Contemporary Publishing Group, Inc.
4255 West Touhy Avenue, Lincolnwood (Chicago), Illinois 60646-1975 U.S.A.
Copyright © 1998, 1993 by NTC/Contemporary Publishing Group, Inc.
All rights reserved. No part of this work may be reproduced, stored in a retrieval system, or transmitted in any form or by any means, electronic, mechanical, photocopying, recording, or otherwise, without the prior permission of NTC/Contemporary Publishing Group, Inc.

Printed and bound in the United States of America

10 9 8 7 6 5 4 3 2

Managing Director and Publisher: Jack Artenstein
Director of Publishing Services: Rena Copperman
Editorial Director, Juvenile: Brenda Pope-Ostrow
Director of Juvenile Development: Amy Downing
Director of Art Production: Bret Perry
Project Editor: Lisa Melton
Design: Brenda Leach
Cover Photo: Ann Bogart
Female Cover Photo Model: Gia Lew

Writing with Flying Colors
(or, How to Use a Thesaurus to Improve Your Writing)

Do you sometimes have  butterflies in your stomach about writing?

Is expanding your vocabulary  an uphill climb?

Well, you don't have to  bend over backward anymore to find just the right word for your writing, because *The Thesaurus for Kids* is here.

What exactly *is* a thesaurus? First and foremost, it's a powerful tool to help you make your writing lively and interesting. That includes the reports and essays you write for school, as well as the stories, poems, and anything else you might write for yourself. A thesaurus is also a great way to expand your speaking and reading vocabularies, and when that happens, your writing will automatically improve.

Like a dictionary, a thesaurus is a list of words in alphabetical order. Each word is called an *entry word*. But while a dictionary tells you the meaning (or meanings) of each entry word, a thesaurus gives you a list of *synonyms*. Synonyms are close in meaning to the entry word, and they are the reason for using a thesaurus in the first place—to find an alternate word for something you want to write or say.

When to Use a Thesaurus

Just as a soccer coach might send in a substitute player to make a game better, you might "send in" substitute words to make your writing better. That's when you should reach for *The Thesaurus for Kids*. For example, let's say you write the following sentence:

The children climbed to the top of the cliff.

Does it sound too ordinary to you? Or perhaps too boring? Well, spice it up! Use your thesaurus and look up the entry word **cliff**. Look over the synonyms, then send in the substitute player!

The children climbed to the top of the *precipice*.

What if you want to improve your sentence further? Look up **climb**.

The children *clambered* to the top of the *precipice*.

Now you know how to put the thesaurus to work for you. You chose more interesting words. Now check to see that your new sentence fits what you want to say.

Choosing the *Right* Synonym

In each entry, the synonyms differ in some way. One synonym may be closer in meaning to the entry word than another. One may be more intense—for example, **famished** means not just "hungry," but "very hungry." Now compare the words **smart** and **ingenious**. Although this thesaurus lists *ingenious* as a synonym for *smart,* most people would agree that an ingenious idea is even smarter than a smart idea. So choose the synonym that best matches the idea you want to communicate! Just how smart is the idea? *You* are the writer—*you* decide!

Try to avoid words that are overused, such as **good** or **big** or **look**. Replace these words with more colorful synonyms, such as **admirable** or **massive** or **glance**. As you write a story or report, also consider *who will* *read it.* For instance, if a story is for your little brother, using the word **pallid** to replace the word **pale** might not be a good idea, but your teacher might like it!

Remember that in choosing the right synonym, you must be careful! Some synonyms are used only in certain contexts. For example, the word **vacant** is shown as a synonym for the entry word **empty**. While **vacant** can be used to describe an empty house, it can't be used to describe an empty glass. The sample phrases provided for many of the entry words will help you determine how a certain synonym may be used.

Special Features of Your Thesaurus

Your thesaurus doesn't stop at providing lists of synonyms for entry words. It also has other special features. These features are summarized in the legend box located on most right-hand pages of the book. Here's what the legend looks like:

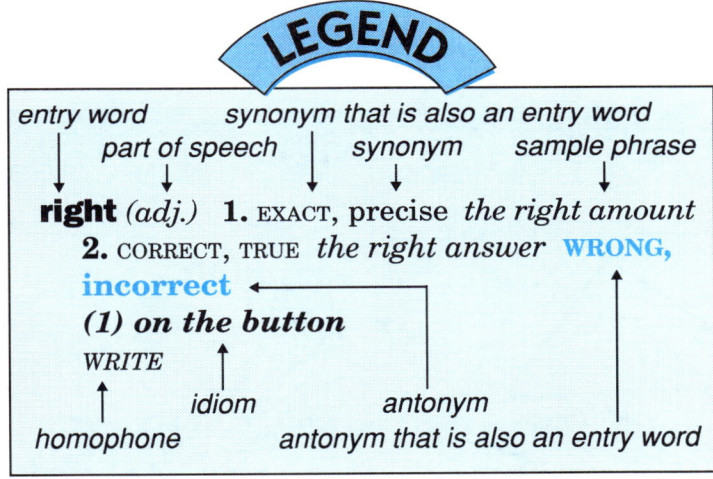

entry word: shown in **boldface** type. When an entry word is listed more than once, it's being used for different parts of speech.

part of speech: shown in *italic*.

synonym: a word close in meaning to the entry word.
When a synonym is CAPITALIZED, it can be looked up as an entry word.

sample phrase: shown in *italic*. When an entry word has more than one meaning, the meanings are numbered and a sample phrase is given for each meaning. The sample phrase shows how the entry word might be used in a phrase or sentence.

antonym: shown in blue type. An antonym is a word opposite in meaning to the entry word.
When an antonym is CAPITALIZED, *it can be looked up as an entry word.*

idiom: shown in ***bold italic.*** An idiom is a colorful phrase whose meaning does not come from the individual words that make it up. Rather, its meaning is close to that of the entry word. When an entry word has more than one meaning, the idiom is numbered to correspond with the set of synonyms to which it belongs.

homophone: shown in CAPITALIZED ITALIC. A homophone is pronounced the same as the entry word but is spelled differently and has a different meaning.

The Thesaurus for Kids also includes two additional features. In one, you get to **Guess the Idiom** that goes with a humorous illustration. The entry word provides a clue. **Go Crazy with Words** shows you illustrated clusters of words that are related in meaning. For instance, **damp**, **wet**, **soaked**, and **drenched** are all related. But which do you think is wetter, damp or drenched? The illustration gives you a clue.

Going on a Word Search

Remember that in searching for the right synonym, only you know what word you want. If you do not find the perfect synonym the first place you look, don't give up. Instead, go on a word search!

A word search works something like this: Say you are writing a story about a big monster. Using your thesaurus, you turn to the entry word **big** to find the perfect synonym. But you do not find one that you like. You see that the synonym **HUGE** is shown in capital letters. Turn to the page where **huge** is included as an entry word. You might find the perfect word there! (How about **colossal**?) If you don't find the word, don't stop your search. Continue until you've found exactly the right word you need to express your thoughts.

A Final Word

Remember that to a writer, there's no better friend than a thesaurus.

And using one is a piece of cake!

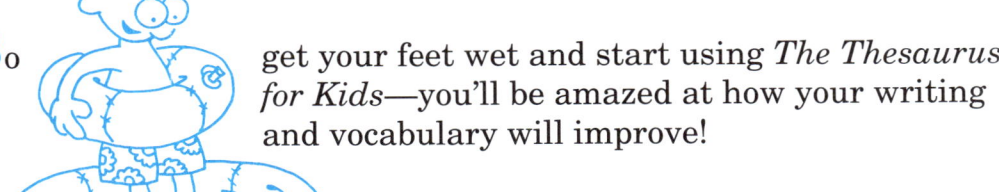

So get your feet wet and start using *The Thesaurus for Kids*—you'll be amazed at how your writing and vocabulary will improve!

abandon • acquire

Aa

abandon (v.) 1. DESERT, forsake, SURRENDER, LEAVE, strand, cede *abandon the ship* **recover** 2. withdraw, RECALL *abandon the argument*

ability (n.) 1. SKILL, TALENT, dexterity, knack, GIFT, aptitude *She had great athletic ability.* **inability** 2. means, POWER, capacity *the ability to pay* **inability**

able (adj.) FIT, talented, skillful, capable, QUALIFIED, practiced, apt, competent, proficient, adept, deft **unable, incompetent** *on the ball*

• Guess the Idiom •

clue: able

answer: on the ball

about (prep.) 1. concerning, regarding *a book about animals* 2. ALMOST, nearly, around, approximately *about five dollars* **exactly, precisely**

above (adv.) over, aloft, beyond **below**

absent (adj.) missing, away, lacking **PRESENT**

absorb (v.) 1. sop, sponge, consume, swallow *absorb the water with a sponge* 2. cushion *absorb the shock*

absurd (adj.) FOOLISH, SILLY, RIDICULOUS, STUPID, idiotic, asinine, inane **rational, reasonable, sensible**

abuse (n.) misuse, mistreatment, deception, injury

abuse (v.) HURT, INJURE, misuse, mistreat, violate, defile *walk all over*

accept (v.) 1. BELIEVE, TRUST, APPROVE, ADMIT, endure *accept the excuse* **mistrust** 2. TAKE, RECEIVE *accept the invitation* **REFUSE, decline** 3. ASSUME, undertake *accept the responsibility* **DENY**

accident (n.) misfortune, mishap, DISASTER, casualty

accurate (adj.) CORRECT, EXACT, precise, sound **INACCURATE, imprecise**

accuse (v.) BLAME, CHARGE, denounce

ache (v.) HURT, throb

achieve (v.) accomplish, REACH, COMPLETE, DO, FULFILL **FAIL**

acquire (v.) OBTAIN, GET, GAIN **LOSE**

act *(n.)* deed, feat, achievement, performance, exploit

act *(v.)* behave, WORK, PERFORM, OPERATE, execute

action *(n.)* movement, gesture, deed, feat, performance

active *(adj.)* **1.** BUSY, ENERGETIC, dynamic, LIVELY, frisky, vigorous *an active puppy* IDLE, LAZY, inactive **2.** ALERT *an active mind* IDLE, inactive

activity *(n.)* ACTION, TASK, chore, WORK, LABOR, undertaking, venture

actual *(adj.)* **1.** TRUE, GENUINE, CERTAIN *an actual flag from the Civil War* imitation, FAKE **2.** REAL, tangible, concrete, material *What's the actual cost of the computer?* IMAGINARY

adapt *(v.)* ADJUST, FIT, SUIT, modify, conform

add *(v.)* **1.** sum up, TOTAL *Add the numbers to get the answer.* SUBTRACT **2.** EXTEND, INCREASE, JOIN, unite, supplement, ENLARGE *We plan to add a room to the house.* DECREASE, REMOVE **3.** complement *The hat adds to the outfit.* detract

adequate *(adj.)* ENOUGH, sufficient, ample, SATISFACTORY inadequate, lacking

adjust *(v.)* CHANGE, modify, regulate, SET, alter

admire *(v.)* appreciate, CHERISH, RESPECT, regard, esteem, venerate

admit *(v.)* **1.** CONFESS, own up, concede, acknowledge, avow *Admit the truth.* DENY **2.** let in, PERMIT, ACCEPT *Admit the visitor.*

adore *(v.)* ADMIRE, LOVE, HONOR, WORSHIP, revere, idolize, venerate HATE, DESPISE, loathe

adorn *(v.)* DECORATE, beautify, enrich, grace

advance *(v.)* **1.** APPROACH, proceed *Advance toward the finish line.* withdraw, retreat **2.** progress, further, BETTER, RISE, thrive, IMPROVE, flourish *Advance within the company.*

adventure *(n.)* EXPERIENCE, exploit, undertaking

advice *(n.)* guidance, counsel, tip, pointer

affect *(v.)* **1.** INFLUENCE, alter, CHANGE, sway, CONCERN, modify *His injury will affect the outcome of the game.* **2.** impress, touch, STIR *The teacher's lectures affect everyone.*

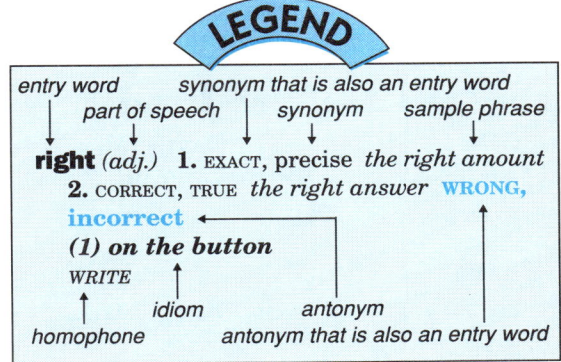

afraid *(adj.)* frightened, scared, fearful, terrified, TIMID, alarmed FEARLESS, **unafraid**, DARING, BOLD, CONFIDENT

after *(prep.)* afterward, following, later, subsequently, behind, next BEFORE

aggravate *(v.)* **1.** IRRITATE, ANNOY, exasperate *He aggravates me.* **2.** intensify, EXAGGERATE, worsen, exacerbate *Don't aggravate the problem.*
(2) rock the boat, add fuel to the fire

agony *(n.)* **1.** PAIN, torment, torture, suffering, distress, pang *the agony of a broken leg* **2.** anguish, misery, heartache, woe *the agony of defeat*

agree *(v.)* concur, CONFIRM, consent, YIELD, APPROVE, PERMIT, SUPPORT, assent DISAGREE, **differ, oppose**

aid *(n.)* HELP, assistance, benefit, RELIEF, service.

aid *(v.)* HELP, ASSIST, SUPPORT, relieve, BACK **hinder, deter**

aim *(n.)* GOAL, PURPOSE, objective, motive, REASON, mission, intention

aim *(v.)* **1.** POINT, DIRECT, target *aim the arrow* **2.** INTEND, MEAN, propose *aim to make good grades*

alarm *(v.)* FRIGHTEN, SCARE, startle, terrify, UPSET COMFORT, CALM, SOOTHE

alert *(v.)* WARN, CAUTION, INFORM, SIGNAL

alert *(adj.)* **1.** attentive, vigilant, AWARE, wary, watchful *The students were alert this morning.* **inattentive** **2.** LIVELY, spry, QUICK, INTELLIGENT *a very alert newborn colt* DULL
(1) on your toes

alike *(adj.)* similar, SAME, like, IDENTICAL, twin, matching DIFFERENT

allow *(v.)* LET, PERMIT, consent, grant, APPROVE, LICENSE **prohibit,** FORBID, **inhibit**
give the green light

almost *(adv.)* nearly, somewhat, approximately, around, ABOUT, roughly

alone *(adj.)* solitary, apart, isolated, LONELY, lone, SINGLE, PRIVATE **accompanied**
out in the cold

♦ **Guess the Idiom** ♦

clue: alone

answer: out in the cold

always *(adv.)* forever, eternally, perpetually, evermore, forevermore NEVER

amaze *(v.)* SURPRISE, THRILL, FASCINATE, stun, bewilder, ASTONISH, astound, captivate bore

amount *(n.)* NUMBER, QUANTITY, score, tally, TOTAL, sum, bulk, capacity, volume

amuse *(v.)* PLEASE, TICKLE, DELIGHT, ENTERTAIN displease

ancient *(adj.)* OLD, aged, antique MODERN, NEW

anger *(n.)* RAGE, fury, wrath, ire

anger *(v.)* AGGRAVATE, IRRITATE, madden, ANNOY
make one's blood boil

angry *(adj.)* annoyed, IRRITABLE, resentful, stormy, furious, infuriated, enraged, raging, antagonistic, indignant, irate, wrathful, livid pleased, gratified
hot under the collar

announce *(v.)* DECLARE, proclaim

annoy *(v.)* DISTURB, nag, pester, BOTHER, displease, TROUBLE, IRRITATE, OFFEND, AGGRAVATE, provoke, exasperate, plague
PLEASE, gratify, appease
get on someone's nerves

annoyed *(adj.)* irritated, bothered, upset, ANGRY, FURIOUS, livid
pleased, gratified, satisfied

answer *(n.)* response, REPLY, explanation, solution, reaction, retort QUESTION, query

answer (v.) RESPOND, REPLY, EXPLAIN, SOLVE, react, retort ASK, QUESTION, query

anxious (adj.) NERVOUS, worried, RESTLESS, concerned, disturbed, uneasy, apprehensive relaxed, CALM

having butterflies in one's stomach

• Guess the Idiom •

clue: anxious

answer: having butterflies in one's stomach

apologize (v.) REGRET, DEFEND, allege, ANSWER

appear (v.) 1. COME, ARRIVE, arise, surface, emerge, SHOW *appear at noon* VANISH, DISAPPEAR 2. SEEM, LOOK *The answer may appear correct.*

appearance (n.) 1. LOOK *She has a nice appearance.* 2. guise, semblance, pretext *Although quite interested, he had a deliberately bored appearance.*

appetite (n.) hunger, craving, DESIRE, longing, thirst, lust, demand

applaud (v.) CHEER, PRAISE, CLAP, APPROVE BOO, disapprove, hiss

appreciate (v.) 1. prize, value, treasure, relish *appreciate one's parents* 2. UNDERSTAND, comprehend, acknowledge *appreciate one's point of view*

approach (v.) 1. ADVANCE, NEAR, APPROXIMATE, impend, converge *Approach the injured dog with caution.* 2. address, propose, INTRODUCE *waiting for a good time to approach the subject*

appropriate (adj.) FIT, suitable, relevant, pertinent unfit, unsuitable, irrelevant

approve (v.) APPLAUD, commend, attest, endorse, ratify DISAPPROVE, dispute

approximate (v.) 1. ADVANCE, NEAR *Approximate the starting line.* 2. ESTIMATE, appraise, compute, figure *Approximate the answer.*

approximate (adj.) NEAR, rough, inexact, CLOSE, imprecise

area (n.) 1. SPACE, REGION, territory, district, quarter *We live in the area.* 2. department, field, sphere *Modern art is her area of interest.*

argue (v.) DISAGREE, QUARREL, quibble, FIGHT, differ, haggle, DEBATE, dispute AGREE **lock horns**

• Guess the Idiom •

clue: argue

answer: lock horns

arrange (v.) ORGANIZE, ORDER, PLACE **disarrange**

arrest (v.) 1. CAPTURE, CATCH, apprehend, detain, nab *Arrest the criminal.* 2. STOP, STAY, CHECK, DELAY, BLOCK, retard, inhibit *By educating people, we hope to arrest the spread of disease.* **promote**

arrive (v.) COME, REACH, APPEAR **LEAVE, DEPART**

artificial (adj.) synthetic, unreal, unnatural, FALSE, counterfeit, FAKE **REAL, genuine**

ashamed (adj.) embarrassed, shamefaced, abashed PROUD

ask (v.) QUESTION, INQUIRE, query, REQUEST, appeal, interrogate, petition, entreat, solicit **RESPOND, ANSWER**

assemble (v.) 1. GATHER, COLLECT, convene *The students assemble in the school auditorium.* SCATTER 2. BUILD, erect, CONSTRUCT, fabricate, MANUFACTURE *Assemble the model car.* **disassemble**

assign (v.) appoint, allot, allocate

assist (v.) HELP, AID, SERVE, relieve, SUPPORT **hinder, impede**

assume (v.) 1. BELIEVE, infer, suppose, presume, SUSPECT *Let's assume we will win the game.* 2. adopt, undertake, shoulder, ACCEPT *He assumed a new position on the team.* **REJECT, REFUSE, decline**

assure (v.) 1. PROMISE, PLEDGE, affirm, attest, guarantee, certify *Assure the safety of the crew.* 2. ENCOURAGE, enthuse, hearten *Assure the worried child.*

astonish (v.) SURPRISE, astound, AMAZE, dazzle, awe, stupefy, SHOCK, overwhelm

attach (v.) JOIN, FASTEN, secure, FIX, adhere, affix **DETACH, SEPARATE**

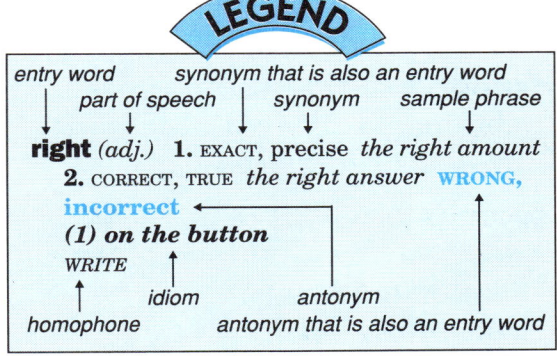

attack *(n.)* RAID, invasion, offense, onslaught retreat

attack *(v.)* RAID, CHARGE, INVADE, STORM, assault, encroach retreat, DEFEND

attempt *(v.)* TRY, undertake, STRUGGLE, strive, toil, AIM, endeavor, venture

attend *(v.)* **1.** VISIT, FREQUENT, haunt *Will you attend the party?* **2.** LISTEN, heed, harken *Attend the teacher.* IGNORE, disregard **3.** nurse, AID, ASSIST *Attend the sick pony.* **4.** escort, chaperone, accompany, usher *Attend to the younger children on Halloween.*

attitude *(n.)* **1.** pose, posture, POSITION, bearing, deportment *The wrestler approached his opponent with an attitude of aggression.* **2.** disposition, presence, air, demeanor *She has a calm attitude.*

attract *(v.)* DRAW, PULL, TEMPT, LURE, COAX, BAIT, charm, allure, entice repel
catch someone's eye

attractive *(adj.)* LOVELY, appealing, BEAUTIFUL, alluring, inviting unappealing, UGLY

available *(adj.)* READY, accessible, obtainable unavailable
at one's fingertips

average *(adj.)* NORMAL, USUAL, REGULAR EXTRAORDINARY, OUTSTANDING, UNUSUAL
run-of-the-mill

avoid *(v.)* DODGE, MISS, ESCAPE, shun, shirk, hedge, elude, evade SEEK

award *(n.)* REWARD, decoration, medal, trophy, medallion

aware *(adj.)* attentive, observant, watchful, ALERT, vigilant unaware, unobservant

awful *(adj.)* dreadful, appalling, frightful, HORRIBLE, shocking, disagreeable, objectionable WONDERFUL, terrific, GREAT

awkward *(adj.)* CLUMSY, cumbersome, inept agile, dexterous
all thumbs

Bb

baby *(n.)* newborn, infant, tot, toddler

back *(n.)* REAR, posterior FRONT, anterior

bad *(adj.)* **1.** NAUGHTY, mischievous, DISHONEST, spoiled, WICKED, EVIL, shady, unfit, IMMORAL, CORRUPT, sinful *a bad character* GOOD **2.** ROTTEN, spoiled *bad meat* FRESH **3.** faulty, defective, dysfunctional, impaired *a bad battery*

baffle *(v.)* PUZZLE, bewilder, CONFUSE, mystify, perplex enlighten, demystify

bag *(n.)* sack, pouch

bait *(v.)* ATTRACT, LURE, snare, entice, entrap

ball *(n.)* **1.** globe, sphere, orb *Catch the ball.* **2.** DANCE, prom, masquerade, reception *Attend the ball.*
BAWL

ban *(v.)* FORBID, prohibit, outlaw, disallow, BAR, EXCLUDE, PREVENT
ALLOW, PERMIT

band *(n.)* **1.** GROUP, GANG *band of musicians* **2.** STRIP, stripe, ribbon, belt *He wore a band around his waist.*

bar *(v.)* STOP, PREVENT, BLOCK, FORBID, EXCLUDE, barricade
ALLOW, PERMIT

bare *(adj.)* **1.** naked, nude, unclothed *a bare body* CLOTHED **2.** EMPTY, PLAIN, barren *a bare landscape* lush
BEAR

bargain *(n.)* **1.** DEAL, buy *Her new shirt was a bargain.* **2.** agreement, CONTRACT, transaction *I have a bargain with my father to make the team.*
(1) a steal

base *(n.)* **1.** BOTTOM, STAND, foundation *the base of the statue* **2.** ROOT, CAUSE, origin *the base of the problem*

basic *(adj.)* ESSENTIAL, fundamental, elementary, primary, rudimentary, SIMPLE

beach *(n.)* shore, seaside, COAST
BEECH

bear *(v.)* **1.** CARRY, TRANSPORT, CONVEY *Bear the flag.* **2.** STAND, suffer, tolerate, endure *Try to bear the pain.* **3.** PRODUCE, YIELD, REPRODUCE, beget, render, procreate, propagate *bear young*
BARE

beat *(n.)* **1.** throb, pulse, pound *the beat of one's heart* **2.** tempo, meter, time, measure *the beat of the music*
BEET

beat *(v.)* **1.** WIN, DEFEAT, overcome, OVERTHROW, CONQUER, vanquish, thwart, surpass, SUCCEED, EXCEED, excel *Beat the team.* LOSE **2.** thrash, WHIP, lash, flog, maul, scourge *In* Oliver Twist, *the orphanage owner beats young Oliver.*
BEET

beautiful *(adj.)* PRETTY, LOVELY, ATTRACTIVE, FAIR, GORGEOUS, ravishing UGLY
a real knockout

beauty *(n.)* splendor, elegance, loveliness ugliness

become *(v.)* GROW, CHANGE, ADAPT

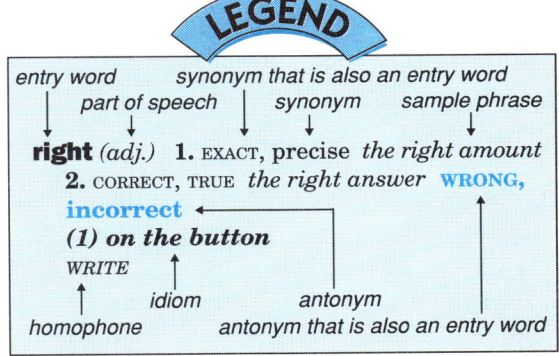

bed (n.) **1.** crib, bunk, berth, cot *sleep in a bed* **2.** patch, garden *plant strawberries in a bed*

before (adv.) prior, preceding, previously, earlier AFTER

beg (v.) plead, appeal, implore, entreat, beseech, petition, solicit, grovel,

begin (v.) START, commence, initiate, OPEN, INTRODUCE, launch, originate, arise END *get the ball rolling, get the show on the road*

beginner (n.) trainee, learner, recruit, novice

beginning (n.) **1.** START, opening, outset, commencement *the beginning of the play* ending **2.** creation, birth, origin, invention, rise, conception, SOURCE *The 1950s marked the beginning of rock 'n' roll.*

behavior (n.) CONDUCT, manner, deportment, ATTITUDE, demeanor, carriage

believe (v.) TRUST, ACCEPT, ADMIT disbelieve *swallow hook, line, and sinker*

belong (v.) FIT, SUIT, befit, pertain

bend (v.) TURN, fold, flex, crease, hinge straighten

best (adj.) greatest, highest, utmost, supreme, CHIEF, paramount worst

bet (v.) RISK, GAMBLE, wager *put money on*

better (adj.) **1.** superior, preferable, improved, greater *look for a better job* worse, INFERIOR **2.** healthier, improving, recovering, mending *She's feeling better now that the surgery is over.* worse

big (adj.) **1.** LARGE, GREAT, HUGE, bulky, massive *a big dog* SMALL, LITTLE **2.** IMPORTANT, significant, influential, OUTSTANDING, momentous *a big moment in history* UNIMPORTANT, insignificant

bill (n.) **1.** beak, nib *the bill of a pelican* **2.** tab, statement, invoice, account *The school paid the bill for the new band uniforms.* **3.** LAW, amendment, measure, proposal *He presented the bill to student government.*

bit (n.) PIECE, SCRAP, speck, mite, particle

• Guess the Idiom •

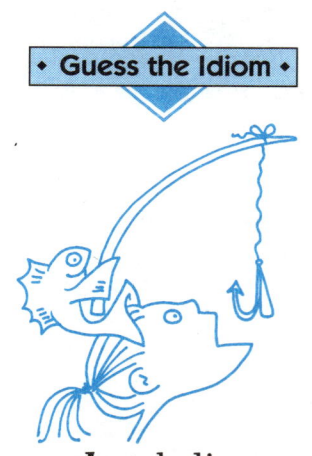

clue: believe

answer: swallow hook, line, and sinker

bite (v.) gnaw, nibble, CHEW, grind

bitter (adj.) SOUR, SHARP, HARSH, acrid sweet

blame (v.) ACCUSE, CHARGE, CONDEMN, DISAPPROVE, convict, CRITICIZE, denounce, chide, rebuke, SCOLD
point a finger at

bland (adj.) tasteless, STALE, flat, DULL, tedious tasty, SPICY

blank (n.) SPACE, void, cavity, HOLE

blank (adj.) 1. EMPTY, vacant *fill in the blank space* FULL 2. bewildered, dazed, confused, astonished *a blank stare*

bleak (adj.) 1. DREARY, DISMAL, cheerless, rainy *It was a bleak day yesterday.* BRIGHT, sunny 2. BARE, barren *a bleak landscape* lush

blend (v.) MIX, COMBINE, merge, mingle SEPARATE

block (v.) hinder, hamper, STOP, obstruct, thwart, impede, oppose, annul, counteract PASS, ALLOW

blow (v.) 1. fan, ruffle *Blow your hair dry.* 2. BOTCH, BUNGLE, flub, fumble, goof *blow the exam*

blue (adj.) 1. azure, sapphire, navy, aquamarine, turquoise *She wore a blue dress.* 2. SAD, GLUM, depressed *feeling blue* HAPPY
BLEW

blunder (n.) MISTAKE, ERROR, slip, oversight

board (n.) 1. plank, WOOD, beam, girder, rafter, timber *Saw the board.* 2. COMMITTEE, council *The Board of Education oversees the school system.*
BORED

boast (v.) BRAG, crow, flaunt, show off
blow one's own horn

body (n.) 1. trunk, torso *The arms extend from the body.* 2. corpse, carcass, cadaver, remains *dissect the body of the frog* 3. TROOP, COMPANY, BAND, association *She is the president of the student body.*

bold (adj.) BRAVE, courageous, unafraid, FEARLESS, VALIANT, intrepid, DARING, CONFIDENT bashful, SHY

boo (v.) hiss, scorn, RIDICULE, DISAPPROVE, deride APPLAUD, PRAISE

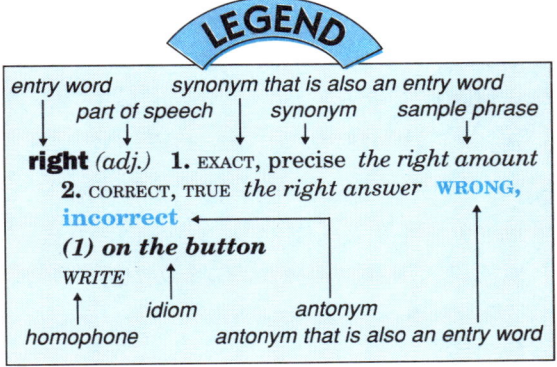

boost *(v.)* **1.** LIFT, RAISE, ELEVATE, hoist *Boost the child up onto the pony.* **2.** expand, INCREASE *boost sales*

border *(n.)* boundary, EDGE, verge, brink, margin, fringe
BOARDER

bored *(adj.)* indifferent, disinterested, apathetic **interested, involved, absorbed**
BOARD

boring *(adj.)* DULL, uninteresting, tiresome, wearisome, humdrum, tedious, monotonous
INTERESTING

boss *(n.)* director, superintendent, overseer, supervisor, manager

botch *(v.)* blunder, misjudge, OVERLOOK, SLIP, flub
put one's foot in one's mouth, bark up the wrong tree

bother *(n.)* TROUBLE, NUISANCE, annoyance, PEST, WORRY
pain in the neck

bother *(v.)* TEASE, ANNOY, UPSET, IRRITATE, pester, nag, DISTURB, disconcert, harass, torment, provoke, vex, exasperate
get in one's hair, drive up the wall

bottom *(n.)* BASE, underside, sole, foot, depths, ground **TOP, head**

bow *(v.)* **1.** BEND, stoop *Bow for the audience.* **2.** YIELD, submit, SURRENDER *Bow to the principal's decision.*
BOUGH

box *(n.)* CHEST, CASE, carton, bin, trunk, crate, parcel, package, hamper, vault

brace *(v.)* SUPPORT, prop, bolster, buttress, fortify, stiffen, steady

brag *(v.)* BOAST, crow, gloat, flaunt
toot one's own horn, pat oneself on the back

brains *(n.)* INTELLIGENCE, intellect, SENSE, REASON, JUDGMENT

branch *(n.)* **1.** bough, limb, shoot, offshoot, STICK *the branch of a tree* **2.** department, PART, portion, SECTION *a branch of the government*

◆ Guess the Idiom ◆

clue: bother

answer: drive up the wall

brave *(adj.)* courageous, FEARLESS, DARING, heroic, VALIANT, GALLANT, adventurous, dauntless, intrepid, undaunted **COWARDLY**

brawl (n.) FIGHT, STRUGGLE, clash, disturbance, tumult

break (v.) **1.** CRACK, snap, FRACTURE, SPLIT, rupture *break your leg* REPAIR **2.** violate, infringe, trespass, transgress *break the law* OBEY **3.** INTERRUPT, STOP, SEPARATE *break the connection* CONNECT, ATTACH
BRAKE

breathe (v.) inhale, exhale, INSPIRE, expire, gasp, puff, wheeze, sniff, BLOW

brief (adj.) SHORT, concise, condensed, compact LONG, lengthy

bright (adj.) **1.** SMART, CLEVER, INTELLIGENT, keen, gifted, ALERT *a bright student* STUPID **2.** BRILLIANT, radiant, sparkling, glittering *a bright light* DIM **3.** vivid *a bright color* DULL

brilliant (adj.) **1.** SMART, INTELLIGENT, BRIGHT, ALERT, gifted, ingenious *a brilliant mind* STUPID, DULL **2.** BRIGHT, sparkling, glittering, SHINY, dazzling *a brilliant star* DIM, DULL

bring (v.) **1.** CARRY, CONVEY, BEAR, DELIVER *Please bring a gift to the party.* take, REMOVE **2.** CAUSE, EFFECT, PRODUCE *A rabbit's foot may bring good luck.*

broad (adj.) **1.** WIDE, expansive *Many football players have broad shoulders.* NARROW **2.** comprehensive, extensive, sweeping *Many actors have a broad background in the arts.* limited, sparse

bruise (v.) INJURE, HURT, WOUND
HEAL

brutal (adj.) CRUEL, MEAN, beastly, savage, fierce, brutish, barbarous KIND, humane

budge (v.) stir, shift, MOVE, GO, advance, proceed, progress

build (v.) MAKE, CONSTRUCT, erect, ASSEMBLE, RAISE, fabricate
DESTROY

building (n.) structure, edifice, construction

bully (n.) tyrant, ruffian, brute, thug, RASCAL, heavy

bully (v.) FORCE, coerce, intimidate, harass, THREATEN, TEASE

bunch (n.) GROUP, bundle, bale, cluster, COLLECTION, SET, PACK

bungle (v.) BOTCH, fumble, bumble, muddle, muff, blunder, SPOIL

burglar (n.) THIEF, ROBBER, intruder

burn (v.) singe, char, scorch, sear, blister, roast, scald

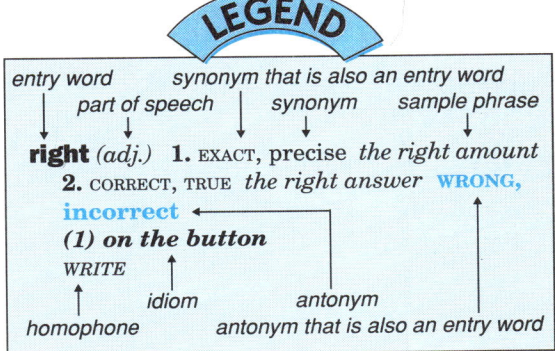

LEGEND
entry word — synonym that is also an entry word
part of speech — synonym — sample phrase
right (adj.) **1.** EXACT, precise *the right amount* **2.** CORRECT, TRUE *the right answer* WRONG, incorrect
(1) on the button
WRITE
homophone — idiom — antonym — antonym that is also an entry word

burst *(v.)* snap, rupture, EXPLODE

bury *(v.)* inter, PLANT, HIDE, CONCEAL UNCOVER, reveal

business *(n.)* **1.** TRADE, occupation, profession, employment, calling, CAREER, pursuit *She started a new business.* **2.** MATTER, CONCERN, affair, INTEREST *He made it his business to learn all the facts.*

busy *(adj.)* ACTIVE, LIVELY, hectic, hardworking, industrious, diligent passive, IDLE
a finger in every pie

buy *(v.)* PURCHASE, ACQUIRE, GET, OBTAIN, invest SELL
BY

Cc

cabin *(n.)* hut, hovel, SHACK, shed, lodge

calculate *(v.)* compute, COUNT, reckon

call *(v.)* **1.** summon, INVITE *Call a friend over.* **2.** CRY, EXCLAIM, SHOUT *Call for help.* **3.** NAME, term, christen *Call him by his nickname.*

calm *(n.)* QUIET, stillness, silence, harmony, concord, serenity, repose disquiet, unrest, turmoil

calm *(v.)* placate, pacify, appease disrupt, DISTURB

calm *(adj.)* **1.** QUIET, STILL, serene, placid, tranquil, restful, PEACEFUL, SMOOTH *a calm day* LOUD, disruptive **2.** composed, collected, unruffled, restrained, dispassionate *a calm mood* unrestrained

cancel *(v.)* ERASE, delete, nullify, repeal, revoke, annul, obliterate, abolish

capital *(n.)* **1.** city, metropolis, municipality *the state's capital* **2.** cash, MONEY, funding, WEALTH, resources, assets, means, investment *raise the capital to build a new gym*
CAPITOL

capital *(adj.)* GOOD, EXCELLENT, first-rate, FINE, CHOICE BAD, third-rate

captain *(n.)* commander, CHIEF, LEADER, skipper

capture *(v.)* **1.** seize, TAKE, arrest, CATCH, apprehend, TRAP, snare, occupy *The police will capture the thief.* RELEASE, FREE **2.** ATTRACT, captivate, enthrall, charm *Our play will capture the audience's attention.*

car *(n.)* VEHICLE, motorcar, automobile, carriage

care *(n.)* safeguard, precaution, forethought, prudence, wariness

care *(v.)* nurture, foster, CHERISH, nourish

career (n.) JOB, profession, occupation, field

careful (adj.) CAUTIOUS, attentive, watchful, wary, conscientious, prudent, meticulous, precise, vigilant, discreet, scrupulous
CARELESS

walking on eggshells

• Guess the Idiom •

clue: careful

answer: walking on eggshells

careless (adj.) negligent, heedless, rash, RECKLESS, inadvertent, accidental, inconsiderate
CAREFUL

cargo (n.) LOAD, freight

carry (v.) BEAR, BRING, TRANSPORT, CONVEY, CONDUCT

cart (n.) wagon, vehicle, dray, wheelbarrow

carve (v.) CUT, chisel, sculpt, engrave, score, hack, hew, dissect

case (n.) 1. BOX, capsule, covering, sheath *a case for the camera* 2. occurrence, instance, ACTION, lawsuit *the case of the missing jewels*

cast (v.) 1. THROW, FLING, sling, lob, hurl, pitch, toss *cast pennies into the fountain* 2. radiate, spread, emit *use a candle to cast light*

castle (n.) 1. palace, mansion, chateau *The queen lives in a castle.* 2. fort, fortress, citadel *defend the castle*

catch (v.) nab, seize, grasp, snatch, grapple, CAPTURE, arrest, entrap, ensnare, apprehend
RELEASE, DROP

category (n.) CLASS, SORT, KIND

cause (n.) REASON, motive, PURPOSE, incentive, AIM, stimulus
EFFECT, RESULT

cause (v.) provoke, incite, PRODUCE, CREATE, kindle, originate

caution (n.) CARE, heed, wariness, discretion, prudence

caution (v.) WARN, ALERT, INFORM, SIGNAL, forewarn, counsel

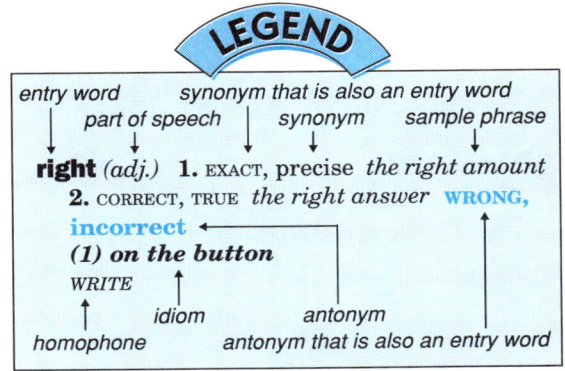

21

cautious *(adj.)* CAREFUL, prudent, wary, watchful, mindful, circumspect CARELESS, RECKLESS

cave *(n.)* cavern, den, burrow, grotto, HOLE

cease *(v.)* STOP, desist, END, QUIT, refrain, suspend, terminate, FINISH START, BEGIN

celebrate *(v.)* rejoice, HONOR, OBSERVE, PRAISE, extol, revel disregard, IGNORE

center *(n.)* MIDDLE, inner, CORE, heart SIDE, BORDER, outskirts

ceremony *(n.)* ritual, rite, service, observance, pomp

certain *(adj.)* SURE, SECURE, POSITIVE, assured, convinced, unfailing uncertain, doubtful **in the bag**

chain *(v.)* shackle, fetter, manacle, handcuff

challenge *(n.)* **1.** summons, dare *I interpreted his look as a challenge.* **2.** TASK *Studying for the history test was quite a challenge.*

challenge *(v.)* protest, OBJECT, dispute, DEFY, DARE

champion *(n.)* HERO, victor, winner, conqueror, master loser

chance *(n.)* **1.** opportunity, occasion, prospect *the chance to succeed* **2.** RISK, HAZARD *take a chance* certainty

chance *(adj.)* RANDOM, lucky, accidental, coincidental, fortuitous, serendipitous contrived, intentional

change *(v.)* **1.** alter, VARY, revise, ADJUST, amend, modify, update, alternate, ADAPT, edit, reform, convert, transform *change the menu in the cafeteria* **2.** replace, SUBSTITUTE, EXCHANGE *change your clothes before gym class* **(1) turn over a new leaf**

character *(n.)* REPUTATION, disposition

characteristic *(n.)* trait, feature, peculiarity, QUALITY

charge *(n.)* **1.** PRICE, COST *What's the charge for the equipment?* **2.** ATTACK, assault *The team captain led the charge.* **3.** accusation *He was jailed on a charge of robbery.*

charge *(v.)* **1.** ATTACK, assault *Charge the fort.* **2.** ACCUSE, BLAME *charge with the crime*

charming *(adj.)* enchanting, bewitching, engaging, fascinating, pleasing, winning

chase *(v.)* HUNT, FOLLOW, track, pursue

cheap *(adj.)* **1.** INEXPENSIVE, low-priced, worthless *a cheap meal* EXPENSIVE **2.** INFERIOR *made of cheap material* quality, VALUABLE **3.** thrifty, frugal, sparing, STINGY, tightfisted, TIGHT *too cheap to pay* GENEROUS CHEEP

cheat *(v.)* swindle, FOOL, DECEIVE, TRICK, mislead, defraud, dupe, hoodwink, delude

check *(v.)* **1.** REVIEW, INSPECT, EXAMINE, monitor, CONFIRM, audit *Check the answers.* **2.** STOP, hinder, curb, obstruct, HALT, restrain *The vaccine will check the spread of the disease.* ALLOW

cheer *(v.)* **1.** APPLAUD, CLAP, salute, root, SUPPORT *Cheer for your favorite team.* BOO **2.** COMFORT, ENCOURAGE, hearten, console *Cheer the team by showing your support.*

cheerful *(adj.)* GLAD, LIVELY, joyful, HAPPY, jolly, MERRY, jubilant, ecstatic SAD

cherish *(v.)* VALUE, treasure, PRIZE, SUPPORT

chest *(n.)* **1.** trunk, torso *The Boy Scout wore a medal on his chest.* **2.** BOX, CASE, trunk, coffer *a treasure chest of coins and jewels*

chew *(v.)* BITE, gnaw, munch, nibble

chief *(n.)* LEADER, chieftain, commander, head, BOSS

chief *(adj.)* MAIN, head, leading, principal, primary

children *(n.)* kids, YOUTH, YOUNG, offspring, juveniles

chill *(v.)* cool, FREEZE, refrigerate

chilly *(adj.)* COLD, COOL, brisk, frigid, frosty HOT, WARM

chip *(n.)* flake, splinter, sliver

choice *(n.)* selection, pick, option, decision

choice *(adj.)* select, FINE, superior, preferred

choke *(v.)* 1. suffocate, gasp, stifle, smother, strangle, asphyxiate *choke on a chicken bone* 2. limit, constrict *The weeds might choke the flowers.*

choose *(v.)* PICK, DECIDE, NAME, select, pluck, appoint, PREFER, nominate, elect, designate **weed out**

chop *(v.)* CUT, mince, dice

chubby *(adj.)* plump, stocky, FAT, fleshy, corpulent SKINNY, THIN

circle *(n.)* RING, halo, hoop, BAND, loop

claim *(n.)* demand, RIGHT, title, assertion

claim *(v.)* DEMAND, REQUIRE, assert, DECLARE

clap *(v.)* APPLAUD, CHEER, PRAISE **give a hand**

class *(n.)* GROUP, CATEGORY, SECTION, department, RANK, ORDER, GRADE, SET, species

clean *(v.)* WASH, WIPE, mop, swab, purify, refine soil **straighten up**

clean *(adj.)* spotless, PURE, IMMACULATE, sterile, sanitary, hygienic DIRTY, SOILED, FILTHY **spic-and-span**

clear *(v.)* 1. REMOVE *Clear the snow from the driveway.* 2. ERASE, void, vindicate, exonerate, absolve *a chance to clear himself*

clear *(adj.)* 1. transparent, see-through *clear water* murky, opaque 2. OBVIOUS, definite, PLAIN, SURE, apparent, evident *a clear victory* questionable, unclear 3. decipherable, graphic, lucid *a clear explanation* ambiguous, VAGUE 4. cloudless, sunny *a clear sky* 5. BARE, OPEN, denuded *a clear path* blocked, obstructed

clever *(adj.)* SMART, QUICK, WISE, WITTY, shrewd, ingenious, deft, skillful, apt SLOW, CLUMSY, incompetent **on the ball, sharp as a tack**

• Guess the Idiom •

clue: clever

answer: sharp as a tack

cliff *(n.)* precipice, crag, bank, bluff

climb *(v.)* scale, RISE, mount, clamber, ascend DESCEND

cling *(v.)* **1.** STICK, adhere, HOLD *Lint often clings to fabric.* **2.** embrace, clasp *cling to one's doll*

clip *(v.)* CUT, trim, snip, DIVIDE, SEPARATE

close *(v.)* SHUT, slam, LOCK, BAR, FASTEN, secure OPEN

close *(adj.)* **1.** NEAR, nearby, adjacent, adjoining, neighboring, proximate *His house is close to school.* FAR, distant, removed **2.** immediate, imminent, impending *The date for our vacation is close.* remote **3.** chummy, FAMILIAR *She's a close friend.* aloof
(1) just a stone's throw away

cloth *(n.)* MATERIAL, fabric, textile

clothes *(n.)* clothing, garment, attire, habit, outfit, SUIT, costume, frock, garb, uniform, apparel, wardrobe

cloudy *(adj.)* **1.** overcast, shadowy, GLOOMY, DIM *a cloudy day* sunny, cloudless **2.** blurred, indistinct, VAGUE, unclear, obscure *a cloudy memory* CLEAR **3.** murky, opaque *cloudy water* transparent

clue *(n.)* HINT, SIGN, EVIDENCE, trace, suggestion, indication

clumsy *(adj.)* AWKWARD, blundering, ungainly, gawky, inept, cumbersome **dexterous, deft**
all thumbs

clutter *(n.)* MESS, disorder, disarray, jumble **arrangement, array**

coach *(v.)* INSTRUCT, TRAIN, DRILL, prompt

coarse *(adj.)* ROUGH, CRUDE FINE
COURSE

coast *(n.)* shore, BEACH, seaside, seashore

coax *(v.)* PERSUADE, CONVINCE, INVITE, ATTRACT, wheedle, cajole

coincidence *(n.)* CHANCE, ACCIDENT, fluke

cold *(adj.)* **1.** CHILLY, chilled, COOL, brisk, frosty, icy, wintry, freezing, raw, arctic, frigid *a cold day* HOT **2.** UNFRIENDLY, distant, aloof *a cold attitude* welcoming, FRIENDLY

collapse *(v.)* FALL, founder, disintegrate

collect *(v.)* GATHER, ASSEMBLE, harvest, hoard, muster, amass, accumulate SCATTER

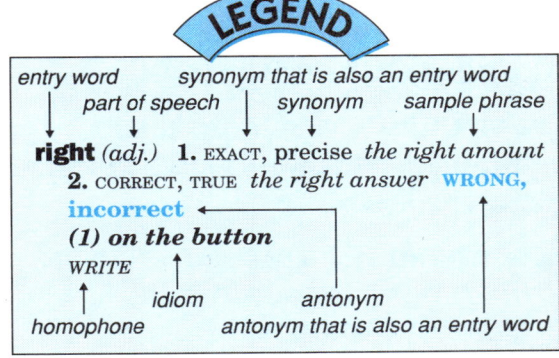

collection (n.) **1.** GROUP, cluster, gathering, hoard, store, PILE, accumulation, assortment *He has a great compact disc collection.* **2.** offering, DONATION, CONTRIBUTION, charity *They took up a collection to help the tornado victims.*

college (n.) university, institute, SCHOOL

color (n.) hue, tint, shade, DYE, tone, tinge, pigment, complexion

combat (n.) FIGHT, battle, conflict, skirmish, CONTEST

combat (v.) RESIST, FIGHT, oppose, battle, contend

combine (v.) JOIN, unite, pool, BLEND, MIX, CONNECT SEPARATE

come (v.) ARRIVE, REACH GO, LEAVE

comfort (n.) EASE, RELIEF, PEACE, REST discomfort

comfort (v.) CHEER, reassure, console, SOOTHE WORRY, ANNOY, DISTURB

comfortable (adj.) **1.** COZY, comfy, snug *a comfortable chair* uncomfortable **2.** EASY, contented, untroubled *a comfortable feeling about the decision* uneasy, discontented

comic (adj.) FUNNY, HUMOROUS, amusing, SILLY, HILARIOUS, droll, farcical SERIOUS

command (v.) LEAD, RULE, GOVERN, INSTRUCT, CONTROL, ORDER, dominate OBEY, comply

comment (n.) REMARK, statement, utterance, SAYING

comment (v.) EXPRESS, utter, REMARK, react, RESPOND

committee (n.) council, BOARD, commission, GROUP, cabinet

common (adj.) **1.** ORDINARY, commonplace, REGULAR, USUAL, habitual, customary, FREQUENT *Jogging is a common activity.* RARE, uncommon **2.** GENERAL, POPULAR, PUBLIC, universal, accepted, prevailing, prevalent *The common opinion is that he's a good president.*
(1) a dime a dozen

communicate (v.) **1.** ANNOUNCE, TELL, disclose, PASS, proclaim, INFORM, impart, reveal *communicate in person* **2.** transmit, CONVEY *communicate over the telephone lines*

community (n.) neighborhood, town, village, district, GROUP, association, society

companion (n.) FRIEND, buddy, mate, comrade, associate

company (n.) **1.** BUSINESS, firm, corporation, partnership, union, alliance *She works at a clothing company.* **2.** guests, visitors *Our company is arriving for dinner at 6:00 P.M.*

compare (v.) liken, match, weigh, relate, equate contrast

compete (v.) oppose, rival, contend

competition (n.) **1.** CONTEST, rivalry, tournament, MATCH *the tennis competition* **2.** rival, competitor *She's your main competition in the school election.*
(2) a run for one's money

complain (v.) protest, OBJECT, CHALLENGE, WHINE, moan, groan, mutter, grumble, dispute

complete (v.) DO, FINISH, CONCLUDE, accomplish, ACHIEVE, END
wrap up

complete (adj.) WHOLE, finished, comprehensive, extensive, BROAD
unfinished, INCOMPLETE

complex (adj.) COMPLICATED, tangled, intricate, ELABORATE **CLEAR, PLAIN, SIMPLE**

complicated (adj.) DIFFICULT, HARD, COMPLEX, tangled, intricate, convoluted, puzzling, perplexing **SIMPLE, EASY**

compliment (n.) PRAISE, HONOR, commendation, endorsement
INSULT
COMPLEMENT

compliment (v.) PRAISE, HONOR, commend, FLATTER, congratulate, CELEBRATE **INSULT, OFFEND, dishonor**
sing one's praises
COMPLEMENT

compose (v.) **1.** WRITE, CREATE, draft, author, conceive *She composed a short story.* **2.** CALM, CONTROL, COLLECT, QUIET, pacify, quell *He composed himself before speaking to the class.*

comprehend (v.) UNDERSTAND, SEE, GET, CONCLUDE, grasp, fathom
get the picture

conceal (v.) HIDE, stash, COVER, mask, screen, DISGUISE, BURY, camouflage **uncover, reveal, divulge**

conceited (adj.) vain, boastful, smug, arrogant, egotistical, showy, ostentatious, pompous, pretentious, bombastic, grandiose **HUMBLE**
too big for one's britches

◆ Guess the Idiom ◆

clue: conceited

answer: too big for one's britches

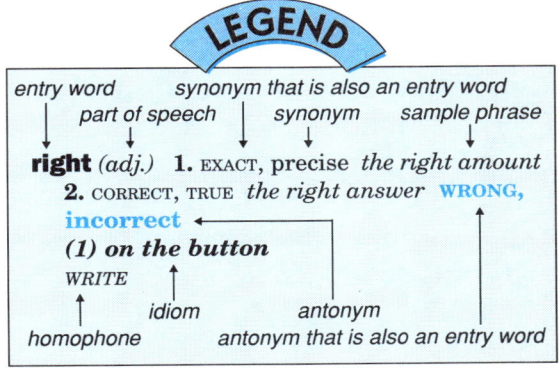

concentrate (v.) **1.** THINK, ponder, focus *Concentrate on your homework.* **2.** COLLECT, GATHER, consolidate *Concentrate the information in one place.* **disperse, DISTRIBUTE 3.** REDUCE, condense, CONTRACT *Concentrate the juice by removing the water.* **dilute, THIN**

concept (n.) IDEA, notion, THOUGHT, theory, impression

concern (n.) **1.** MATTER, BUSINESS, PROBLEM, affair, consequence *not your concern* **2.** CARE, WORRY, consideration, regard, THOUGHT, ANXIETY, FEAR *concern for the poor* **indifference, apathy**

concern (v.) **1.** TROUBLE, BOTHER, WORRY, disquiet, preoccupy, DISTURB, perturb *Her behavior concerns her parents.* **2.** AFFECT, INCLUDE, implicate *The situation concerns you.*

conclude (v.) **1.** END, FINISH, terminate, CLOSE, complete, CEASE, wrap up *conclude the lesson* **BEGIN 2.** determine, deduce, infer, GATHER, REASON, JUDGE, presume, UNDERSTAND *conclude the defendant is innocent*
(1) bring down the curtain

condemn (v.) **1.** BLAME, DISAPPROVE, denounce, CRITICIZE, rebuke, berate *Don't condemn my thinking.* **APPLAUD, PRAISE 2.** sentence, JUDGE, convict, damn, doom *Condemn the criminal to life imprisonment.* **FORGIVE, PARDON 3.** FORBID, outlaw, proscribe *condemn the actions* **SUPPORT, BACK, endorse, ALLOW**

condition (n.) **1.** STATE, situation *The book is in good condition.* **2.** plight, predicament, illness, SICKNESS *His condition is improving.*

conduct (n.) BEHAVIOR, actions, manners, demeanor

conduct (v.) **1.** LEAD, DIRECT, GUIDE, MANAGE, GOVERN, OPERATE *Conduct the orchestra.* **2.** GUIDE, LEAD, CONVEY, TRANSPORT, usher *Conduct the child out of the theater.* **3.** ACT, BEHAVE *Conduct yourself in a polite manner.*

confess (v.) **1.** TELL, STATE, ADMIT, concede, acknowledge *confess one's guilt* **withhold 2.** affirm, avow, profess, DECLARE *He confessed his religious beliefs.*

confidence (n.) **1.** self-assurance, assurance, dignity, poise, aplomb *She has confidence in her abilities.* **2.** FAITH, TRUST *place confidence in friendship* **DOUBT, apprehension**

confident (adj.) SURE, assured, CERTAIN, positive, hopeful **unsure, doubtful**

confidential (adj.) SECRET, PRIVATE, restricted, personal, privy

confirm (v.) **1.** verify, establish, authenticate, substantiate, validate, ASSURE *confirm a doctor's appointment* **2.** strengthen, fortify, establish, SUPPORT, reinforce, corroborate *confirm an argument* **disprove, refute**

confuse (v.) BAFFLE, PUZZLE, bewilder, mystify, confound, mislead, DISTURB **clarify** *throw someone for a loop*

connect (v.) JOIN, unite, COMBINE, link, couple **SEPARATE, DISCONNECT**

conquer (v.) BEAT, overcome, subdue, vanquish, quell **succumb, SURRENDER, YIELD**

conscious (adj.) **1.** ALIVE, AWAKE, ALERT, AWARE, sensible *She was conscious and breathing after the accident.* **unconscious** **2.** purposeful, intentional *a conscious decision*

conserve (v.) PRESERVE, SAVE, KEEP, safeguard, maintain, sustain, support **squander, waste**

consider (v.) EXAMINE, STUDY, regard, ponder, muse, REFLECT, speculate, deliberate, JUDGE *turn over in one's mind*

considerate (adj.) KIND, WISE, NICE, COURTEOUS, THOUGHTFUL, WARM, discreet, prudent **inconsiderate, THOUGHTLESS, UNKIND**

consistent (adj.) CONSTANT, STEADY, REGULAR, unchanging, STABLE, FIRM, uniform **inconsistent, discrepant**

conspicuous (adj.) apparent, PLAIN, CLEAR, noticeable, distinct, OBVIOUS, evident, visible, manifest, prominent **inconspicuous** *plain as day, plain as the nose on one's face*

constant (adj.) **1.** CONSISTENT, SET, fixed, FIRM, STABLE, REGULAR, unchanging *a constant problem* **intermittent** **2.** FAITHFUL, LOYAL, steadfast, TRUE, DEVOTED *The soldiers remained constant.* **disloyal, traitorous**

construct (v.) **1.** BUILD, erect, RAISE, fabricate, MANUFACTURE *construct a model* **RAZE** **2.** CREATE, forge, FASHION *construct an argument*

consult (v.) confer, ADVISE, DISCUSS

contagious (adj.) infectious, catching, communicable, transmissible

contain (v.) INCLUDE, embody, comprise, HOLD

contaminate (v.) POLLUTE, POISON, taint, INFECT, defile, corrupt **purify**

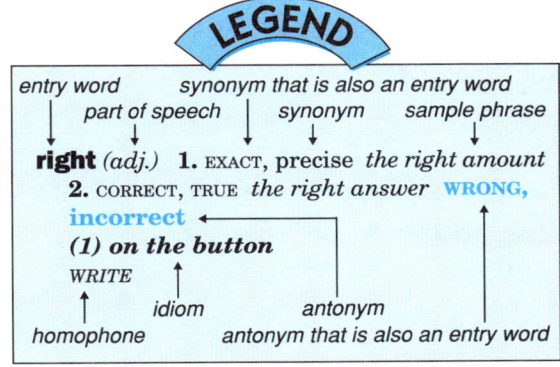

content *(adj.)* satisfied, HAPPY, pleased, appeased **discontented, UNHAPPY**

contest *(n.)* **1.** COMPETITION, GAME, tournament, MATCH *a swimming contest* **2.** STRUGGLE, conflict, rivalry *a contest of wills*

continue *(v.)* persist, endure, MAINTAIN, LAST, persevere **desist, CEASE** *keep the ball rolling*

contract *(n.)* agreement, BARGAIN, treaty, DEAL, pact, covenant

contract *(v.)* SHORTEN, LESSEN, DECREASE, diminish, SHRINK, condense **EXPAND, lengthen**

contribute *(v.)* **1.** GIVE, grant, bestow, SUPPLY, DONATE *contribute to charity* **2.** FURNISH, PROVIDE, SUPPLY *contribute your time*

contribution *(n.)* GIFT, DONATION, offering, grant, bestowal

control *(v.)* **1.** DIRECT, MANAGE, dominate, master, COMMAND *The president controls the meeting.* **2.** regulate, curb, CHECK, restrain *control the water flow*

convenient *(adj.)* timely, opportune, APPROPRIATE, suitable, USEFUL, HANDY **INCONVENIENT, bothersome**

conversation *(n.)* TALK, CHAT, discussion, COMMUNICATION

convey *(v.)* **1.** CARRY, BEAR, BRING, TRANSPORT *convey the freight* **2.** COMMUNICATE, divulge, reveal, disclose, transmit *convey the truth*

convince *(v.)* PERSUADE, INFLUENCE, URGE, COAX, goad, spur, induce, entice

cook *(v.)* fry, bake, grill, boil, brew, stew, simmer, broil, sauté, roast, PREPARE

cool *(adj.)* **1.** COLD, CHILLY, brisk *a cool wind* **WARM, HOT 2.** UNFRIENDLY, apathetic, unexcited, distant, lukewarm, discourteous, insolent *disappointed by the cool reception* **FRIENDLY, welcoming 3.** GOOD, NEAT, keen *He bought cool sunglasses for the beach.*

cool *(adv.)* CALM, collected, composed **NERVOUS, agitated**

cooperate *(v.)* collaborate, unite **oppose** *put your heads together*

copy *(n.)* **1.** DUPLICATE, reproduction, replica *Before turning in his report, he made a copy of it.* **original 2.** imitation, counterfeit, FAKE, phony *They discovered the painting was just a copy of the original.* **original**

copy *(v.)* DUPLICATE, REPRODUCE, mimic, FOLLOW, IMITATE, recreate, transcribe, REPEAT, pirate, ape, impersonate

core (n.) **1.** CENTER, MIDDLE *the core of the apple* **2.** essence, heart, gist, substance *the core of the problem*

correct (v.) IMPROVE, BETTER, amend, rectify, remedy, revise, reform

correct (adj.) **1.** ACCURATE, EXACT, precise *the correct answer* **INCORRECT, WRONG** **2.** APPROPRIATE, FIT, fitting, JUST, PROPER *correct behavior* **IMPROPER**
(1) on the nose

clue: correct

answer: on the nose

corrupt (adj.) **1.** dishonest, degenerate, depraved, rotten, villainous, CROOKED, WICKED, EVIL *a corrupt soul* **HONEST, MORAL, GOOD** **2.** CROOKED, unethical, immoral, shady, double-dealing, unscrupulous, underhanded *a corrupt politician* **ethical, scrupulous, upright, dependable, trustworthy**

cost (n.) PRICE, VALUE, CHARGE, expense, FEE, expenditure

count (v.) tally, compute, calculate, ESTIMATE, reckon

country (n.) **1.** nation, STATE *Pledge allegiance to your country.* **2.** backwoods, farmland, outback *They lived on a farm in the country.* **city**

country (adj.) RURAL, rustic, pastoral, SIMPLE, PLAIN **urban**

courage (n.) bravery, nerve, daring, valor, pluck, SPIRIT, prowess, fortitude **FEAR, COWARDICE, timidity**

course (n.) **1.** ROUTE, WAY, TRACK, ROAD *a safe course across the mountains* **2.** direction, bearing, itinerary *stay on course* **3.** SUBJECT, program, STUDY, CLASS *She took a biology course.* **4.** process, PLAN, METHOD, procedure *a course of action*
COARSE

courteous (adj.) POLITE, gracious, obliging, refined, accommodating **IMPOLITE, RUDE**

cover (n.) canopy, roof, SHELTER

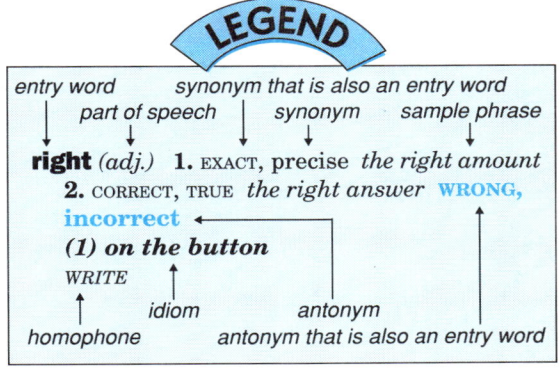

cover (v.) CONCEAL, HIDE, mask, screen, DISGUISE, cloak UNCOVER, EXPOSE, DISPLAY

coward (n.) weakling, chicken, deserter, scaredy-cat HERO

cowardly (adj.) TIMID, shrinking, fearful, AFRAID, BRAVE, heroic, courageous, VALIANT

cozy (adj.) **1.** snug, comfortable, SOFT *a cozy chair* uncomfortable **2.** intimate, FAMILIAR *The room was a cozy setting for a party.* STRANGE, unfamiliar

crack (n.) BREAK, FRACTURE, cleft, fissure, rupture

cram (v.) JAM, SQUEEZE, stuff, gorge, glut, FILL, ram, PRESS, FORCE

crash (n.) collision, impact, ACCIDENT

crash (v.) collide, SMASH, clash

crazy (adj.) MAD, insane, lunatic, demented, deranged SANE
bats in one's belfry

create (v.) MAKE, PRODUCE, FORM, INVENT, render, forge, originate COPY

creature (n.) animal, being, organism

crime (n.) felony, wrongdoing, offense, transgression, breach, violation

criminal (n.) crook, hoodlum, outlaw, convict, VILLAIN, rogue, TRAITOR, renegade, rebel, felon, miscreant, fugitive

critical (adj.) **1.** disapproving, faultfinding, derogatory *a critical speech* uncritical, supportive **2.** DANGEROUS, hazardous, RISKY, precarious, perilous *in critical condition* **3.** CRUCIAL, decisive, IMPORTANT *a critical bit of information* UNIMPORTANT, trivial

criticize (v.) SCOLD, reprimand, chastise, reprove, JUDGE, censor, CONDEMN PRAISE, APPROVE, endorse
tear one to pieces

crooked (adj.) bent, awry, curved, angled, twisted, irregular, asymmetrical, askew STRAIGHT

cross (v.) **1.** span, traverse, REACH, intersect *cross the river* **2.** betray, double-cross *cross the enemy* **3.** CANCEL, STRIKE, MARK *cross it out* **4.** crossbreed, interbreed, hybridize *When you cross an orange with a tangerine, you get a tangelo.*
(2) *bite the hand that feeds one*

cross (adj.) IRRITABLE, testy, peevish, MOODY, surly, somber, sulky, sullen, morose
a chip on one's shoulder

crouch (v.) squat, stoop, cower, cringe STAND

crowd *(n.)* MOB, multitude, swarm, throng, horde

crucial *(adj.)* SEVERE, trying, decisive, acute, distressing

crude *(adj.)* IMPOLITE, COARSE, RAW, unpolished, RUDE, vulgar POLITE, well-mannered

cruel *(adj.)* ruthless, merciless, heartless, BRUTAL, SAVAGE merciful

crumble *(v.)* DECAY, decompose, disintegrate, degenerate, deteriorate

crush *(v.)* 1. SMASH, pound, compress, pulverize *Crush the nut with the nutcracker.* 2. overpower, CONQUER, subdue, stifle, suppress *crush a rebellion*

cry *(v.)* 1. WEEP, sob, tear, wail, whimper, WHINE, snivel, blubber, bawl, mourn, grieve, lament *Cry when you are sad.* LAUGH, SMILE 2. CALL, SHOUT, squeal *Cry for help.*

cuddle *(v.)* HUG, embrace, snuggle, caress, nuzzle

cunning *(adj.)* crafty, skillful, artful, SLY, wily, shrewd, foxy naive, SIMPLE

cure *(n.)* remedy, treatment, antidote

cure *(v.)* HEAL, TREAT, remedy, restore, preserve

curious *(adj.)* 1. inquisitive, investigative, prying, NOSY *She was curious about the customs of other countries.* detached, uninterested, unresponsive 2. STRANGE, UNUSUAL, ODD, peculiar, bizarre, UNIQUE *a curious happening in the old house*

curse *(v.)* SWEAR, cuss, blaspheme bless

custom *(n.)* tradition, HABIT, ritual, practice, routine, usage, folklore, convention

customer *(n.)* purchaser, buyer, patron, client

cut *(n.)* WOUND, gash, laceration

cut *(v.)* CLIP, snip, slice, dissect, sever, cleave, PART, SPLIT, SEPARATE, DISCONNECT, DETACH, DIVIDE, mince, CARVE, whittle, chisel, engrave, CHOP, hew, crop, hack, lance, prune, trim

cute *(adj.)* adorable, delightful, appealing, DAINTY

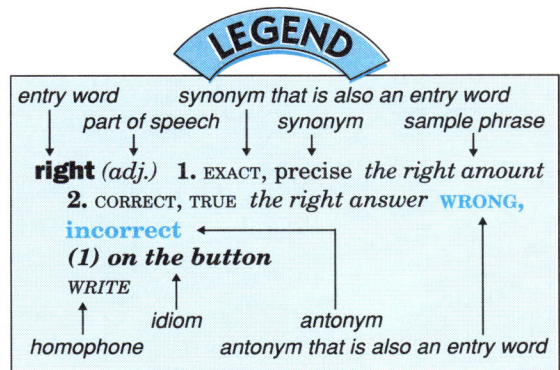

Dd

dainty (adj.) DELICATE, elegant, fragile, petite, frail

damage (n.) injury, HARM, MISCHIEF, ruin

damage (v.) HARM, INJURE, impair, spoil, RUIN, ABUSE REPAIR, FIX

damp (adj.) WET, moist, dank, humid, soaked, drenched DRY

dance (n.) prom, BALL, ballet

danger (n.) HAZARD, peril, RISK, jeopardy, threat SAFETY, security
thin ice

dangerous (adj.) hazardous, risky, unsafe, DIFFICULT, perilous, jeopardous, formidable, precarious SAFE, SECURE, HARMLESS

dare (v.) brave, face, CHALLENGE, DEFY, risk cower
take the bull by the horns

daring (adj.) BRAVE, BOLD, adventurous, FEARLESS, heroic

dark (adj.) dim, dusky, shady, shadowy, murky, GLOOMY, overcast, CLOUDY, obscure, opaque LIGHT

Go CRAZY with WORDS! — damp

darling *(adj.)* pet, DEAR, beloved, PRECIOUS, cherished, FAVORITE

dash *(v.)* RUSH, HURRY, scurry, scuttle, scamper, SPEED, RACE, bolt, charge dally, LINGER

date *(n.)* **1.** engagement, appointment, rendezvous *We went out on a date.* **2.** escort, boyfriend, girlfriend *My date took me to a movie.*

daze *(v.)* dazzle, blind, bewilder, SURPRISE, CONFUSE, stun, AMAZE, stupefy
DAYS

dead *(adj.)* **1.** deceased, lifeless, finished, defunct, EXTINCT *a dead snake* alive **2.** obsolete, outdated, passé, outmoded *a dead style of clothing*

deadly *(adj.)* **1.** lethal, toxic, poisonous, noxious, malignant, baneful *deadly fumes* healthful, HEALTHY, wholesome **2.** FATAL, mortal, murderous, lethal *a deadly car accident* HARMLESS

deal *(n.)* agreement, treaty, pact, concord, union, trade, negotiation, transaction

deal *(v.)* **1.** TRADE, BARGAIN *deal with another company* **2.** DISTRIBUTE, DIVIDE, allot *Deal the cards.*

dear *(adj.)* **1.** beloved, PRECIOUS, DARLING, cherished, prized *a dear child* **2.** EXPENSIVE, costly, priceless, PRECIOUS, VALUABLE *one of a kind at a dear price* CHEAP, INEXPENSIVE
DEER

debate *(v.)* DISCUSS, argue, dispute, DEMONSTRATE, PROVE, contend, quarrel agree, concur

debt *(n.)* due, obligation, liability, deficit

decay *(v.)* ROT, SPOIL, decompose, molder, perish, decline, wither, disintegrate
go to pot

deceive *(v.)* CHEAT, TRICK, FOOL, delude, dupe, hoax, hoodwink, betray, beguile

decide *(v.)* CHOOSE, determine, CONCLUDE, settle hesitate, vacillate
make up one's mind

declare *(v.)* SAY, STATE, announce, proclaim, affirm

decorate *(v.)* ADORN, garnish, embellish

decrease *(v.)* LESSEN, diminish, dwindle, wane, REDUCE, curtail INCREASE

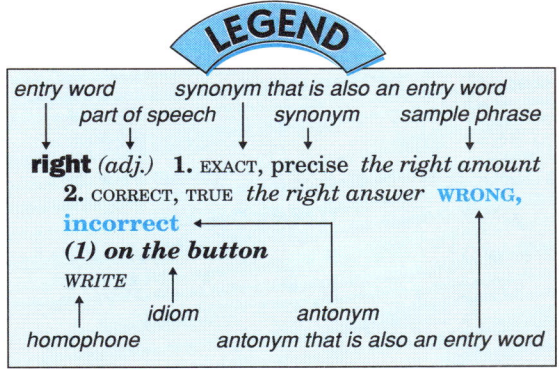

deep *(adj.)* **1.** bottomless, abysmal, cavernous *a deep lake* shallow **2.** profound, complex *a deep thought* EASY, SIMPLE, CLEAR **3.** SERIOUS, grave, grievous *in deep trouble*

defeat *(v.)* BEAT, OVERTHROW, overcome, CONQUER

defect *(n.)* flaw, blemish, FAULT, weakness, drawback

defect *(v.)* ABANDON, LEAVE, DESERT, forsake, renounce, abscond STAY

defend *(v.)* PROTECT, shield, GUARD, secure ATTACK

defense *(n.)* **1.** protection, GUARD, bulwark *The army provides defense against the enemy.* offense **2.** REPLY, ANSWER, retort *She presented her defense in the debate.*

define *(v.)* EXPLAIN, DESCRIBE, clarify, interpret, ascertain

defy *(v.)* RESIST, CHALLENGE, DISOBEY, disregard OBEY

degree *(n.)* **1.** level, GRADE, STEP, STAGE, extent *the degree of danger* **2.** REWARD, GRADE, HONOR *a degree from college*

delay *(n.)* PAUSE, WAIT, interval

delay *(v.)* PAUSE, WAIT, HESITATE, postpone, slacken, detain, stall, dawdle continue, proceed, prolong, hasten, expedite *drag your feet, put on hold, put on ice*

delicate *(adj.)* **1.** DAINTY, frail, TENDER *a delicate child* **2.** precarious, CRITICAL *a delicate situation* **3.** subtle, slight *a delicate scent*

delicious *(adj.)* tasty, luscious, juicy, palatable, savory tasteless, flavorless, BLAND

delight *(n.)* JOY, happiness, enjoyment, gladness, PLEASURE, ecstasy DISAPPOINTMENT

delight *(v.)* **1.** PLEASE, entice, ATTRACT, captivate *delight the child with stories* displease, disgust **2.** SATISFY, enliven *delight the senses*

deliver *(v.)* **1.** SEND, transfer, CONVEY, PASS, DIRECT *deliver a letter* **2.** PRONOUNCE, EXPRESS, ADVANCE, COMMUNICATE *deliver a speech*

demand *(v.)* REQUIRE, ORDER, COMMAND, summon

♦ Guess the Idiom ♦

clue: delay

answer: put on ice

demonstrate *(v.)* **1.** SHOW, ILLUSTRATE, DISPLAY, EXHIBIT *demonstrate the science experiment* CONCEAL, HIDE, DISGUISE, camouflage **2.** PROVE, TEST, TRY, authenticate, validate *The attorneys will demonstrate that the defendant is innocent.*

dense *(adj.)* **1.** THICK, compact, CLOSE, crowded, lush, impenetrable *a dense forest* sparse **2.** STUPID, DULL, FOOLISH, IGNORANT, moronic, thick-headed *a dense person* QUICK, INTELLIGENT, BRIGHT

deny *(v.)* **1.** disclaim, renounce, repudiate, refute, DISMISS *Don't deny you're at fault.* admit, acknowledge **2.** REFUSE, decline *Deny the request.* grant, permit, allow

depart *(v.)* **1.** LEAVE, GO, part *Depart on the next plane.* ARRIVE **2.** DIE, PASS, perish, expire *depart from this life*

depend *(v.)* rely, TRUST

depressed *(adj.)* SAD, dejected, GLOOMY, discouraged, disheartened, BLUE, melancholy HAPPY, joyous

descend *(v.)* FALL, SINK, DROP, plunge, slip RISE, ascend

describe *(v.)* EXPLAIN, clarify, DEFINE, interpret, recount, relate, report, narrate

desert *(v.)* LEAVE, forsake, ABANDON, QUIT, DEFECT, EVACUATE *bail out*
DESSERT

deserve *(v.)* EARN, merit, entitle, warrant

desire *(n.)* WISH, NEED, longing, craving

desire *(v.)* WISH, WANT, crave, covet
set your heart on

desperate *(adj.)* hopeless, despondent, despairing, forlorn

despise *(v.)* HATE, detest, scorn, spurn, disdain LIKE, LOVE

destination *(n.)* GOAL, target, END, objective

destroy *(v.)* RUIN, RAZE, demolish, sack, ravage, annihilate, devastate, eradicate, exterminate CREATE

detach *(v.)* SEPARATE, SPLIT, disjoin, DISCONNECT, sever, DIVIDE ATTACH

detail *(n.)* feature, PART, aspect, trait, particular

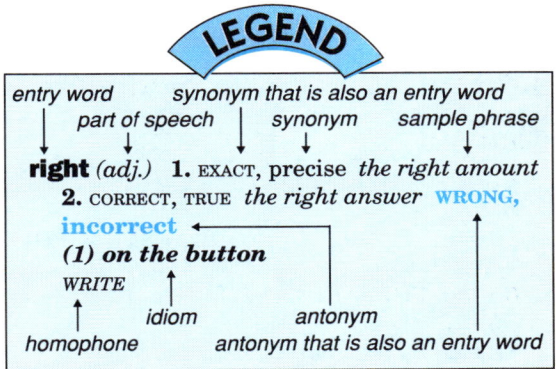

detect *(v.)* FIND, DISCOVER, SPOT, expose, catch, ascertain

determined *(adj.)* firm, decided, resolved, resolute, steadfast, relentless

develop *(v.)* **1.** GROW, CHANGE, mature, evolve *develop into an adult* **2.** EXPAND, INCREASE, promote *develop skills* **3.** CREATE, formulate, synthesize *develop a plan*

device *(n.)* INSTRUMENT, MACHINE, GADGET, TOOL, apparatus, contraption

devoted *(adj.)* **1.** FAITHFUL, dutiful, devout, LOYAL, CONSTANT, ardent *a devoted fan* **unfaithful, disloyal** **2.** loving, affectionate, attentive *a devoted parent*

die *(v.)* expire, CEASE, perish, decease **LIVE, survive** *bite the dust, kick the bucket* DYE

difference *(n.)* **1.** contrast, variation, distinction, diversity *the difference between two colors* **similarity** **2.** disagreement, misunderstanding, opposition *a difference of opinion* **agreement, accord**

different *(adj.)* **1.** unlike, dissimilar, varying, diverse *different habits* **SAME** **2.** uncommon, UNUSUAL, SPECIAL, ODD, EXTRAORDINARY, distinct *a different hairstyle* **COMMON** **(2)** *off the beaten track*

difficult *(adj.)* HARD, trying, COMPLICATED, COMPLEX, tangled, intricate, arduous, laborious, formidable, irksome **EASY, SIMPLE** *easier said than done, no picnic, an uphill climb*

• Guess the Idiom •

clue: difficult

answer: an uphill climb

dig *(v.)* burrow, hollow, scoop, mine, quarry, excavate, delve

dilapidated *(adj.)* decayed, ruined, SHABBY, run-down, deteriorated, neglected, unkempt

dim *(adj.)* DARK, DULL, shadowy, FAINT, unclear, WEAK, obscure, VAGUE, indistinct, faded **BRIGHT**

dine *(v.)* EAT, consume, feast, gorge

dingy *(n.)* DIRTY, soiled, sullied, dull, dusky **CLEAN**

direct *(v.)* ORDER, COMMAND, INSTRUCT, AIM, POINT, SHOW *call the shots*

directions *(n.)* instructions, formula, prescription, GUIDE, COURSE

dirt (n.) soil, earth, land, GROUND, mud, muck, dust, sediment, grime, soot

dirty (adj.) 1. unclean, FILTHY, soiled, grimy, impure, FOUL, vile, GROSS, contaminated, polluted, squalid *dirty water* PURE, CLEAN 2. obscene, indecent, smutty, offensive *dirty language*
(2) off-color

disadvantage (n.) handicap, drawback, obstacle, hindrance, inconvenience ADVANTAGE

disagree (v.) REJECT, oppose, CHALLENGE, DENY, dispute AGREE, concur

disappear (v.) VANISH, FADE, evaporate, DISSOLVE, vaporize APPEAR

disappoint (v.) dissatisfy, FRUSTRATE, foil, FAIL PLEASE

disappointment (n.) frustration, setback, FAILURE, DEFEAT, unfulfillment, dissatisfaction

disapprove (v.) REJECT, CONDEMN, censure, OBJECT, oppose, protest, dispute APPROVE, ACCEPT
take a dim view of, take exception to

disaster (n.) mishap, misfortune, mischance, tragedy, catastrophe, calamity

discard (v.) REJECT, scrap, eliminate, exclude, jettison KEEP, retain

disconnect (v.) SEPARATE, disjoin, sever, DETACH, disengage CONNECT

discourage (v.) 1. dishearten, depress, deject, unnerve *The high cost of supplies will discourage us.* encourage 2. dissuade, deter, obstruct, inhibit, BLOCK, prevent *Placing land mines will discourage the advance of the enemy.*
(2) throw cold water on

discover (v.) FIND, reveal, UNCOVER, LEARN

discuss (v.) TALK, negotiate, deliberate

disease (n.) SICKNESS, ailment, malady

disgrace (n.) disfavor, SHAME, dishonor, infamy, scandal, contempt, humiliation HONOR

disgrace (v.) defile, SHAME, smirch HONOR
drag through the mud

disguise (n.) costume, mask, guise, camouflage

disguise (v.) masquerade, CONCEAL, mask, HIDE, camouflage

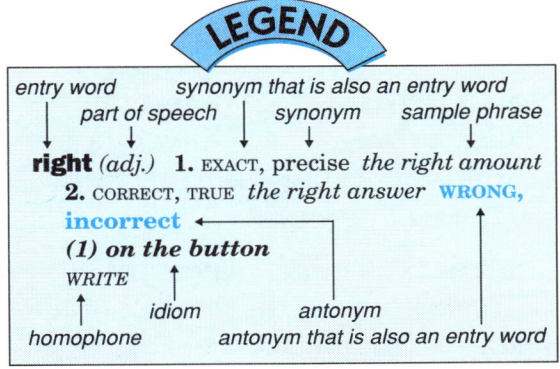

39

disgusting *(adj.)* repulsive, distasteful, offensive, CRUDE, revolting, repellent, loathsome, vulgar

dishonest *(adj.)* lying, untruthful, deceitful, mendacious, CROOKED, CORRUPT, fraudulent, unprincipled HONEST, **truthful** *two-faced*

dislike *(v.)* disfavor, DISAPPROVE, HATE, loathe, detest LIKE

dismal *(adj.)* cheerless, GLOOMY, DARK, DULL, dreary, depressing

dismiss *(v.)* **1.** fire, DISCHARGE, unseat, RELEASE *dismiss an employee* HIRE, EMPLOY **2.** DISCARD, REJECT, expel, decline *dismiss an idea* ACCEPT, HOLD, **retain, embrace**

disobey *(v.)* DEFY, disregard, IGNORE, neglect, REJECT, rebel, revolt, OFFEND, transgress, infringe OBEY

display *(n.)* **1.** exhibition, exposition, pageant, fanfare *a display of jewelry* **2.** exhibition, SHOW *a display of affection*

display *(v.)* EXHIBIT, SHOW, publicize COVER, HIDE, CONCEAL

dissolve *(v.)* **1.** liquefy, MELT, thaw, soften *The sugar dissolves in hot water.* **2.** END, terminate, discontinue, annul, invalidate, repeal *dissolve a partnership* FORM

distract *(v.)* divert, avert, sidetrack, CONFUSE, bewilder, befuddle, confound, PUZZLE

distress *(n.)* **1.** PAIN, AGONY, anguish, GRIEF, woe, torment *He felt distress over the loss of his job.* **2.** TROUBLE, WORRY, adversity *financial distress*
(1) a heavy heart

distribute *(v.)* **1.** dispense, allot, issue, disperse, allocate, DIVIDE, apportion *Distribute the funds.* **2.** SCATTER, SPREAD, disperse, sprinkle *Distribute the seeds.* GATHER, COLLECT

disturb *(v.)* INTERRUPT, TROUBLE, disquiet, ALARM, disrupt, unsettle, perturb, disconcert CALM **kick up a storm, rock the boat**

ditch *(n.)* trench, trough, channel, moat, gully

dive *(v.)* plunge, submerge, immerse

divide *(v.)* **1.** SPLIT, CUT, sever, slice, cleave, PART, SEPARATE, rend *The river divides the land.* **unite** **2.** SHARE, DISTRIBUTE, apportion *Divide the pizza among the guests.*

divine *(adj.)* **1.** HOLY, RELIGIOUS, blessed, godlike, heavenly, spiritual *a divine experience* **2.** EXCELLENT, delightful, SUPER, admirable *a divine dinner*

dizzy *(adj.)* unsteady, staggering, unstable, hazy, giddy

do (v.) PERFORM, FINISH, COMPLETE, enact, ACT, ACHIEVE, commit, execute, EFFECT, perpetrate undo *carry out*
DEW, DUE

dodge (v.) AVOID, MISS, ESCAPE, evade, elude, hedge

dog (n.) hound, canine, pooch, mongrel, mutt, puppy

donation (n.) contribution, offering, alms, dole, GIFT, PRESENT, gratuity

door (n.) entrance, entry, EXIT, gate, threshold, portal

doubt (n.) CONCERN, anxiety, uncertainty, skepticism, distrust certainty

doubt (v.) QUESTION, distrust, mistrust, SUSPECT, dispute *think something sounds fishy, take with a grain of salt, call into question*

doze (v.) SLEEP, slumber, NAP, drowse

drab (adj.) DREARY, DULL, DINGY, flat BRIGHT, vivid

drag (v.) 1. PULL, haul, DRAW, tug, tow *Drag the cart up the hill.* 2. LINGER, dawdle, loiter, poke *The day dragged when he had little to do.* 3. lengthen, EXTEND, prolong *Drag out the argument.* *(2) go at a snail's pace*

draw (v.) 1. SKETCH, illustrate, PICTURE, portray, REPRESENT, draft, depict *Draw a picture.* 2. REMOVE, TAKE *Draw water from the well.* 3. PULL, drag *Draw the curtains.* 4. ATTRACT, LEAD, induce, elicit, provoke *draw attention to oneself*

dread (n.) FEAR, ALARM, awe, TERROR, apprehension

dream (n.) 1. vision, fantasy, ILLUSION, nightmare *a frightening dream in the middle of the night* 2. GOAL *Her dream is to be a doctor.*

dreary (adj.) 1. GLOOMY, DARK, DISMAL, cheerless, depressing, forlorn *a dreary day* sunny, BRIGHT 2. BORING, DULL, tedious, tiresome *a dreary time doing yard work*

dress (n.) CLOTHES, attire, apparel

drill (v.) bore, PIERCE, poke, puncture, perforate, penetrate

drink (v.) sip, swallow, gulp *wet your whistle*

drive (v.) 1. GUIDE, OPERATE, DIRECT, CONTROL *drive a car* 2. FORCE, INFLUENCE, pressure, PRESS, compel *We must drive the committee to make a decision.*

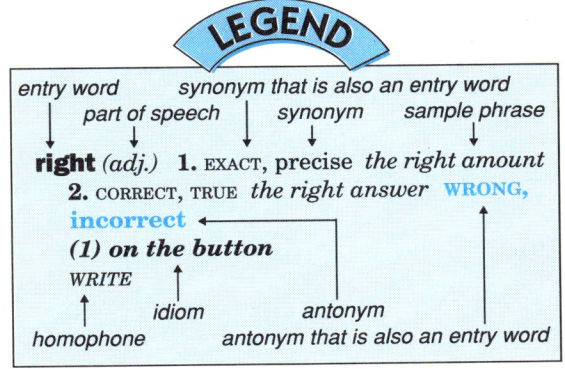

droop *(v.)* wither, wilt, FADE, sag, slouch, slump

drop *(v.)* **1.** FALL, TUMBLE, COLLAPSE *drop to the floor* **2.** lower, REDUCE, decline, dwindle, SINK *Car sales may drop.* INCREASE **3.** OMIT, ELIMINATE, discontinue, ABANDON, forsake, DESERT, REJECT *Drop the project from the schedule.* adopt, ACCEPT

drunk *(adj.)* tipsy, inebriated, intoxicated SOBER

dry *(v.)* wither, parch, shrivel WET

dry *(adj.)* parched, barren, waterless, arid, thirsty WET

due *(adj.)* **1.** owed, unpaid, payable, OUTSTANDING, unsatisfied *Pay the amount due.* **2.** PROPER, FIT, suitable, deserved, warranted *He received due punishment for the crime.* **3.** expected, awaited, anticipated, scheduled *The report is due on Friday.*

dull *(adj.)* **1.** blunt, WEAK *a dull knife* **2.** BORING, uninteresting, STALE, trite, COMMON, tedious *a dull movie* INTERESTING, exciting **3.** DIM, flat, DRAB, muted, lackluster *a dull color* BRIGHT, BRILLIANT, luminous

dumb *(adj.)* IGNORANT, STUPID, uneducated, DULL, FOOLISH, idiotic, illiterate, fatuous SMART, BRIGHT, QUICK

dunk *(v.)* dip, plunge, douse, submerge, immerse

duplicate *(n.)* COPY, reproduction, replica, likeness, twin ORIGINAL

duplicate *(v.)* COPY, reproduce, imitate, double, REPEAT

duty *(n.)* **1.** TASK, obligation, responsibility *He felt it was his duty to help the needy.* **2.** tax, toll, CUSTOM *Pay the duty on imported goods.*

dwell *(v.)* LIVE, INHABIT, occupy, STAY, reside, abide

dye *(n.)* pigment, tint, COLOR, STAIN, tinge DIE

dye *(v.)* COLOR, tint, STAIN DIE

Ee

eager *(adj.)* ENTHUSIASTIC, zealous, avid, keen, fervent, ardent reluctant, hesitant

early *(adj.)* **1.** timely, premature *an early arrival* LATE **2.** former, previous, preceding, prior *the early years* latter

earn *(v.)* GAIN, GET, ACQUIRE, merit, WIN, DESERVE

earnest *(adj.)* DETERMINED, ardent, EAGER, fervent, passionate, SINCERE, SERIOUS

ease (n.) 1. REST, repose, QUIET, COMFORT, contentment, HAPPINESS, relaxation, security, well-being *She felt at ease when on vacation.* **discomfort, disquiet, WORRY, vexation, tension** 2. knack, facility, readiness, effortlessness *She completed the test with ease.* **difficulty**

ease (v.) COMFORT, SOOTHE, QUIET, console, relieve, alleviate **worsen, exacerbate**

easy (adj.) SIMPLE, effortless, elementary **DIFFICULT** *a piece of cake*

clue: easy

answer: a piece of cake

eat (v.) DINE, consume, devour, munch, CHEW, nibble, swallow, gobble, gorge **abstain, fast**

echo (v.) REPEAT, REFLECT, resound, IMITATE, mimic, reverberate

edge (n.) BORDER, boundary, LIMIT, brink, brim, RIM, lip, SIDE, verge, margin **CENTER, MIDDLE**

educate (v.) TEACH, INSTRUCT, TRAIN, discipline, EXPLAIN, inform, cultivate

effect (n.) RESULT, consequence, issue, outcome **CAUSE**

effect (v.) PRODUCE, realize, accomplish, induce **CAUSE**

effort (n.) 1. TASK, chore, STRUGGLE, STRAIN *a physical effort* 2. ATTEMPT, trial, endeavor, undertaking, venture *the athlete's best effort*

elaborate (adj.) 1. decorated, ornate, detailed, intricate *an elaborate design* **PLAIN** 2. COMPLICATED, involved, DIFFICULT *He tackled the elaborate problem.* **SIMPLE**

elegant (adj.) refined, GRACEFUL, polished, FINE, genteel **CLUMSY, unpolished**

elevate (v.) 1. RAISE, LIFT, hoist *Elevate the crane.* **lower, deflate, depress** 2. promote, upgrade, advance, BOOST, heighten *elevate to a higher-paying job* **demote, downgrade, lower**

eliminate (v.) OMIT, REMOVE, expel, exclude, abolish, cancel **INCLUDE**

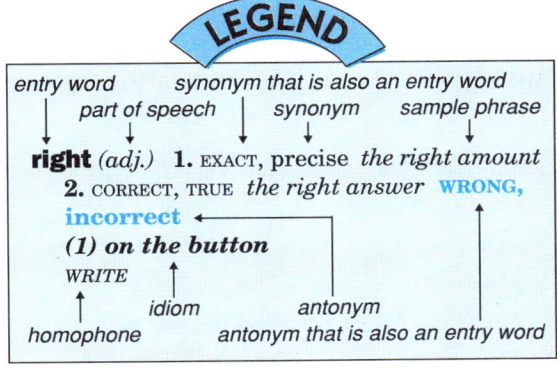

embarrass (v.) SHAME, HUMILIATE, degrade, mortify, abash *put down, cause to lose face*

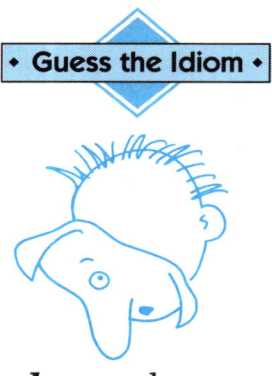

• Guess the Idiom •

clue: embarrass

answer: cause to lose face

emergency (n.) crisis, dilemma, PROBLEM, predicament, difficulty

emotion (n.) FEELING, passion, sentiment, impression

employ (v.) 1. HIRE, engage, CONTRACT, enlist, sign up *employ students for the summer* 2. USE, utilize, wield, apply *employ a new tool for road building*

empty (adj.) 1. unfilled *an empty glass* FULL 2. vacant, uninhabited, deserted, void *an empty house* occupied 3. BARE, BLANK, desolate, devoid, barren *an empty landscape* lush

enclose (v.) SURROUND, encircle, envelop, WRAP, encompass

encounter (n.) 1. meeting, joining, rendezvous, appointment *She had a chance encounter with a friend.* 2. BATTLE, conflict, FIGHT, CONTEST, clash, bout, FEUD *an encounter with the enemy*

encounter (v.) MEET, confront, FACE AVOID, MISS *run across, stumble upon*

encourage (v.) 1. hearten, COMFORT, ASSURE, reassure, revitalize, INSPIRE, embolden *They encouraged the runner to finish the race.* DISCOURAGE, dishearten 2. SUPPORT, foster, advocate, advance *encourage recycling* oppose, hinder
(1) give one a shot in the arm

end (n.) 1. LIMIT, boundary *the end of the road* 2. conclusion, finale, outcome, RESULT *the end of the book* beginning 3. GOAL, PURPOSE *the means to an end*

end (v.) STOP, FINISH, lapse, discontinue, COMPLETE, CONCLUDE, CLOSE, CHECK, suspend, arrest, abort, terminate, culminate, annul BEGIN, START, open *pull the plug*

• Guess the Idiom •

clue: end

answer: pull the plug

endanger (v.) RISK, DARE, imperil, jeopardize PROTECT

endless (adj.) boundless, limitless, infinite, continuous limited, finite

enemy (n.) FOE, RIVAL, OPPONENT, competitor, antagonist, opposition, adversary FRIEND

energetic (adj.) vigorous, ACTIVE, vital, spirited, LIVELY inactive, LAZY

energy (n.) SPIRIT, vitality, force, STRENGTH, POWER, MIGHT, efficiency, vigor, vim

enhance (v.) IMPROVE, INCREASE, enrich, APPRECIATE detract

enjoy (v.) LIKE, APPRECIATE
have a ball

enlarge (v.) GROW, bulge, SWELL, INCREASE, EXPAND, EXTEND, amplify, magnify REDUCE

enormous (adj.) HUGE, monstrous, IMMENSE, GIGANTIC, VAST tiny, minute

enough (adj.) plenty, ADEQUATE, sufficient, ample, FULL, SATISFACTORY, abundant, PLENTIFUL wanting, lacking, unsatisfactory

enrage (v.) ANGER, madden, infuriate, inflame, vex, AGGRAVATE, provoke
make one's blood boil

enter (v.) 1. penetrate, INVADE, INTRUDE *Enter the abandoned house.* EXIT, LEAVE 2. inscribe, register, RECORD, INTRODUCE *Enter the information into the computer.* ERASE, delete
(1) set foot in

entertain (v.) AMUSE, PLEASE, CHEER, divert bore

enthusiasm (n.) eagerness, INTEREST, fervor, passion, ZEAL apathy

enthusiastic (adj.) EAGER, avid, passionate, fervent, zealous, ardent, keen, vehement reluctant
all fired up

entire (adj.) WHOLE, COMPLETE, FULL, intact partial, INCOMPLETE

environment (n.) surrounding, atmosphere, neighborhood, scene, circumstances

envy (n.) jealousy, resentment, covetousness, malice, SPITE

envy (v.) covet, begrudge

episode (n.) occurrence, incident, circumstance, happening, EVENT, occasion

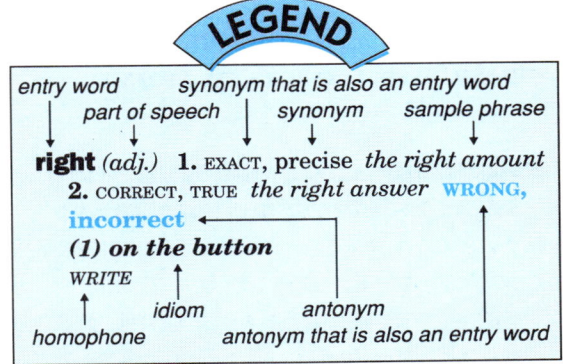

equal (adj.) 1. LIKE, ALIKE, SAME, IDENTICAL, EQUIVALENT, duplicate *They have equal athletic ability.* **unequal, dissimilar** 2. FAIR, impartial, JUST, nondiscriminatory, unbiased *The judge gave equal consideration to both people.* **inequitable, unfair**

equip (v.) FURNISH, PROVIDE, arm, rig, SUPPLY, prepare

equipment (n.) gear, apparatus, implement, paraphernalia

equivalent (adj.) EQUAL, SAME, matching, ALIKE, identical, interchangeable, synonymous **unequivalent, unequal, dissimilar, DIFFERENT**

erase (v.) delete, REMOVE, CANCEL, obliterate, nullify, annul ADD

erode (v.) corrode, WEAR, abrade

errand (n.) mission, TASK, CHORE, JOB, duty, assignment

error (n.) MISTAKE, FAULT, shortcoming, failing, fallacy

escape (v.) flee, AVOID, evade, elude, abscond
fly the coop

essential (adj.) NECESSARY, vital, IMPORTANT, fundamental, key, BASIC **unnecessary, unrequired**

establish (v.) 1. found, originate, START *establish a colony in the New World* 2. PROVE, SUPPORT, substantiate, verify *He will establish his argument before we ask questions.*
(2) *lay the foundation*

estimate (n.) 1. approximation, GUESS *His estimate is that the bike is worth about $200.* 2. appraisal, valuation, PRICE *The mechanic will give us an estimate to repair the damage.*
(1) *a ballpark figure*

estimate (v.) value, appraise, assess, COUNT, APPROXIMATE, round, round off, reckon, calculate

evacuate (v.) LEAVE, ABANDON, DESERT, relinquish FILL, occupy

• Guess the Idiom •

clue: escape

answer: fly the coop

even *(adj.)* **1.** SMOOTH, LEVEL, FLAT, HORIZONTAL *an even surface* **2.** CALM, placid, unruffled *an even temper* **3.** STEADY, REGULAR, CONSISTENT, unchanging, CONSTANT, unvarying, uniform, monotonous *an even flow of water* **irregular** **4.** EQUAL, EQUIVALENT, LIKE *an even score* **uneven, unequal, disparate**

event *(n.)* happening, occasion, occurrence, performance, EPISODE, opportunity, EXPERIENCE, affair, INCIDENT

evidence *(n.)* PROOF, testimony, facts

evil *(adj.)* BAD, WICKED, sinful, sinister, DISHONEST, CROOKED, shady, CORRUPT, IMMORAL, villainous, depraved, unprincipled, unscrupulous **GOOD, MORAL**

exact *(adj.)* CORRECT, precise, ACCURATE, absolute **inexact, APPROXIMATE**
to the letter

exaggerate *(v.)* overstate, MAGNIFY, ENLARGE, amplify **understate**
make a mountain out of a molehill, blow out of proportion

examine *(v.)* INSPECT, analyze, scan, INVESTIGATE, EXPLORE, SEARCH, probe, scrutinize
go over with a fine-tooth comb

• Guess the Idiom •

clue: examine

answer: go over with a fine-tooth comb

example *(n.)* SAMPLE, model, PATTERN, specimen, standard, norm, paradigm

exceed *(v.)* **1.** BEAT, surpass, excel, outpace, top *The cyclist exceeds her opponent by half a mile.* **2.** dominate, outdo *This trial run exceeds my ability.*
(1) leave in the dust

excellent *(adj.)* GREAT, FINE, superior, SUPERB, SPLENDID, MARVELOUS, CHOICE, admirable, EXTRAORDINARY **mediocre, INFERIOR, ORDINARY**

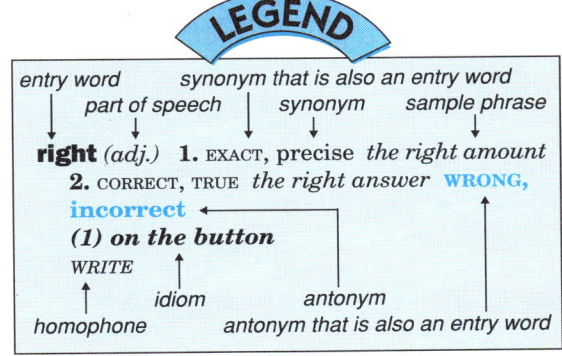

exchange (v.) TRADE, swap, barter, SUBSTITUTE, interchange

excite (v.) stimulate, provoke, ENCOURAGE, URGE, incite, animate bore

exclaim (v.) YELL, SHOUT, CALL, DECLARE, blurt out

exclude (v.) BAR, prohibit, OMIT, disallow, FORBID, banish, REJECT, spurn, blackball, DROP INCLUDE

excuse (n.) REASON, plea, apology, DEFENSE, justification

excuse (v.) 1. FORGIVE, PARDON, exempt, condone *Please excuse the mistake.* REWARD, PRAISE, PUNISH 2. FREE, RELEASE *The teacher will excuse us from class.* detain
(1) look the other way

exhaust (v.) 1. expend, USE, DRAIN, consume, SPEND, FINISH *exhaust the food supply* replenish 2. weaken, FATIGUE, wind, tire, WEAR, tax, sap, strain *The runner exhausted himself.* invigorate, revive
(1) scrape the bottom of the barrel

exhibit (n.) exhibition, fair, DISPLAY, SHOW, presentation, exposition, performance, spectacle

exhibit (v.) DISPLAY, SHOW, DEMONSTRATE, PRESENT, disclose

exist (v.) BE, LIVE, subsist, SURVIVE, BREATHE, abide

exit (n.) DOOR, gate entrance

exit (v.) LEAVE, GO, DEPART, MOVE, migrate, emigrate ENTER

expand (v.) 1. STRETCH, ENLARGE, INCREASE, SWELL, dilate, distend *Expand the size of the vegetable garden.* CONTRACT 2. DEVELOP, INCREASE, elaborate, STRENGTHEN, SPREAD, accelerate *expand the business* REDUCE, DECREASE

expect (v.) anticipate, await, HOPE

expensive (adj.) costly, DEAR, pricey CHEAP, INEXPENSIVE

experience (n.) 1. happening, EVENT *a horrible experience* 2. PRACTICE, KNOWLEDGE, SKILL, background *He has experience teaching.*

expert (n.) authority, master, veteran, specialist BEGINNER, novice

expert (adj.) ABLE, experienced, masterful, skillful, competent, deft, proficient amateurish, inept

explain (v.) 1. DESCRIBE, DEFINE, clarify, interpret, TRANSLATE *He explained the assignment to his students.* 2. SOLVE, decipher, decode, resolve *Try to explain the puzzle.*
(1) spell out

explode (v.) BURST, detonate, rupture, erupt

explore (v.) SEARCH, INVESTIGATE, probe, INSPECT, EXAMINE

expose (v.) 1. UNCOVER, BARE *expose the wound to the air* COVER, HIDE 2. DISCOVER, disclose, reveal *expose the truth*

express (v.) SPEAK, utter, STATE, TELL, DECLARE

extend (v.) 1. STRETCH, REACH, EXPAND, elongate *extend a cord* contract, condense 2. lengthen, prolong *extend a rehearsal* shorten

extinct (adj.) DEAD, defunct, finished, gone, ended, vanished living

extra (adj.) additional, surplus, SPARE, reserve, remnant, UNNECESSARY, redundant, excessive, needless, superfluous

extraordinary (adj.) 1. UNUSUAL, uncommon, RARE, ODD, peculiar, bizarre *an extraordinary event* commonplace, ORDINARY 2. striking, remarkable, amazing, astonishing, glorious, miraculous, wondrous *the extraordinary beauty of nature* 3. noteworthy, eminent, IMPORTANT, impressive, exceptional *recognized for one's extraordinary talent*

Ff

fabulous (adj.) MARVELOUS, SUPERB, GREAT, WONDERFUL, amazing, astounding, remarkable, exceptional, legendary

fact (n.) TRUTH, reality, certainty fiction

fade (v.) 1. discolor, pale, bleach *The book's paper faded over time.* 2. weaken, wither, DIE *The flowers faded in the sun.*

fail (v.) 1. flunk, bomb *The student failed the class.* SUCCEED, triumph 2. DISAPPOINT, neglect *fail his friends* 3. weaken, decline, deteriorate *Her health failed.*

failure (n.) 1. DEFEAT, frustration, BLUNDER, ERROR, SLIP *the failure of a business* SUCCESS 2. loser, lemon, dud *a failure in life* 3. delinquency, negligence, default, oversight, dereliction *failure to respond to the summons*

faint (v.) swoon, COLLAPSE, crumple, DROP

faint (adj.) 1. DIM, PALE, faded, muted, blurred, fuzzy, muffled, mild *a faint signal* bright 2. dizzy, woozy, FEEBLE *a faint feeling*

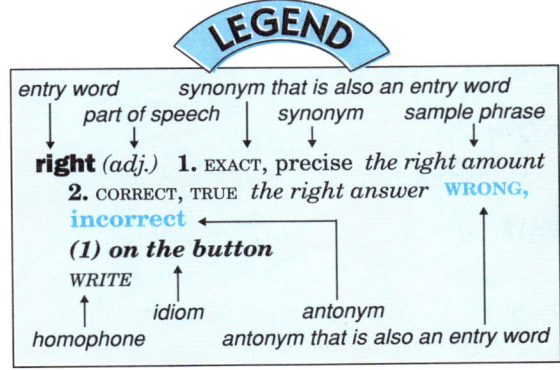

fair (n.) exhibition, gathering, exposition, bazaar, FESTIVAL, carnival
FARE

fair (adj.) **1.** JUST, unbiased, RIGHT, HONEST, truthful, STRAIGHT, upright, SOUND, lawful, reasonable, impartial, equitable, neutral, rational, virtuous, diligent, conscientious, scrupulous *a fair verdict* **unfair 2.** sunny *fair weather* **RAINY 3.** BEAUTIFUL *a fair maiden* **UGLY 4.** LIGHT *a fair complexion* **DARK**
FARE

fairy (n.) elf, pixie, sprite, naiad, nymph

faith (n.) **1.** belief, TRUST, CONFIDENCE *The jurors showed faith in the judge.* **DOUBT 2.** creed, religion, belief, doctrine, persuasion, denomination *free to worship in one's faith*

faithful (adj.) trustworthy, LOYAL, TRUE, DEVOTED **unfaithful, traitorous**

fake (n.) fraud, forgery, imitation, sham, IMPOSTOR, charlatan **original**

fake (adj.) ARTIFICIAL, FALSE, synthetic, unreal, IMAGINARY, unnatural, fraudulent, bogus, counterfeit, spurious **REAL, authentic**

fall (v.) **1.** DROP, plunge, DESCEND, topple, TUMBLE *fall from the cliff* **2.** overturn, COLLAPSE *The government in power will fall.* **3.** DECREASE, SINK, diminish, REDUCE, subside *The temperature will fall.* **INCREASE**

false (adj.) **1.** UNTRUE, incorrect, WRONG, erroneous, inaccurate *The rumor I heard was false.* **TRUE, factual 2.** counterfeit, FAKE, bogus, spurious *a false gem* **GENUINE, authentic**

fame (n.) renown, HONOR, GLORY, repute, distinction, eminence **obscurity**

familiar (adj.) CLOSE, FRIENDLY, intimate, COMMON, well-known **unfamiliar**

family (n.) relatives, kin, ancestors, clan, tribe

famous (adj.) celebrated, well-known, popular, noted, notable, renowned, distinguished, eminent, illustrious, prominent **unknown**

fan (n.) admirer, follower, supporter, enthusiast, devotee

fancy (adj.) **1.** decorated, ELABORATE, ornate, embellished *a fancy sweater* **PLAIN 2.** ELEGANT, FINE, lavish, refined *a fancy restaurant*

fantastic (adj.) **1.** INCREDIBLE, WONDERFUL, MARVELOUS *That was a fantastic concert.* **2.** fictitious, fictional, fanciful, IMAGINARY, unreal, unbelievable, incredible, farfetched *a fantastic tale* **realistic, ORDINARY**

far *(adj.)* remote, distant, removed NEAR, CLOSE

fascinate *(v.)* CHARM, enchant, DELIGHT, intrigue, transfix

fashion *(n.)* STYLE, trend, mode, CUSTOM

fashion *(v.)* MAKE, BUILD, CONSTRUCT, PRODUCE, CREATE, FORM, SHAPE

fast *(adj.)* **1.** QUICK, RAPID, swift, speedy, fleeting *a fast swimmer* SLOW **2.** SUDDEN, INSTANT *a fast reaction*

fast *(adv.)* **1.** rapidly, swiftly, speedily, quickly *Walk fast.* **2.** suddenly, instantly *happen fast* **3.** tightly *Hold fast to the rope.*

fasten *(v.)* **1.** TIE, hook, clasp, ATTACH, JOIN, SECURE, FIX, bind *Fasten the pin to the blouse.* unfasten, undo **2.** CONCENTRATE, FOCUS, direct, train *Fasten your mind on the lesson.*

fat *(adj.)* plump, CHUBBY, chunky, portly, stocky, stout, HUSKY, burly, obese, corpulent, rotund SKINNY, THIN

fatal *(adj.)* DEADLY, lethal, murderous, ruinous, disastrous life-giving, beneficial

fatigue *(n.)* weariness, exhaustion, drowsiness, ENERGY, vitality

fault *(n.)* **1.** DEFECT, blemish, flaw *Repair the fault in the plumbing.* **2.** ERROR, MISTAKE, blame, guilt, offense *It's not my fault.*

favor *(n.)* **1.** KINDNESS, deed, benefit, HELP, SUPPORT *Will you do me a favor?* **2.** regard, admiration, esteem, RESPECT *The principal held the student in good favor.* disfavor

favor *(v.)* PREFER, APPROVE

favorite *(adj.)* preferred, DEAR, pet, esteemed, beloved, adored, cherished
the apple of one's eye

• Guess the Idiom •

clue: favorite

answer: the apple of one's eye

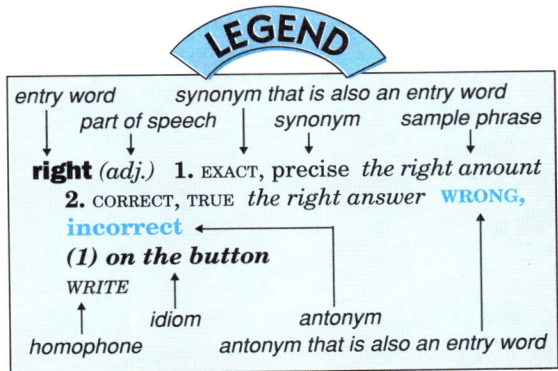

fear *(n.)* **1.** FRIGHT, dismay, terror, HORROR, ALARM, panic, apprehension *control one's fear* **fearlessness, COURAGE 2.** phobia, distaste, DREAD, aversion *He has a fear of the dark.*
(1) cold feet

• Guess the Idiom •

clue: fear

answer: cold feet

fearless *(adj.)* BRAVE, BOLD, DARING, courageous, intrepid, undaunted **COWARDLY, chicken**

fee *(n.)* **1.** CHARGE, BILL, toll, fare, payment *He paid a fee to enter the zoo.* **2.** REWARD, compensation *She charged a fee to paint the house.*

feeble *(adj.)* **1.** WEAK, frail, infirm, DELICATE, sickly, unhealthy *He was feeble after his illness.* **2.** ineffective, futile, USELESS, hopeless *A feeble attempt is likely to fail.*

feed *(v.)* nourish, nurture, nurse **starve**

feel *(v.)* **1.** TOUCH, HANDLE, grope *Feel the softness.* **2.** SENSE, perceive, UNDERSTAND, EXPERIENCE *Feel the heat.*

feeling *(n.)* EMOTION, sensation, impression, sentiment

fellow *(n.)* MAN, chap, guy, MATE, COMPANION, comrade

ferocious *(adj.)* WILD, fierce, SAVAGE, VIOLENT, BRUTAL, barbarous, bestial **GENTLE, TAME, MILD**

festival *(n.)* feast, holiday, celebration, CEREMONY, rite, ritual

feud *(n.)* QUARREL, argument, dispute, spat, FIGHT, squabble

fight *(n.)* QUARREL, BATTLE, argument, dispute, clash, conflict, tussle, scuffle, outbreak, fray, BRAWL, RIOT, row, fracas

fight *(v.)* **1.** QUARREL, DISAGREE, squabble, quibble, FEUD, wrangle, bicker, BATTLE, BOX, STRUGGLE, wrestle, spar, BRAWL *a fight for freedom and equality* **2.** RESIST, COMBAT, oppose, withstand *fight an illness*
(1) take up arms

• Guess the Idiom •

clue: fight

answer: take up arms

figure *(n.)* **1.** FORM, SHAPE, outline, configuration, PATTERN *a beautiful figure* **2.** numeral, digit *Write the figure on the line.* **3.** sum, TOTAL, AMOUNT, PRICE, COST *Calculate the final figures.* **4.** diagram, PICTURE, representation, IMAGE *Refer to Figure A in your math book.*

figure *(v.)* CALCULATE, COUNT, reckon, cipher, TOTAL, appraise, assess

fill *(v.)* **1.** LOAD, PACK, heap, pile, stuff, stock *Fill the truck with supplies.* **2.** SATISFY, fulfill, meet *Fill the requirements of the class.*

filthy *(adj.)* **1.** DIRTY, NASTY, FOUL, squalid, sordid, slovenly, contaminated, polluted *a filthy room* **CLEAN** **2.** obscene, indecent, foul, DIRTY, vile, sordid, smutty, offensive *filthy language*

final *(adj.)* LAST, latest, conclusive, closing, ultimate, terminal **FIRST, initial**

find *(v.)* LOCATE, DISCOVER, UNCOVER, unearth, EXPOSE, DETECT, ascertain **LOSE, misplace**

fine *(n.)* penalty, punishment, FEE

fine *(adj.)* **1.** EXCELLENT, admirable, select *He did a fine job.* **2.** TINY, minute *fine grains of sand*

finish *(v.)* DO, COMPLETE, accomplish, ACHIEVE, REACH, END, STOP, STAY, CEASE, desist, terminate, arrest **BEGIN**

fire *(n.)* blaze, flame, flare, GLOW, BURN

firm *(adj.)* **1.** fixed, SET, unchanging, unyielding, definite, STEADY, steadfast, STABLE *a firm decision* **fluctuating, wavering** **2.** solid, HARD *firm muscles* **SOFT**

first *(adj.)* **1.** beginning, earliest, leading, FRONT *the first chapter of the book* **LAST** **2.** ORIGINAL, initial, novel, NEW, primary *the first Thanksgiving*

fit *(n.)* outburst, tantrum, seizure

fit *(adj.)* **1.** APPROPRIATE, suitable, pertinent, relevant *a house fit for a king* **2.** HEALTHY *feeling fit*

fix *(v.)* **1.** MEND, REPAIR, PATCH *Let's fix the car.* **2.** restore, IMPROVE, HEAL, CURE, remedy *The doctor will fix the broken bone.* **BREAK, DESTROY** **3.** FASTEN, ATTACH *Fix the picture to the wall.*

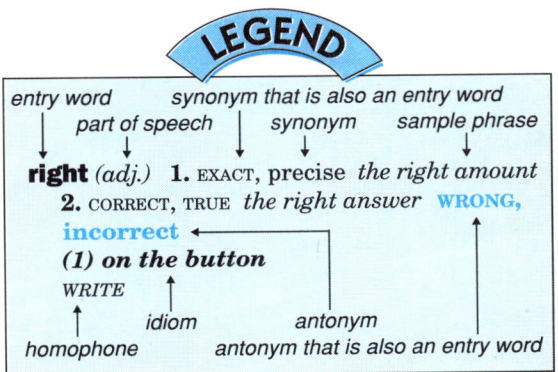

flag (*n.*) pendant, banner

flat (*adj.*) **1.** horizontal, prone, prostrate, recumbent *Lie flat on the ground.* **2.** LEVEL, SMOOTH, even, flush *a flat surface* ROUGH

flatter (*v.*) PRAISE, humor, COMPLIMENT, cajole, laud, extol CRITICIZE
lay it on thick

flavor (*n.*) TASTE, season

flexible (*adj.*) **1.** bendable, supple, pliable, pliant *a flexible hose* RIGID **2.** adaptable, EASY, affable, versatile *a flexible employee*

flimsy (*adj.*) **1.** WEAK, frail, FRAGILE, SHABBY, ramshackle, rickety, DILAPIDATED, SORRY *a flimsy ladder* STRONG **2.** POOR, immaterial, frivolous, trivial, INADEQUATE, worthless *a flimsy argument* SUBSTANTIAL **3.** THIN, SHEER, LIGHT *a flimsy fabric* THICK

fling (*v.*) THROW, CAST, TOSS, PITCH, hurl, sling, heave

floor (*n.*) ground, deck, STORY

flow (*v.*) stream, RUN, gush, surge, cascade, spout

fluster (*v.*) CONFUSE, rattle, disconcert, baffle, startle

fly (*v.*) soar, glide, hover

foe (*n.*) ENEMY, adversary, OPPONENT, antagonist, RIVAL, contender FRIEND, **teammate**

follow (*v.*) **1.** pursue, track, trail, CHASE, HUNT *Follow the criminal's trail.* **2.** SUCCEED, ensue *A discussion will follow the lecture.* **3.** OBEY, heed, comply, submit, OBSERVE *Follow the rules.* DISOBEY

food (*n.*) fare, rations, provisions, nourishment

fool (*n.*) simpleton, dunce, ninny, nincompoop, blockhead, buffoon, booby, moron, dullard, ignoramus, bore, cretin, imbecile, oaf

fool (*v.*) CHEAT, hoax, DECEIVE, dupe, delude
pull the wool over one's eyes

foolish (*adj.*) SILLY, STUPID, RIDICULOUS, senseless, idiotic, ABSURD, unreasonable, shallow, daft, fatuous, frivolous, trifling, imprudent, inept WISE, **sensible**

forbid (*v.*) BAN, prohibit, disallow, hinder, DENY, REFUSE, veto, taboo ALLOW, PERMIT

force (*v.*) DRIVE, URGE, compel, coerce, oblige, impel, constrain

foreign (*adj.*) alien, STRANGE, unfamiliar, peculiar, exotic, outlandish **native**

foreigner (*n.*) STRANGER, alien, outsider, immigrant, newcomer

forget (*v.*) disregard, neglect REMEMBER
draw a blank, slip one's mind

forgive *(v.)* EXCUSE, PARDON, RELEASE, OVERLOOK, CLEAR, acquit, absolve BLAME, CHARGE
bury the hatchet, let off the hook

form *(n.)* **1.** FIGURE, SHAPE, structure *a carved form of Benjamin Franklin* **2.** KIND, SORT, METHOD *a form of punishment* **3.** STYLE, MANNER, mode *His tennis game is in good form.*

form *(v.)* MAKE, SHAPE, FIGURE, mold, sculpt, contrive

formal *(adj.)* prim, dignified, precise, solemn, ceremonial **informal, casual**

fortunate *(adj.)* LUCKY, blessed, favorable
on top of the heap

fortune *(n.)* **1.** LUCK, CHANCE, FATE, happenstance, serendipity *It was her good fortune to find her lost puppy.* **misfortune**
2. WEALTH, riches, affluence, opulence *He left his fortune to the children.*
(1) *how the ball bounces, how the cookie crumbles*

foul *(adj.)* **1.** decayed, stinking, ROTTEN, NASTY, vile, rancid, putrid *foul meat* FRESH
2. stormy, RAINY *foul weather* FOWL

fraction *(n.)* PART, portion, fragment, PIECE, segment, division WHOLE

fracture *(n.)* BREAK, CRACK, rupture, cleavage, fissure

fracture *(v.)* BREAK, CRACK, rupture, SPLIT, cleave, shatter

fragile *(adj.)* frail, WEAK, DELICATE, tenuous **STRONG, durable**

free *(v.)* RELEASE, untie, liberate, discharge, extricate **constrain, imprison**

free *(adj.)* **1.** gratis, gratuitous, complimentary *a free sample* **costly** **2.** emancipated, untied, LOOSE, liberated, discharged, unrestricted, unfettered, INDEPENDENT *a free citizen* **imprisoned, incarcerated, bound**
(1) *on the house*

freedom *(n.)* **1.** LIBERTY, liberation, release, independence, emancipation, autonomy *freedom from slavery* **2.** RIGHT, privilege, LICENSE, authorization *the freedom to make one's own decisions*

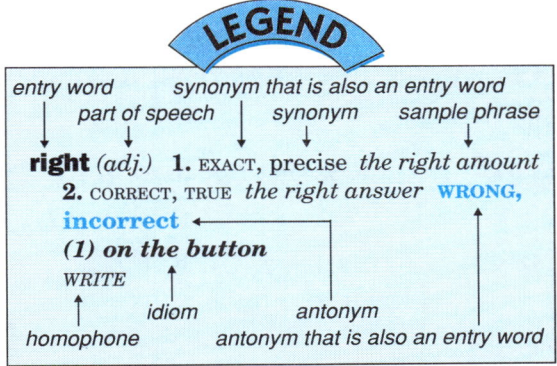

freeze *(v.)* **1.** CHILL, ice, congeal, numb, refrigerate *Freeze the meat.* **2.** STOP, HESITATE *Freeze in your tracks.*

frequent *(v.)* hang out, hang around, VISIT, haunt, ATTEND **avoid**

frequent *(adj.)* **1.** COMMON, OFTEN, customary, everyday, daily *a frequent sight* **RARE, uncommon** **2.** recurrent, repeated, PERSISTENT, numerous *frequent visits to the hospital*

fresh *(adj.)* **1.** NEW, sweet *fresh bread* **OLD, STALE** **2.** PURE *fresh air* **3.** vigorous, HEALTHY *fresh from a good night's sleep* **4.** NEW, novel, ORIGINAL, recent *Are there any fresh data from the lab?*

friend *(n.)* buddy, pal, MATE, chum, COMPANION, partner, comrade, associate, crony **ENEMY, FOE, OPPONENT**

friendly *(adj.)* SOCIAL, welcoming, CHEERFUL, personable, hospitable, affable, amicable, congenial **UNFRIENDLY, belligerent**

fright *(n.)* FEAR, ALARM, TERROR, dismay, PANIC

frighten *(v.)* SCARE, ALARM, SHOCK, terrify, daunt, THREATEN, menace, intimidate

front *(n.)* face, facade, fore, anterior **BACK**

frown *(v.)* pout, scowl, mope, grieve, SULK, despair **SMILE**

frustrate *(v.)* **1.** IRRITATE, BAFFLE, DISCOURAGE, torment, tantalize *Her actions frustrate me.* **2.** BLOCK, foil, thwart, DEFEAT, annul, nullify *The new law frustrated his plans.* ENCOURAGE
(2) take the wind out of one's sails

fulfill *(v.)* **1.** COMPLETE, FINISH *fulfill the requirements for graduation* **2.** realize, accomplish, ACHIEVE *fulfill a dream* **3.** OBEY, OBSERVE, FOLLOW, MIND, heed, acknowledge, RESPECT *fulfill the letter of the law*

full *(adj.)* **1.** filled, loaded, stuffed *the full glass* EMPTY **2.** COMPLETE, total, WHOLE, ENTIRE *the full story* INCOMPLETE

fun *(n.)* cheer, glee, merriment, amusement, enjoyment, mirth

funny *(adj.)* HUMOROUS, laughable, amusing, entertaining, comical, WITTY, droll, HILARIOUS, farcical, ludicrous, jovial SAD, BORING, DULL

furious *(adj.)* ANGRY, raging, infuriated, fuming, wrathful, irate, frantic CALM, **unruffled**

furnish *(v.)* GIVE, SUPPLY, PROVIDE, EQUIP, outfit, stock

fuss *(n.)* **1.** WORRY, disquiet, unrest *a lot of fuss over what to wear* **2.** ARGUMENT, dispute, QUARREL, squabble *They had a fuss over who was right.*

fuss *(v.)* COMPLAIN, fret, WORRY
make a mountain out of a molehill

fussy *(adj.)* **1.** fidgety, fretful, RESTLESS, IMPATIENT, cranky *Calm the fussy baby.* **2.** particular, choosy, DIFFICULT, CRITICAL, finicky, discriminating, fastidious *a fussy eater*

Gg

gadget *(n.)* appliance, contraption, INSTRUMENT, DEVICE, TOOL

gain *(v.)* **1.** GET, ACQUIRE, OBTAIN, REACH, attain, EARN, WIN, secure *gain knowledge* **2.** profit, IMPROVE, benefit, ADVANCE *gain understanding from the experience*

gallant *(adj.)* BRAVE, valiant, courageous, heroic, intrepid, noble, chivalrous, courteous, dashing

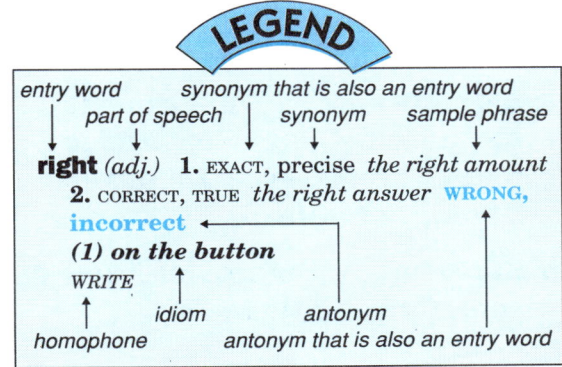

gamble (n.) RISK, CHANCE, speculation, venture *a shot in the dark*
GAMBOL

gamble (v.) 1. RISK, BET, wager *gamble at a casino* 2. speculate *I'll gamble she'll show up at the dance tonight.*
GAMBOL

game (n.) 1. MATCH, CONTEST, COMPETITION, sport, amusement, diversion, recreation *Play the game.* 2. PREY, quarry *hunting for big game*

gang (n.) GROUP, MOB, PACK, crew, BAND, clan, PARTY, herd, clique

garbage (n.) TRASH, rubbish, WASTE, litter, REFUSE, JUNK, salvage, debris

gather (v.) COLLECT, PICK, ASSEMBLE, accumulate, harvest, reap, muster, garner SCATTER *round up*

gaze (v.) STARE, gape, regard

general (adj.) 1. COMMON, USUAL, universal, conventional, prevalent, POPULAR *general opinion* 2. VAGUE, inexact, indefinite, abstract *a general explanation of how it works* specific

generous (adj.) giving, charitable, unselfish, KIND, benevolent, philanthropic STINGY, CHEAP *a heart of gold*

genius (n.) brilliance, intelligence, ingenuity, TALENT

gentle (adj.) HARMLESS, MILD, docile, INNOCENT, innocuous, inoffensive VIOLENT, ROUGH

genuine (adj.) 1. authentic, REAL, actual, valid, guaranteed *a genuine diamond* IMITATION, FAKE 2. SINCERE, heartfelt, natural, HONEST *genuine concern*

get (v.) 1. fetch, procure, net, GAIN, annex, requisition *Go and get the tickets.* GIVE, relinquish 2. RECEIVE, ACQUIRE, OBTAIN, EARN, CLEAR, attain, accomplish *We need to get a computer.* LOSE

ghastly (adj.) 1. HORRIBLE, frightening, hideous, grisly, horrendous *a ghastly accident* 2. shocking, unforgivable, odious, appalling *a ghastly deed that hurt me*

ghost (n.) SPIRIT, phantom, specter, vision, spook, apparition

giant (n.) MONSTER, behemoth, ogre, colossus

giant (adj.) HUGE, ENORMOUS, GIGANTIC, VAST, monstrous, gargantuan, colossal TINY, SMALL

gift (n.) 1. PRESENT, PRIZE, AWARD *a birthday gift* 2. DONATION, gratuity, offering, blessing, legacy, bequest *a generous gift of money* 3. talent, SKILL, ABILITY, aptitude *She was born with a gift for music.*

gigantic (adj.) GIANT, HUGE, ENORMOUS, IMMENSE, jumbo, colossal, staggering, king-size SMALL, TINY, minute

give *(v.)* **1.** grant, PRESENT, donate, CONTRIBUTE, DISTRIBUTE, endow, bestow, confer, allot, allocate *Give her my skates.* TAKE, RECEIVE **2.** SUPPLY, PROVIDE, FURNISH *give advice* GET **3.** BUDGE, MOVE *The door would not give.*

glad *(adj.)* HAPPY, pleased, contented, delighted, CHEERFUL, tickled, elated, jubilant UNHAPPY

gloom *(n.)* **1.** sadness, depression, melancholy, SORROW, woe, doldrums, grief *the gloom caused by separation* **2.** darkness, SHADE, shadow, dusk, murkiness *the gloom of a rainy day*

gloomy *(adj.)* **1.** DARK, dusky, shadowy, DIM, DINGY *a gloomy day* **2.** cheerless, UNHAPPY, depressed, SAD, GLUM, DISMAL, melancholy *a gloomy mood*

glory *(n.)* FAME, HONOR, renown, repute

glow *(v.)* SHINE, gleam, glimmer, blaze

glum *(adj.)* GLOOMY, sullen, MOODY, grumpy, dejected, pessimistic

go *(v.)* ADVANCE, MOVE, CONTINUE, LEAVE, TRAVEL, DEPART, proceed, PASS, progress, BUDGE, STIR STAY, COME, ARRIVE, REMAIN
beat it

goal *(n.)* AIM, PURPOSE, objective, target, intent, intention, OBJECT, END, DESTINATION

good *(adj.)* **1.** SATISFACTORY, ADEQUATE, alright, acceptable *The shoes are a good fit.* **2.** MORAL, upright, virtuous, PLEASANT *a good person* BAD **3.** CORRECT, fitting, APPROPRIATE, JUST, valid, SOUND, USEFUL *a good answer*

gorgeous *(adj.)* BEAUTIFUL, ATTRACTIVE, ravishing, dazzling, radiant, impressive, MAGNIFICENT, resplendent UGLY

gossip *(n.)* hearsay, RUMOR, chatter, tattle, scandal

govern *(v.)* LEAD, RULE, reign, CONTROL, MANAGE, COMMAND, oversee
be in the driver's seat

grab *(v.)* seize, clutch, grasp, CATCH, clasp, clench, CAPTURE, snatch

graceful *(adj.)* ELEGANT, tasteful, FINE, refined, cultured, polished, suave, mannerly AWKWARD

grade *(n.)* **1.** CLASS, CATEGORY, DEGREE *a fine grade of meat* **2.** MARK *a good grade on a test* **3.** SLOPE, gradient, incline *an uphill grade*

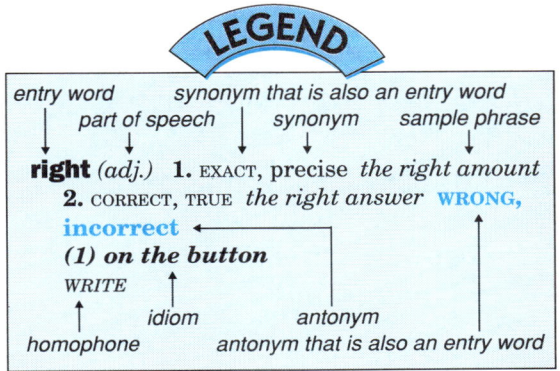

gradual *(adj.)* SLOW, continuous *at a snail's pace*

grand *(adj.)* stately, ROYAL, MAJESTIC, MAGNIFICENT HUMBLE

grateful *(adj.)* THANKFUL, indebted, APPRECIATIVE ungrateful

grave *(n.)* vault, crypt, tomb, sepulcher, catacomb

grave *(adj.)* **1.** solemn, SOBER, staid, sedate *a grave occasion* **2.** SERIOUS, IMPORTANT, weighty, CRITICAL *a grave piece of evidence in court* UNIMPORTANT

great *(adj.)* **1.** LARGE, tremendous *a great monument* LITTLE, SMALL **2.** NOBLE, exalted, mighty, notable, distinguished, eminent *a great leader*
GRATE

greedy *(adj.)* SELFISH, avaricious, rapacious, covetous GENEROUS

greet *(v.)* MEET, WELCOME, address, salute, hail

grief *(n.)* SORROW, woe, sadness, anguish, MISERY, heartache, AGONY, REGRET, DISTRESS

grim *(adj.)* **1.** HORRIBLE, AWFUL, hideous, appalling, dire, dreadful, grisly *a grim task* **2.** stern, HARSH, SEVERE, unyielding *He fought on with grim resolve.*

gross *(adj.)* DISGUSTING, repulsive, loathsome, distasteful, revolting, sickening, CRUDE, offensive, FOUL, lewd honorable

ground *(n.)* land, PLOT, field, meadow, tract

group *(n.)* **1.** BUNCH, SET, bundle, bale, cluster, COLLECTION, store, PILE *a group of stamps* **2.** PARTY, assembly, association, organization, society, club, COMMITTEE, congregation, forum, clan, clique, RING, league, gathering, CROWD, COMPANY, squad, TEAM, BAND, tribe, FAMILY *a group of people*

grow *(v.)* **1.** mature, DEVELOP, evolve, flourish *grow to adulthood* **2.** cultivate, PRODUCE, RAISE *grow crops*

growth *(n.)* INCREASE, enlargement, development, maturation, expansion, extension

grumpy *(adj.)* MOODY, sullen, GLUM, GLOOMY, temperamental, churlish, PESSIMISTIC CHEERFUL

guard *(v.)* PROTECT, WATCH, shield, DEFEND, SUPPORT

guess *(n.)* conjecture, supposition, ESTIMATE

guess *(v.)* ESTIMATE, surmise, PREDICT, RECKON *take a shot at*

guest *(n.)* visitor, caller, COMPANY

guide *(n.)* LEADER, director, pilot, escort

guide *(v.)* **1.** LEAD, DIRECT, pilot, CONDUCT, STEER, SHOW *guide an expedition* mislead **2.** administer, supervise *The teacher guides the students.*
(1) hold the reins

guilty *(adj.)* **1.** RESPONSIBLE, culpable, blameworthy *a guilty criminal* INNOCENT **2.** SORRY, remorseful, regretful, contrite, penitent, repentant *a guilty feeling about not helping*

gun *(n.)* weapon, firearm, pistol, rifle, revolver, carbine, musket

gyp *(v.)* CHEAT, mislead, TRICK, DECEIVE, bamboozle, swindle, dupe

Hh

habit *(n.)* CUSTOM, practice, mannerism, tradition, routine, trait, idiosyncrasy

halt *(v.)* **1.** STOP, CEASE, PAUSE *halt at the border* proceed **2.** ARREST, curb, terminate, END, quell *halt the abuse*

handle *(v.)* TOUCH, FEEL, grasp

handsome *(adj.)* good-looking, ATTRACTIVE, becoming UGLY

handy *(adj.)* skillful, CLEVER, dexterous, adroit CLUMSY

hang *(v.)* **1.** suspend, dangle, sling *Hang up your coat.* **2.** ATTACH, hook, tack *Hang the picture on the wall.* **3.** hover, float *The clouds hang over the shore.*

happen *(v.)* arise, occur, befall, ensue, DEVELOP, transpire

happiness *(n.)* JOY, enjoyment, merriment, mirth, bliss, contentment, rapture sadness

happy *(adj.)* **1.** CHEERFUL, GLAD, joyous, MERRY, festive, lighthearted, delighted, jolly, jubilant, ecstatic *He's in a happy mood.* UNHAPPY, SAD, downcast, mournful, sorrowful **2.** contented, satisfied *She's happy with the travel plans.* dissatisfied
(1) walking on air

clue: happy

answer: walking on air

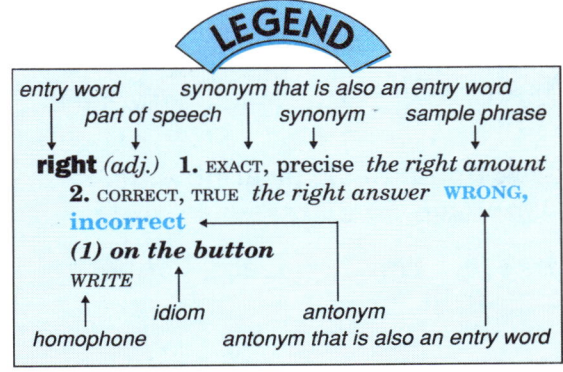

hard *(adj.)* **1.** FIRM, solid, RIGID *a hard surface* SOFT, limp **2.** DIFFICULT, COMPLICATED, COMPLEX, tangled, rigorous, INTENSE, intricate, laborious, arduous, irksome *a hard problem to solve* EASY, SIMPLE **3.** insensitive, unfeeling, callous, severe, stern, HARSH *a hard coach* SENSITIVE, GENTLE, KIND

harm *(n.)* injury, DAMAGE, wrong, wickedness, maltreatment

harm *(v.)* **1.** DAMAGE, sabotage, vandalize *harm the relief supplies* **2.** HURT, INJURE, maltreat, impair, ABUSE, victimize *harm the child*

harmful *(adj.)* DANGEROUS, hurtful, ruinous, destructive, injurious HARMLESS, HELPFUL, beneficial

harmless *(adj.)* INNOCENT, unoffending, unobjectionable, inoffensive HARMFUL, hurtful

harsh *(adj.)* **1.** abrupt, blunt, stern, SEVERE, RUDE, discourteous, unmannerly, gruff, churlish *a harsh voice* **2.** desolate, stark, BARE, barren, RUGGED, BLEAK, EMPTY *The Arctic tundra is a harsh environment.*

hasty *(adj.)* **1.** QUICK, swift, RAPID, fleet, FAST *a hasty eater* SLOW **2.** immediate, prompt, expeditious *a hasty response* delayed

hat *(n.)* cap, headgear, bonnet, helmet, hood

hate *(n.)* malice, rancor, SPITE, resentment, enmity, antagonism LOVE

hate *(v.)* DISLIKE, DESPISE, scorn, spurn, disdain, detest, loathe, abhor, abominate LOVE

hazard *(n.)* DANGER, peril, jeopardy, threat, CHANCE, RISK

heal *(v.)* CURE, restore, revive, IMPROVE, FIX, remedy, recover

healthy *(adj.)* WELL, SOUND, robust, hearty, vigorous ILL

hear *(v.)* LISTEN, heed, ATTEND, harken, regard
learn through the grapevine

♦ Guess the Idiom ♦

clue: hear

answer: learn through the grapevine

heavy *(adj.)* **1.** weighty, bulky, hefty, unwieldy, cumbersome *The weights are too heavy to lift.* LIGHT **2.** DIFFICULT, troublesome, imposing, oppressive, overwhelming, burdensome *The news is heavy.*

help *(n.)* AID, assistance, RELIEF, SUPPORT **hindrance**

help *(v.)* AID, ASSIST, SERVE, SUPPORT, relieve, benefit, abet, ally, COOPERATE **hinder, obstruct, oppose**
lend a hand, pitch in

helper *(n.)* COMPANION, ally, assistant, partner, colleague

helpful *(adj.)* **1.** USEFUL, beneficial, practical, pragmatic, utilitarian *a helpful tool* USELESS **2.** FRIENDLY, neighborly, KIND, benevolent, philanthropic *a helpful neighbor* **unfriendly**

helpless *(adj.)* **1.** WEAK, dependent *A newborn baby is helpless.* INDEPENDENT **2.** powerless, unarmed, vulnerable, unprotected, unguarded *The town was helpless during the storm.* **guarded,** SAFE

hero *(n.)* CHAMPION, victor, winner, idol

hesitate *(v.)* PAUSE, DELAY, waver, DOUBT, demur
drag one's feet

hidden *(adj.)* concealed, covered, masked, unexplained, obscure
CONSPICUOUS, **visible**

hide *(v.)* COVER, CONCEAL, screen, mask, BURY, obscure, DISGUISE **DISCOVER, reveal, disclose, unmask**

high *(adj.)* **1.** TALL, lofty, elevated *a high mountain* LOW **2.** shrill, SHARP, piercing, acute, piping *a high scream* LOW

hilarious *(adj.)* FUNNY, comical, MERRY, mirthful, jolly, jocund

hill *(n.)* SLOPE, incline, SLANT, mound, knoll, gradient

hint *(n.)* SIGN, tip, CLUE, indication, inkling, suggestion
a bug in one's ear

• Guess the Idiom •

clue: hint

answer: a bug in one's ear

hint *(v.)* SUGGEST, MENTION, imply, insinuate, intimate, allude, prompt

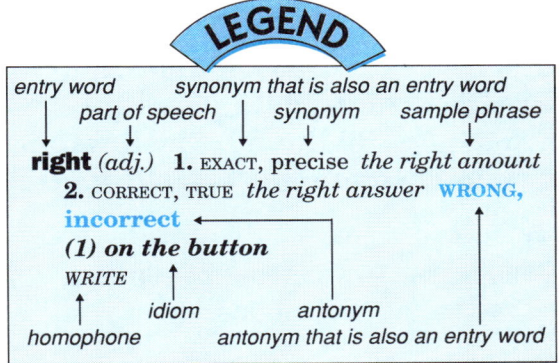

hire *(v.)* USE, EMPLOY, engage, CONTRACT, enlist fire

hit *(v.)* STRIKE, assault, BEAT, WHIP, lash, thrash, flog, ram, pound, whack, smack, collide, smite

hobo *(n.)* tramp, loafer, vagrant, beggar, outcast, vagabond

hold *(v.)* 1. grip, grasp, clutch, clasp, KEEP, BEAR, CARRY, cradle, possess *Hold the camera in your hand.* 2. CONTAIN, STORE, accommodate *What does the box hold?* 3. KEEP, SAVE, STAY, retain, reserve, arrest *Hold back your anger.* 4. convene, ORGANIZE *hold a meeting*

hole *(n.)* 1. pit, WELL, hollow, burrow, lair, cavity *The squirrel dug a hole in the ground.* 2. opening, outlet, aperture, perforation, void *a hole in the wall* WHOLE

hollow *(adj.)* 1. EMPTY, unfilled, excavated, concave, indented, vacant *a hollow tree* 2. FALSE, INSINCERE, hypocritical, deceptive *hollow promises* 3. USELESS, fruitless, profitless, worthless *hollow actions* 4. muffled, DULL, flat *a hollow sound*

holy *(adj.)* RELIGIOUS, spiritual, sacred, blessed, godly, saintly, virtuous, hallowed, consecrated, pious, devout unholy, ungodly

home *(n.)* HOUSE, dwelling, lodging, quarters, apartment, SPACE, abode, residence

honest *(adj.)* truthful, trustworthy, GENUINE, FAIR, MORAL, upright, frank, righteous, reliable, dependable, respectable, honorable, JUST, GOOD, virtuous, diligent, conscientious, scrupulous, reputable DISHONEST, deceitful, unfair
above board

honesty *(n.)* TRUTH, sincerity, frankness, veracity deception

honor *(n.)* integrity, virtue, principle, esteem, regard, admiration, RESPECT, rectitude
a feather in one's cap

• Guess the Idiom •

clue: honor

answer: a feather in one's cap

honor *(v.)* RESPECT, esteem, regard, venerate DISGRACE

hop *(v.)* JUMP, LEAP, SPRING, vault, bound

hope *(n.)* WISH, DESIRE, longing, anticipation, aspiration

hope *(v.)* WISH, EXPECT, DESIRE, anticipate
look on the sunny side

horrible *(adj.)* TERRIBLE, AWFUL, dreadful, dire **WONDERFUL, TERRIFIC**

horrid *(adj.)* frightful, ghastly, alarming, horrifying, hideous, dreadful, gruesome

horror *(n.)* TERROR, FEAR, FRIGHT, DREAD, awe, panic, ALARM

horse *(n.)* steed, charger, mount, nag, pony, stallion, mare, gelding, foal, filly, colt, yearling, equine
HOARSE

hostile *(adj.)* **1.** antagonistic, contrary, adverse, opposed, aggressive, warlike, belligerent *Two hostile countries fought a war.* **2.** UNFRIENDLY, unkind, COLD, MEAN, malicious, malevolent *a hostile look* **KIND, hospitable, FRIENDLY**

hot *(adj.)* **1.** WARM, burning, scorching, blazing, fiery, torrid, sweltering, sizzling *hot to the touch* **COLD, icy** **2.** SPICY, biting, pungent, piquant *a hot chili pepper* **BLAND, MILD**

Go **CRAZY** with **WORDS!** — hot

house *(n.)* HOME, SHELTER, dwelling, apartment, SPACE, lodging, residence, quarters, abode

hug *(v.)* **1.** caress, embrace, snuggle, coddle, CLING, enfold *hug a child* **2.** near, APPROACH *The boats hug the shore.*

huge *(adj.)* tremendous, GIGANTIC, ENORMOUS, VAST, IMMENSE, monstrous, colossal, massive

humble *(adj.)* modest, unassuming, unpretentious **arrogant**

humiliate *(v.)* SHAME, EMBARRASS, mortify, degrade, humble

humorous *(adj.)* FUNNY, amusing, WITTY, comical, laughable, RIDICULOUS **SERIOUS, solemn**

hungry *(adj.)* starving, famished, ravenous **FULL, satiated**

hunt *(n.)* quest, pursuit

hunt *(v.)* pursue, SEARCH, SEEK, stalk, CHASE, FOLLOW, track

hurry *(v.)* **1.** RUSH, hasten, quicken, SPEED, accelerate, RACE, SCURRY, PRESS, hustle *hurry to work* **DELAY, dawdle, LINGER 2.** expedite, precipitate *You cannot hurry the vote count.* **SLOW, prolong**
(1) shake a leg, race against the clock

hurt *(v.)* **1.** INJURE, cripple, wound, BRUISE, mistreat, ABUSE, HARM, disable, maim, mutilate, disfigure *Did you hurt your hand in a fall?* **2.** ACHE, sting, throb, smart *His broken leg hurts.*

husky *(adj.)* **1.** hoarse, grating, rough, HARSH *a husky voice* **2.** STURDY, RUGGED *The man had a husky build.*

hustle *(v.)* **1.** HURRY, RUSH, SPEED, hasten, scurry, DASH *Hustle down the street.* **2.** prompt, URGE, goad, accelerate, pressure, compel, FORCE, coerce *Hustle everyone into the room.*

hut *(n.)* shed, shack, shanty, CABIN, hovel

hysterical *(adj.)* **1.** HILARIOUS, sidesplitting *a hysterical laugh* **2.** MAD, crazed, excitable, raving, frantic, WILD, berserk *hysterical behavior*

Ii

idea *(n.)* **1.** THOUGHT, notion, belief, CONCEPT, OPINION, fancy, PLAN, theory, VIEW, supposition, conception, perception, inspiration, impression *a good idea for a show* **2.** topic, theme, SUBJECT *the main idea of the story*

ideal *(adj.)* perfect, faultless, exemplary **average, normal, typical**

identical *(adj.)* SAME, ALIKE, indistinguishable, DUPLICATE, twin **dissimilar, DIFFERENT, distinctive**

identify *(v.)* **1.** RECOGNIZE, distinguish, discern *identify the lost child* **2.** relate, CONNECT, ally *identify with her feelings*
(2) walk in another's shoes, see through another's eyes

idiot *(n.)* FOOL, dunce, clod, oaf, dolt, buffoon, jester

idle *(adj.)* **1.** LAZY, inactive, sluggish, indolent, dawdling, slothful *an idle person* **industrious, diligent, hardworking, active** **2.** unoccupied, vacant, EMPTY *After the family moved, their house stood idle.* **BUSY** **3.** FOOLISH, vain, UNNECESSARY, unproductive, ineffective, ineffectual *He made an idle attempt to stop the horse as it ran by.*
IDOL

idol *(n.)* **1.** deity, god, IMAGE, STATUE, icon, effigy *worship a false idol* **2.** favorite, HERO, heroine, star, celebrity *a teenage idol*
IDLE

ignite *(v.)* LIGHT, BURN, inflame, kindle **extinguish**

ignorant *(adj.)* uneducated, illiterate, unaware, unconscious, uninformed **educated, knowing, AWARE**
in the dark

ignore *(v.)* disregard, neglect, OVERLOOK, snub, slight, OMIT, DEFY, RESIST, REJECT **COMPREHEND, REALIZE, RECOGNIZE**
bury one's head in the sand

clue: ignore

answer: bury one's head in the sand

ill *(adj.)* **1.** SICK, sickly, ailing, unhealthy, unsound, indisposed, unwell *care for the ill child* **WELL, HEALTHY** **2.** BAD, EVIL, WICKED, WRONG, CORRUPT *ill intentions* **GOOD, respectable**
(1) under the weather

illegal *(adj.)* unlawful, forbidden, criminal, unconstitutional **LEGAL, authorized**
under the table

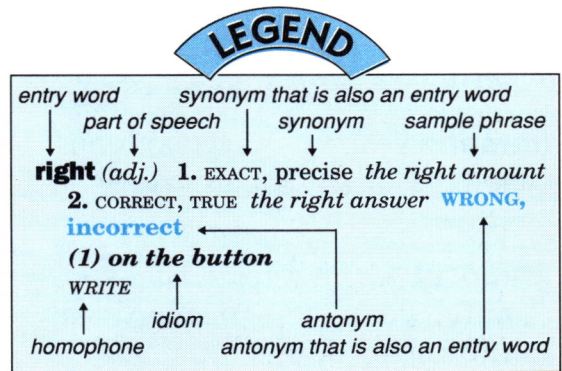

illusion *(n.)* vision, hallucination, mirage, delusion

illustrate *(v.)* **1.** DRAW, PICTURE, portray, depict *illustrate the flowers* **2.** DEMONSTRATE, SHOW, EXPLAIN, elucidate *illustrate how the heart works*

image *(n.)* **1.** likeness, representation, reproduction, FORM *the spitting image of one's mother* **2.** CONCEPT, IDEA, THOUGHT, notion, fancy *the image of a world without hunger*

imaginary *(adj.)* unreal, illusory, supposed, fanciful, visionary REAL, ORDINARY, SIMPLE

imagine *(v.)* THINK, fancy, picture, suppose, conceive, presume, ASSUME, envisage, surmise

imitate *(v.)* COPY, DUPLICATE, REPRODUCE, FOLLOW, mimic, mock, REFLECT, mirror, parody, ape

immaculate *(adj.)* spotless, stainless, CLEAN, NEAT, TIDY DIRTY, FILTHY

immediately *(adv.)* promptly, instantaneously, STRAIGHTAWAY, directly, spontaneously, instinctively, impulsively **slowly, deliberately** *at the drop of a hat*

immense *(adj.)* VAST, ENORMOUS, HUGE, colossal SMALL, TINY, **minute**

immoral *(adj.)* WRONG, WICKED, sinful, CORRUPT, BAD, depraved, unprincipled, unscrupulous, warped, perverted MORAL, **righteous**

immortal *(adj.)* eternal, undying, ENDLESS **mortal, perishable**

immune *(adj.)* protected, invulnerable, inoculated, SAFE **vulnerable, susceptible**

impatient *(adj.)* **1.** uneasy, ANXIOUS, RESTLESS, jittery *feeling impatient before the big game* **tolerant, lenient** **2.** testy, IRRITABLE, fretful, SHORT, RUDE, brusque, hotheaded *impatient because of one's headache* **3.** EAGER, keen, excited *impatient to get the project started* **unhurried**

impolite *(adj.)* RUDE, discourteous, boorish, brash, insolent, inconsiderate, tactless POLITE, COURTEOUS

important *(adj.)* **1.** NECESSARY, ESSENTIAL, weighty, GRAVE, vital, significant, staple, momentous, SERIOUS, monumental, urgent, imperative, pressing *an important announcement* **insignificant** **2.** FAMOUS, VALUABLE *an important government official*

impossible *(adj.)* unattainable, inconceivable, unworkable, unimaginable, hopeless, ABSURD POSSIBLE, LIKELY, **probable** *out of one's reach*

impostor *(n.)* impersonator, pretender, quack, phony, charlatan *wolf in sheep's clothing*

improper *(adj.)* inappropriate, indiscreet, tactless

improve (v.) ENHANCE, BETTER, ADVANCE, CORRECT, FIX, rectify, reform

inaccurate (adj.) incorrect, WRONG, inexact, imprecise, unsound ACCURATE, CORRECT, precise
off base, full of hot air

inadequate (adj.) insufficient, unsatisfactory, deficient, lacking ADEQUATE, sufficient, ENOUGH

incapable (adj.) **1.** incompetent, unable, unqualified, inept *incapable of doing a good job* competent, skilled **2.** powerless, impotent, HELPLESS, defenseless, WEAK *incapable of defending oneself* POWERFUL
(1) not cutting the mustard

incident (n.) EVENT, occurrence, occasion, happening, proceeding, experience

include (v.) **1.** INVOLVE *include in the game* EXCLUDE **2.** CONTAIN, ENCLOSE, comprise, embrace *What does the packet include?*

income (n.) wages, revenue, proceeds

incomplete (adj.) **1.** partial, unfinished *an incomplete story* COMPLETE, finished **2.** deficient, lacking, defective, wanting *an incomplete thought* thorough, conclusive

inconvenient (adj.) AWKWARD, untimely, inopportune, cumbersome, annoying CONVENIENT, suitable, HANDY

increase (v.) GAIN, GROW, ENLARGE, MAGNIFY, amplify, RISE, mount, MULTIPLY, EXPAND, STRETCH, ADVANCE, EXTEND DECREASE, LESSEN, REDUCE, DROP

incredible (adj.) **1.** unbelievable, unrealistic, improbable, fictitious, suspect, doubtful, preposterous *an incredible lie* **2.** FANTASTIC, WONDERFUL, MARVELOUS, EXTRAORDINARY *an incredible trip to Greece*

independent (adj.) **1.** FREE, self-reliant, unrestricted, free-thinking *an independent person* **2.** self-governing, autonomous *an independent country*

inexpensive (adj.) CHEAP, low-priced, reasonable, economical, budget EXPENSIVE, costly

infect (v.) CONTAMINATE, taint, pollute, CORRUPT, AFFECT disinfect

inferior (adj.) **1.** BAD, AWFUL, POOR, shoddy, RANK *an inferior job* superior, supreme **2.** MINOR, insignificant, UNIMPORTANT *an inferior work of art* MAJOR, higher

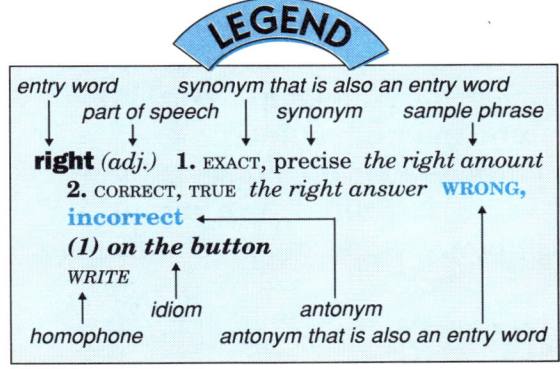

influence (n.) **1.** POWER, force, potency, STRENGTH, WEIGHT, CONTROL, leadership, guidance, DIRECTION *his influence on the presidential race* **2.** importance, prestige, standing *reach a level of influence in the community*

influence (v.) **1.** CONTROL, DIRECT, GOVERN, MANAGE, LEAD, GUIDE *influence the crowd* **2.** AFFECT, sway, modify, CHANGE, alter, transform *influence the outcome of the game*

inform (v.) TELL, ADVISE, notify, relate, apprise, brief

information (n.) facts, data, KNOWLEDGE, news, tidings

inhabit (v.) occupy, reside, abide, DWELL, SETTLE, LOCATE

injure (v.) HURT, WRONG, BRUISE, sprain, strain, wrench, DAMAGE, impair, ABUSE, maltreat

innocent (adj.) guiltless, HARMLESS, naive, ingenuous, unaffected GUILTY
wet behind the ears

inquire (v.) ASK, QUESTION, query, quiz, INVESTIGATE, interrogate

insecure (adj.) **1.** unsafe, untrustworthy, unreliable, precarious, DANGEROUS, perilous, endangered, vulnerable *an insecure hiding place* SECURE, SAFE **2.** TIMID, SHY, hesitant, unsure, apprehensive, diffident, NERVOUS *an insecure feeling about the future* CONFIDENT, CERTAIN

insincere (adj.) DISHONEST, deceitful, underhanded, hypocritical SINCERE, HONEST
full of bologna

• Guess the Idiom •

clue: insincere

answer: full of bologna

insist (v.) DEMAND, STRESS, PRESS, pressure, compel, prompt
put one's foot down

• Guess the Idiom •

clue: insist

answer: put one's foot down

inspect (v.) EXAMINE, STUDY, evaluate, VIEW, REVIEW, survey, scrutinize, peruse, appraise

inspire (v.) 1. ENCOURAGE, enliven, stimulate, invigorate *The coach must inspire the players.* 2. inhale, BREATHE, gasp *inspire two deep breaths* 3. prompt, instigate, incite *inspire a change in one's attitude*

instant (n.) moment, second, flash, jiffy

instant (adj.) immediate, SUDDEN, abrupt, instantaneous, expeditious
in the twinkling of an eye

instinct (n.) 1. intuition, impulse, inclination, leaning *follow one's instinct* 2. TALENT, GIFT, ABILITY, aptitude, flair, knack *a natural instinct for fixing things*

instruct (v.) TEACH, tutor, INFORM, TRAIN, EDUCATE, enlighten

instrument (n.) 1. DEVICE, TOOL, implement, utensil, GADGET *a medical instrument* 2. means, WAY, mover, catalyst *an instrument of destruction*

insult (v.) OFFEND, ABUSE, RIDICULE, HUMILIATE, jeer, mock, taunt, snub, outrage, affront   COMPLIMENT, FLATTER
fling dirt at

intelligent (adj.) BRIGHT, QUICK, CLEVER, ALERT, quick-witted, knowing   STUPID, IGNORANT

intend (v.) MEAN, signify, propose, PLAN, contemplate

intense (adj.) 1. SEVERE, extreme, acute, HARSH, cutting *intense pain* 2. EAGER, EARNEST, ENTHUSIASTIC, ardent, fervent, zealous, passionate *an intense fan*

interest (n.) 1. attention, regard, engagement, consideration *an interest in the arts* 2. SHARE, PART, portion, PIECE *buy an interest in the company* 3. benefit, profit, advantage *an interest in the property deal*

interest (v.) 1. ATTRACT, engage, engross, ABSORB, captivate, mesmerize *interest the audience* 2. CONCERN, INVOLVE, AFFECT *Her problems do not interest me.*
(1) catch one's eye

interesting (adj.) absorbing, fascinating, entertaining, amusing, compelling   BORING, DULL, uninteresting

interfere (v.) 1. meddle, intervene, INTRUDE *interfere in their relationship* 2. obstruct, hamper, BLOCK, FRUSTRATE *interfere with getting one's job done*
(1) put one's two cents in

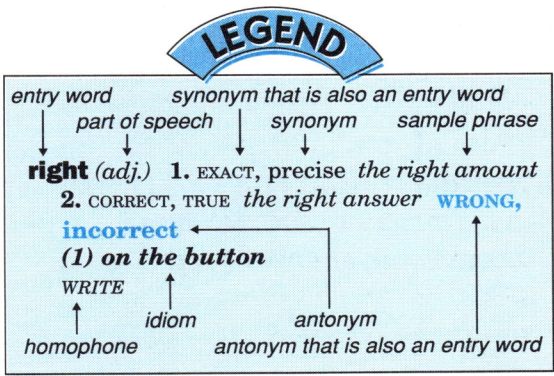

interrupt (v.) **1.** STOP, suspend, discontinue, sever, DISCONNECT, DISTURB, hinder *interrupt progress* **2.** INTERFERE, INTRUDE *interrupt with an emergency call*

introduce (v.) **1.** PRESENT, acquaint *introduce someone to your parents* **2.** START, ANNOUNCE, commence, initiate, precipitate *introduce the program* CONCLUDE **3.** insert, interject *introduce harmful substances into the air*
(1) give the floor to

◆ Guess the Idiom ◆

clue: introduce

answer: give the floor to

intrude (v.) **1.** trespass, INTERFERE, meddle *intrude in someone else's business* **2.** INVADE, infringe, encroach *intrude on one's privacy*

invade (v.) **1.** ATTACK, overrun, assault, RAID, STORM, assail *invade the enemy camp* **2.** INTRUDE, INTERRUPT, intervene *invade the private meeting*

invent (v.) originate, CREATE, conceive, concoct, devise

investigate (v.) RESEARCH, EXPLORE, EXAMINE, INSPECT, scrutinize, STUDY, probe

invisible (adj.) HIDDEN, concealed, indiscernible, imperceptible VISIBLE, OBVIOUS

invite (v.) **1.** REQUEST, ASK, beckon, summon *invite to a party* **2.** ATTRACT, entice, TEMPT, LURE *invite trouble*
(2) leave the door open

involve (v.) **1.** CONCERN, AFFECT *a situation that does not involve you* **2.** INCLUDE, CONTAIN, comprise *What does the job involve?* **3.** ABSORB, engage, preoccupy, commit *involve oneself in one's work*

irritable (adj.) testy, peevish, touchy, GRUMPY, cranky, grouchy, cantankerous, IMPATIENT, crabby, MOODY

irritate (v.) **1.** chafe, inflame *irritate the skin* **2.** provoke, ANNOY, BOTHER, pester, exasperate, ruffle, DISTURB, needle *irritate one's teacher*
(2) tread on one's toes, get one's goat

item (n.) article, DETAIL, feature, component, ingredient

Jj

jail (n.) prison, lockup, dungeon

jail (v.) confine, imprison, commit, incarcerate **FREE, RELEASE**

jam (v.) **1.** crowd, SQUEEZE, ram, wedge, sandwich, CRAM *jam clothes into the suitcase* **2.** obstruct, BLOCK, plug, hinder *jam the exit door*

jar (n.) bottle, urn, vase, crock, pot, jug, flask

jealous (adj.) resentful, envious, covetous
green with envy

jerk (n.) IDIOT, FOOL, moron, booby, simpleton, clod, nerd, numskull, goof

jerk (v.) jolt, PULL, twitch, SHAKE

job (n.) WORK, occupation, employment, profession, craft, calling, vocation

join (v.) **1.** UNITE, COMBINE, ATTACH, CONNECT, merge, cement, splice, graft, link, couple, adhere *join the pieces together* **SEPARATE, DISCONNECT** **2.** ally, associate *join the club* **QUIT, RESIGN**

joke (n.) gag, jest, TRICK, hoax, prank, deception, antic

journey (n.) TRIP, VOYAGE, venture, expedition, jaunt, excursion, passage

joy (n.) DELIGHT, HAPPINESS, pleasure, CHEER, excitement, bliss, rapture, elation, felicity **grief, dejection, pessimism**

judge (n.) referee, umpire, arbitrator

judge (v.) CONSIDER, regard, scrutinize, sentence, CONDEMN

judgment (n.) intelligence, discrimination, tact, discernment, diplomacy, understanding

jump (v.) **1.** HOP, LEAP, SPRING, vault, SKIP, bound *Jump over the log.* **2.** DIVE, plunge *The diver jumped off the platform.* **3.** startle, flinch, START *She jumped in surprise.*

jungle (n.) thicket, forest, bush

junk (n.) SCRAP, TRASH, salvage, rubbish, GARBAGE, WASTE, litter, debris, REFUSE

just (adj.) **1.** RIGHT, FAIR, lawful, legitimate, justified, reasonable, impartial *a just decision* **2.** deserved, earned, DUE, APPROPRIATE *one's just punishment*

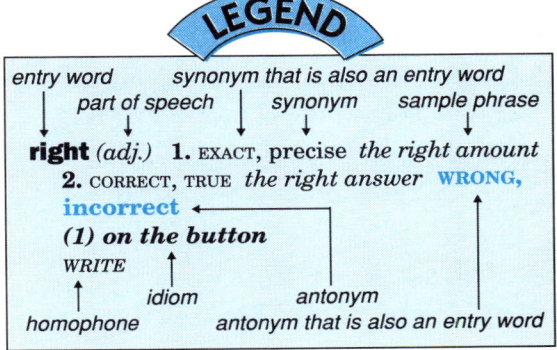

justice (n.) fairness, impartiality, legitimacy

justify (v.) **1.** DEFEND, FORGIVE, absolve, exonerate, acquit *justify one's actions* **2.** SUPPORT, warrant, authorize, legitimize, substantiate *information that would justify his decision to quit*

Kk

keep (v.) **1.** SAVE, HOLD, SECURE, reserve, PRESERVE, CONSERVE *keep the doll* **DISCARD, REJECT** **2.** MAINTAIN, tend, PROTECT, GUARD *keep the lawn mowed* **3.** detain, retain, confine *keep from escaping* **RELEASE**

kill (v.) execute, MURDER, slay, slaughter, butcher, smother, annihilate, exterminate, massacre, assassinate **SPARE**

kind (n.) GROUP, SORT, TYPE, CLASS, species

kind (adj.) FRIENDLY, loving, NICE, COURTEOUS, CONSIDERATE, HELPFUL, PLEASANT, sympathetic, compassionate, affectionate, THOUGHTFUL, TENDER, WARM, liberal, cordial, DEVOTED, EARNEST, humane, charitable, ardent, benevolent **MEAN, UNFRIENDLY, HOSTILE**

kindness (n.) tenderness, sympathy, compassion **brutality**

king (n.) RULER, sovereign, monarch, majesty

kingdom (n.) realm, province, REGION, domain

kiss (n.) smooch, embrace

kit (n.) tools, EQUIPMENT, outfit, COLLECTION

knife (n.) dagger, blade, dirk, stiletto, SWORD, saber, cutlass, rapier, scimitar

knock (v.) tap, rap, HIT, STRIKE, bang, thump

know (v.) UNDERSTAND, COMPREHEND, perceive, RECOGNIZE, discriminate, fathom, gather, surmise
get the picture
NO

knowledge (n.) learning, understanding, WISDOM, JUDGMENT, INFORMATION, intelligence
ignorance

Ll

labor (n.) **1.** WORK, employment, JOB, occupation, living, livelihood, chore, ERRAND, DUTY *earn the fruits of one's labor* **2.** WORKERS, employees, hands *We'll hire extra labor to finish the job.*

labor (v.) WORK, toil

lack *(n.)* WANT, NEED, shortage, shortcoming, sparsity, scarcity, dearth, void

lack *(v.)* NEED, REQUIRE, MISS

language *(n.)* SPEECH, dialect, tongue

large *(adj.)* BIG, BROAD, VAST, extensive, roomy, spacious, HUGE, IMMENSE, ENORMOUS, GIANT, GIGANTIC, colossal SMALL, miniature

last *(v.)* CONTINUE, STAY, REMAIN, endure, persist, abide

last *(adj.)* **1.** FINAL, latter, hindmost, terminal, closing, ultimate *the last act of the play* FIRST, foremost **2.** recent, latest *the last time you went to the movies*

late *(adj.)* tardy, behind, delayed, slack EARLY, ahead

laugh *(v.)* giggle, titter, snigger, cackle, chuckle, guffaw, snicker CRY, lament
crack up, roll in the aisles

law *(n.)* RULE, regulation, ORDER, mandate, standard, principle, doctrine, statute, decree, tenet, ordinance, edict

lay *(v.)* **1.** PUT, place, SET, rest, deposit, plant, park *lay the book on the table* **2.** ASSIGN, attribute, ascribe *lay blame* **3.** MAKE, devise, PREPARE *lay a plan*

lazy *(adj.)* IDLE, sluggish, inactive, passive, lifeless, slack, indolent, slothful industrious, ACTIVE, ALERT, EAGER

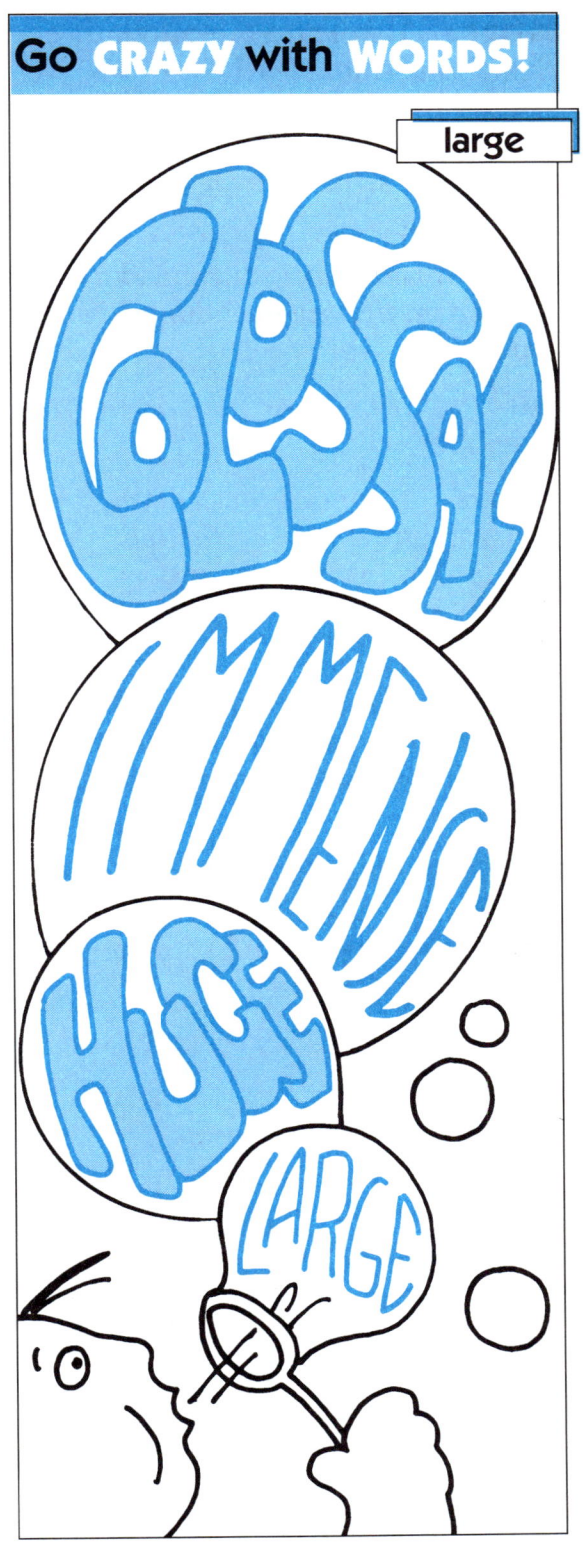

Go **CRAZY** with **WORDS!**

large

75

lead (v.) **1.** COMMAND, GOVERN, RULE, CONTROL *lead the army* **2.** GUIDE, DIRECT, pilot, STEER *lead the way* FOLLOW
call the shots, be in the driver's seat

leader (n.) BOSS, CHIEF, head, director, manager, GUIDE, principal follower

leak (v.) trickle, seep, ooze, drip, dribble

lean (v.) **1.** incline, SLANT, tilt, SLOPE, bank *lean to the left* **2.** DEPEND, rely *lean on for support*

lean (adj.) **1.** THIN, gaunt, SLIM, SKINNY *a lean figure* FAT **2.** nonfat *lean meat* **3.** POOR, deficient, nonproductive *lean years* productive, teeming

leap (v.) JUMP, SPRING, bound, vault, HOP

learn (v.) master, MEMORIZE, DISCOVER, ACQUIRE, grasp, REMEMBER, ascertain

least (adj.) smallest, tiniest, feeblest, slightest most

leave (v.) **1.** DEPART, EXIT, PART, vacate, SCRAP, ABANDON, DESERT, forsake, migrate, emigrate, EVACUATE *leave the area* ARRIVE, REACH, JOIN **2.** QUIT, retire, withdraw, RESIGN *leave one job for another* **3.** will, bequeath, PROMISE *She'll leave her jewelry to her daughter.*
(1) take a powder

lecture (n.) TALK, address, LESSON, discourse, sermon

legend (n.) fable, myth, TALE

lend (v.) **1.** LOAN, GIVE, ADVANCE *lend one's baseball mitt to one's best friend* **2.** FURNISH, PROVIDE, CONTRIBUTE *lend some help*

lessen (v.) DECREASE, REDUCE, SHRINK, condense, compress, CONCENTRATE, diminish, dwindle, deduct, SUBTRACT, ELIMINATE, taper, narrow, wane, ebb, subside, abridge INCREASE, EXPAND, BUILD
cut short
LESSON

lesson (n.) **1.** assignment, exercise, PRACTICE, teaching, recitation *The guitar lesson begins at noon.* **2.** warning, admonition *learn a lesson from stealing* LESSEN

let (v.) ALLOW, PERMIT, consent, grant, APPROVE FORBID, prohibit

level (v.) **1.** flatten, equalize *level the ground for planting* **2.** DESTROY, demolish, RAZE *The tornado might level the town.*

level (adj.) **1.** FLAT, HORIZONTAL, EVEN, SMOOTH, *skate on a level surface* **2.** EQUAL, balanced *level competition* **3.** CALM, even-tempered, collected, composed, unruffled *a level head*

liberty (*n.*) **1.** FREEDOM, independence, autonomy *They fought for liberty.* **2.** privilege, RIGHT, LICENSE, PERMISSION *the liberty to stand up for one's rights*

license (*n.*) PERMIT, consent, authorization, approval

license (*v.*) PERMIT, ALLOW, consent, authorize, sanction, warrant

lick (*v.*) lap, TASTE, moisten

lie (*n.*) untruth, STORY, falsehood, fib, prevarication, fabrication

lie (*v.*) **1.** recline, REST, lounge, repose *lie on the couch* **2.** fib, slander, defame, prevaricate *lie to her mother*
(2) break one's word, stretch the truth

life (*n.*) **1.** being, existence, ENERGY, SPIRIT, viability *lose one's life in a car accident* **2.** NATURE, creation *protect all of life*

lift (*v.*) **1.** RAISE, BOOST, hoist, ELEVATE, SUPPORT *lift the box* **lower** **2.** IMPROVE, BOOST, promote, exalt *lift one's spirits* **depress** **3.** END, revoke *lift the blockade*

light (*v.*) **1.** brighten, illuminate, illumine *The flashlight will light our way.* **2.** IGNITE, BURN, kindle, fire *Light the fire.*

light (*adj.*) **1.** PALE, white, wan, FAINT, pallid *a light complexion* **DARK, black, dim** **2.** portable, movable, buoyant *light enough to carry* **HEAVY**

like (*v.*) ADMIRE, VALUE, APPRECIATE, APPROVE, prize, ENJOY, RESPECT, PREFER, esteem, relish **DISLIKE, HATE, loathe**
get a kick out of, stuck on

likely (*adj.*) probable, POSSIBLE, apt, promising

limit (*n.*) boundary, BORDER, perimeter

limit (*v.*) **1.** bound, confine, restrict, curb, prohibit, STAY *limit progress* **2.** determine, specify, fix, demarcate *limit the area that can be used*
(2) clip one's wings

linger (*v.*) WAIT, STAY, REMAIN, loiter, DELAY, tarry, dawdle, procrastinate, lollygag, loaf **DEPART, vacate**

list (*n.*) register, ROLL, index, catalog

list (*v.*) RECORD, register, chronicle, catalog, index

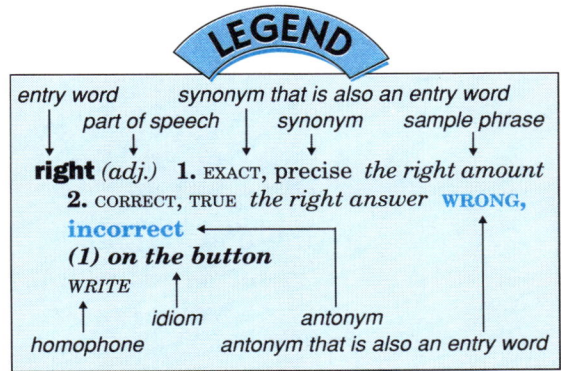

listen *(v.)* **1.** HEAR, harken, ATTEND *listen to the speech* **2.** OBEY, MIND, heed *listen to your mother's advice*
(1) lend an ear

little *(adj.)* SMALL, TINY, minute, miniature, slight, petite, wee, microscopic, puny **BIG, HUGE, colossal**

live *(v.)* **1.** STAY, DWELL, INHABIT, occupy, REMAIN *live in a white house* **2.** EXIST, survive, be, abide, endure, subsist, persist *live for eighty years* **DIE**

lively *(adj.)* ACTIVE, nimble, spirited, brisk, QUICK, agile, spry **DULL, sluggish**

load *(n.)* CARGO, freight, burden, shipment

loan *(n.)* ADVANCE, credit

loan *(v.)* LEND, ADVANCE, credit

locate *(v.)* **1.** PLACE, FIX *locate the house far from the road* **2.** FIND, DISCOVER, UNCOVER, unearth *locate the missing keys* **3.** SETTLE, occupy *locate in a different state*
(2) put one's fingers on
(3) hang up one's hat

lock *(v.)* padlock, latch, bolt, FASTEN, secure **unlock**

lofty *(adj.)* **1.** HIGH, TALL, elevated, towering, soaring *a lofty mountain* **LOW, SHORT, sunken** **2.** GRAND, distinguished, noted, eminent *a lofty career* **3.** PROUD, haughty, arrogant, vain, snotty, snobbish *lofty ideals* **MODEST**
(3) on one's high horse

lonely *(adj.)* lone, ALONE, solitary, apart, SEPARATE, desolate

long *(v.)* DESIRE, WANT, pine, hanker
set one's heart on

long *(adj.)* lengthy, protracted, extended, outstretched

look *(v.)* **1.** glance, glimpse, peep, peer, STARE, gape, GAZE, WATCH, regard *look at the bird* **2.** EXAMINE, INSPECT, INVESTIGATE, scrutinize *look it over* **3.** SEARCH, SEEK, HUNT *look for your notebook* **4.** APPEAR, SEEM *look good in blue*
(1) have your eye on

loose *(adj.)* hanging, limp, slack **TIGHT**

lose *(v.)* **1.** mislay, misplace *lose your watch* **FIND, LOCATE** **2.** FAIL, forfeit, relinquish, forgo, sacrifice, YIELD *lose the game* **WIN, triumph**

lost *(adj.)* **1.** missing, disappeared *a lost ship* **2.** forgotten *a lost memory* **3.** hopeless, irreversible, irretrievable *a lost cause* **4.** wasted, squandered, misspent *make up for lost time* **5.** confused, perplexed, baffled *lost by the explanation*

loud *(adj.)* NOISY, blaring, shrill, boisterous, clamorous, rowdy, vociferous, thunderous **QUIET, SOFT, STILL**

love *(n.)* affection, adoration, fondness, devotion

love *(v.)* ADMIRE, ADORE, WORSHIP, HONOR, CHERISH, esteem, revere
HATE, DESPISE
think the world of

lovely *(adj.)* **1.** BEAUTIFUL, ATTRACTIVE *a lovely girl* **2.** delightful, INTERESTING *a lovely song* **3.** MAGNIFICENT, scenic *a lovely view*

low *(adj.)* **1.** sunken, unelevated *low land* HIGH, elevated **2.** SHORT *a low ceiling* **3.** shallow, reduced, diminished, decreased, lessened *low tide, low funds* **4.** FEEBLE, WEAK, FRAGILE, DELICATE, sickly *in low health* **5.** SAD, depressed, dejected, dispirited *in a low mood*

loyal *(adj.)* FAITHFUL, TRUE, DEVOTED, CONSTANT, unchanging, STABLE, PERMANENT, staunch
disloyal, traitorous

loyalty *(n.)* devotion, allegiance

luck *(n.)* FATE, RISK, CHANCE, FORTUNE, happenstance, serendipity, prosperity, FAVOR, SUCCESS

lure *(v.)* ATTRACT, entice, decoy, TEMPT

luxury *(n.)* splendor, opulence, abundance

luxurious *(adj.)* RICH, plush, extravagant, lavish, SPLENDID, opulent

Mm

machine *(n.)* appliance, DEVICE, TOOL, implement

mad *(adj.)* **1.** CROSS, ANGRY, fretful, testy, IRRITABLE, annoyed, cranky, grouchy, exasperated, ornery, disgruntled, enraged, petulant, peevish *mad at a friend* **2.** CRAZY, insane *The man was mad.* SANE, rational

magic *(n.)* **1.** sorcery, wizardry, incantation, voodoo, conjury, hocus-pocus *an act of magic* **2.** SPELL, INFLUENCE, charm, trance *under one's magic*

magical *(adj.)* enchanting, CHARMING, fascinating, entrancing, mystical, incantational

magnificent *(adj.)* **1.** GRAND, SPLENDID, resplendent, glorious *a magnificent palace* **2.** NOBLE, MAJESTIC, imposing, stately, regal *a magnificent leader*

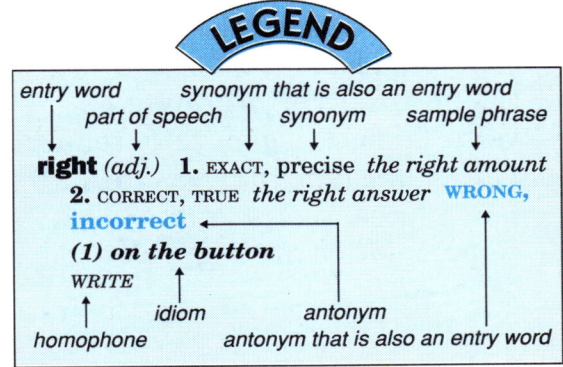

magnify (v.) **1.** ENLARGE, amplify, INCREASE *Magnify the size of the object.* REDUCE **2.** EXAGGERATE, overstate *magnify the truth* understate **3.** intensify, heighten, STRENGTHEN, AGGRAVATE, worsen *magnify the problem* de-escalate

maid (n.) attendant, servant, domestic, HELP, employee
MADE

main (adj.) MAJOR, foremost, CHIEF, principal, primary, leading, IMPORTANT, essential
MANE

maintain (v.) **1.** SUPPORT, KEEP, sustain, PRESERVE, nurse *maintain the garden* **2.** DECLARE, assert, profess *maintain his innocence* **3.** CONTINUE, persist, persevere *maintain one's course*

majestic (adj.) regal, ROYAL, stately, SPLENDID, MAGNIFICENT

major (adj.) **1.** CHIEF, IMPORTANT, primary, principal *a major piece of evidence* **2.** greater, larger, higher, utmost *a major influence*

make (v.) **1.** BUILD, CONSTRUCT, erect, MANUFACTURE, ASSEMBLE, concoct, devise, PRODUCE, FORM, FASHION, CREATE, originate, INVENT, fabricate, generate, render *Let's make a birdhouse.* demolish, WRECK, DESTROY **2.** FORCE, compel *Make the dog well-behaved.*

manage (v.) **1.** HANDLE, manipulate, wield *manage the controls* **2.** supervise, administer, GUIDE, CONDUCT, superintend *manage the team*

manner (n.) **1.** METHOD, mode, FASHION, WAY, STYLE *a manner of speaking* **2.** behavior, aspect, APPEARANCE *a polite manner*
MANOR

manor (n.) estate, mansion
MANNER

manufacture (v.) MAKE, PRODUCE, CONSTRUCT, BUILD, fabricate

many (adj.) numerous, PLENTIFUL, countless, various, bountiful, innumerable, abundant, profuse
few, infrequent, scant

march (v.) **1.** WALK, STEP, pace, parade *march in the parade* **2.** ADVANCE, proceed *march on an enemy*

mark (n.) **1.** STAIN, smudge, notch, score, trace, smear *erase the mark* **2.** stamp, brand, seal, imprint, endorsement *the king's mark*

marry (v.) wed, espouse, betroth, unite, JOIN
tie the knot
MERRY

marvelous (adj.) WONDERFUL, amazing, astonishing, wondrous, EXTRAORDINARY, exceptional,
AWFUL, HORRIBLE

match (n.) GAME, CONTEST, COMPETITION, trial

mate (n.) 1. FRIEND, associate, COMPANION *a good mate* 2. spouse, wife, husband, partner *Choose a mate.*

mate (v.) MARRY, match, breed

material (n.) 1. MATTER, substance, STUFF *an unknown material* 2. fabric, textile *She bought material to make a dress.*

matter (n.) 1. substance, MATERIAL, MEDIUM *The three forms of matter are solid, liquid, and gas.* 2. difficulty, TROUBLE, DISTRESS, ailment, WORRY, PROBLEM, predicament, dilemma, quandary *What's the matter?*

mature (adj.) adult, grown, grown-up, ripe **immature, YOUNG**

maybe (adv.) perhaps, possibly, perchance, conceivably **surely, certainly**

meal (n.) feast, banquet, spread, snack, repast

mean (v.) indicate, signify, denote, imply, INTEND, EXPRESS

mean (adj.) unkind, CRUEL, heartless, bad-tempered, aggressive, EVIL, merciless, beastly, HOSTILE, SAVAGE, fierce, ruthless, atrocious, despicable, antagonistic, malicious **KIND, GENTLE, sympathetic, FRIENDLY**

meaning (n.) 1. significance, SENSE, essence, explanation, gist *The meaning is clear.*
2. PURPOSE, AIM, OBJECT, import, intention, design *the meaning of his actions*

measure (n.) SIZE, gauge, rule, extent, dimension

measure (v.) rule, gauge, appraise, ESTIMATE

medicine (n.) DRUG, ointment, potion, lozenge, PILL, tablet, antidote, salve

medium (adj.) middle, mean, AVERAGE, mediocre

meet (v.) 1. ASSEMBLE, congregate, convene, muster *The club will meet on Monday.* 2. ENCOUNTER, GREET, address, WELCOME, converge *Meet me at the corner later today.*
(2) run across
MEAT

melt (v.) thaw, defrost, liquefy, DISSOLVE **harden, jell, FREEZE**

memorize (v.) REMEMBER, NOTE, commit FORGET
learn by heart

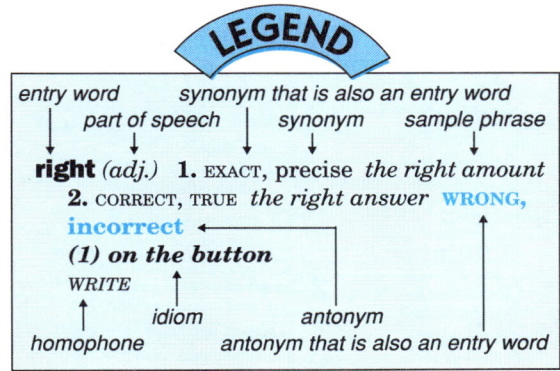

entry word — synonym that is also an entry word
part of speech — synonym — sample phrase
right (adj.) 1. EXACT, precise *the right amount* 2. CORRECT, TRUE *the right answer* WRONG, incorrect
(1) on the button
WRITE — idiom — antonym
homophone — antonym that is also an entry word

memory *(n.)* **1.** recollection, remembrance, retention, RECALL *lose one's memory in the accident* **2.** SOUVENIR, memento, token *He kept the coin as a memory of his trip.*

mention *(v.)* DECLARE, TELL, STATE

mercy *(n.)* PITY, pardon, forgiveness, compassion, charity, sympathy, clemency

merry *(adj.)* HAPPY, CHEERFUL, sprightly, blithe, jolly, jovial somber, SOBER, GLOOMY, SAD

mess *(n.)* **1.** CLUTTER, disorder, disarray, chaos *clean up the mess* **2.** PROBLEM, jam, plight, difficulty, confusion, muddle, predicament, mayhem, snafu *in a real mess*

message *(n.)* dispatch, communication, letter, NOTE, news, tidings

messenger *(n.)* carrier, courier, envoy

messy *(adj.)* untidy, disordered, DIRTY, jumbled, muddled, disheveled CLEAN, TIDY, neat, orderly

method *(n.)* system, technique, WAY, COURSE, mode, MANNER, means, operation

middle *(n.)* CENTER, CORE, interior, heart

middle *(adj.)* **1.** central, interior, inside *the middle house on the block* EDGE **2.** neutral, intermediate *to stand on middle ground in an argument*

might *(n.)* POWER, STRENGTH, force, potency

mild *(adj.)* GENTLE, meek, TENDER, placid, BLAND, nonabrasive stormy, VIOLENT, SPICY

mimic *(adj.)* IMITATE, mime, COPY, copycat, ape, mock

mind *(n.)* intellect, intelligence

mind *(v.)* **1.** regard, MARK, monitor *Mind your manners.* disregard **2.** OBEY, heed *Mind your mother.* DISOBEY, DEFY **3.** GUARD, WATCH, PROTECT, ATTEND *Mind the store while I'm away.*
(3) keep an eye on

• Guess the Idiom •

clue: mind

answer: keep an eye on

minor *(n.)* child, YOUTH

minor *(adj.)* smaller, lesser, INFERIOR, UNIMPORTANT, insignificant, petty, trite MAJOR, significant

miracle *(n.)* marvel, WONDER, prodigy, phenomenon, SIGN, omen

mischief (n.) **1.** naughtiness, roguery, prankishness *involved in mischief* **2.** HARM, injury, DAMAGE *repair the mischief*

miserable (adj.) **1.** UNHAPPY, wretched, forlorn, distressed *a miserable mood* HAPPY, elated **2.** POOR, worthless, valueless *miserable living conditions*

misery (n.) DISTRESS, anguish, heartache, woe, unhappiness, suffering, GRIEF, SORROW DELIGHT, JOY, rapture

miss (v.) **1.** SKIP, OMIT, disregard, IGNORE, blunder *miss an opportunity* **2.** WANT, yearn *miss your best friend*

(1) go in one ear and out the other

♦ Guess the Idiom ♦

clue: miss

answer: go in one ear and out the other

mistake (n.) ERROR, SLIP, BLUNDER, oversight, offense, failing, ACCIDENT, FAULT, BUNGLE

mix (n.) mixture, VARIETY, medley, hodgepodge, BLEND, composite

mix (v.) mingle, COMBINE, merge, JOIN, BLEND, scramble, churn, agitate

mob (n.) CROWD, horde, throng

modern (adj.) recent, LATE, NEW, novel, FRESH, present old-fashioned, outmoded, ANCIENT

modest (adj.) HUMBLE, PLAIN, SIMPLE, unpretentious, bashful meek, reserved boastful, arrogant, PROUD

money (n.) currency, coins, FEE, wages, compensation, salary, cash, funds, WEALTH, riches

monster (n.) demon, fiend, VILLAIN, ogre, brute, colossus

mood (n.) humor, NATURE, TEMPER, temperament, disposition, SPIRIT, vein

moody (adj.) CROSS, sullen, sulky, GLOOMY, dismal, somber, morose CHEERFUL, good-natured, HAPPY

moral (adj.) GOOD, JUST, virtuous, upright, HONEST IMMORAL, DISHONEST, BAD

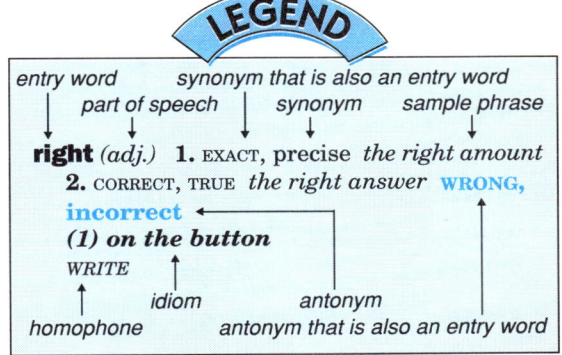

83

morning *(n.)* sunrise, dawn, daybreak

motion *(n.)* **1.** movement, action, gesture *a hand motion* **2.** proposal, suggestion *make a motion before student council*

move *(v.)* GO, proceed, pass, advance, continue, shift, march, stir, BUDGE, depart, travel, relocate STAY, REMAIN

multiply *(v.)* **1.** INCREASE, GAIN, GROW, augment *The problems may multiply.* DECREASE **2.** reproduce, breed, procreate, propagate *Rabbits multiply quickly.*

mumble *(v.)* mutter, murmur, slur
swallow one's words

• Guess the Idiom •

clue: mumble

answer: swallow one's words

murder *(n.)* slaying, killing, homicide, massacre, execution, assassination, carnage

murder *(v.)* KILL, slay, butcher, massacre, execute, assassinate, exterminate, slaughter

mystery *(n.)* SECRET, PUZZLE, RIDDLE, QUESTION, PROBLEM, dilemma, predicament, enigma

Nn

name *(n.)* label, term, title, head, heading, designation, caption

name *(v.)* **1.** label, term, entitle *Name the child.* **2.** MENTION, LIST, designate, cite *Name the winners.*

nap *(v.)* SLEEP, snooze, DOZE, slumber
catch forty winks

narrow *(adj.)* slender, THIN, SLIM, CLOSE, tight, confined WIDE, BROAD, roomy

nasty *(adj.)* **1.** DIRTY, FILTHY, FOUL, unclean, polluted, contaminated *nasty water* **2.** disagreeable, unpleasant, distasteful, OBNOXIOUS *a nasty disposition*

nature *(n.)* **1.** QUALITY, CHARACTERISTIC *Explain the nature of the problem.* **2.** personality, MOOD, disposition, temperament *a pleasant nature*

naughty *(adj.)* mischievous, disobedient, unruly, defiant, noncompliant, BAD GOOD, OBEDIENT

near *(adj.)* CLOSE, NEXT, adjacent, neighboring, immediate, proximate, adjoining FAR, remote, distant

neat *(adj.)* TIDY, CLEAN, spotless, orderly, uncluttered, spruce, STRAIGHT, SMART untidy, cluttered, DIRTY

necessary *(adj.)* required, essential, unavoidable, indispensable, obligatory UNNECESSARY, needless

need *(n.)* necessity, requirement, demand, LACK, urgency, requisite, exigency

need *(v.)* REQUIRE, LACK, WANT KNEAD

nervous *(adj.)* ANXIOUS, worried, disturbed, RESTLESS, jittery, uneasy, TENSE, concerned, apprehensive CALM, relaxed *on pins and needles*

new *(adj.)* **1.** unused, FRESH, untouched, recent, mint *a shiny new penny* OLD, ANCIENT, STALE **2.** novel, MODERN, LATE, latest, innovative, pioneering, unprecedented *a new computer* old-fashioned, outmoded GNU, KNEW

next *(adj.)* impending, approaching, forthcoming, CLOSE, imminent

nice *(adj.)* **1.** COURTEOUS, FRIENDLY, KIND, WARM, PLEASANT, affable, amiable, cordial *a nice salesclerk* offensive, MEAN, UNFRIENDLY **2.** MILD, sunny, WARM, PLEASANT *a nice day*

noble *(adj.)* dignified, upright, stately, ROYAL, MAJESTIC, regal, lordly, aristocratic, imperial, GALLANT, VALIANT, chivalrous ignoble, COMMON, barbaric

noise *(n.)* SOUND, signal, tone, hubbub, bustle, RACKET, ruckus, flurry, commotion, uproar, disturbance, din, clamor, tumult, turmoil, upheaval QUIET, stillness, silence

• Guess the Idiom •

clue: nervous

answer: on pins and needles

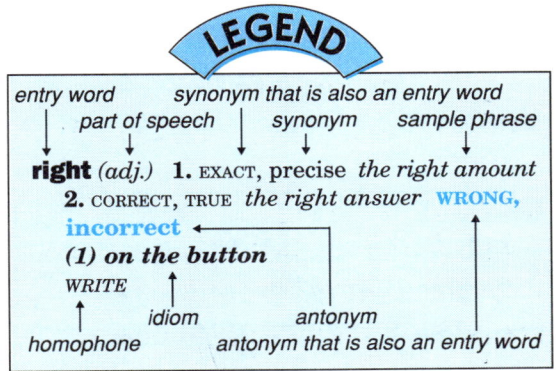

noisy *(adj.)* LOUD, rowdy, disorderly, boisterous, vociferous, clamorous QUIET, silent

nonsense *(n.)* gibberish, drivel, twaddle, rubbish, balderdash, folly, absurdity SENSE

normal *(adj.)* natural, ORDINARY, REGULAR, established, USUAL, typical, standard, COMMON, commonplace, legitimate, customary UNUSUAL, irregular, unnatural, uncommon, abnormal, ODD

nosy *(adj.)* CURIOUS, inquisitive, prying

note *(n.)* 1. NOTICE, memo, memorandum, RECORD, COMMENT, LETTER *Write a note.* 2. tone *Sing a high note.*

note *(v.)* 1. NOTICE, OBSERVE, heed, ATTEND *Note the date.* 2. jot, WRITE, RECORD, inscribe *Note when the assignment is due.*

notice *(n.)* NOTE, poster, SIGN, advertisement, ad, flyer

notice *(v.)* SEE, perceive, regard, OBSERVE, heed, discern MISS, OVERLOOK, IGNORE

now *(adv.)* IMMEDIATELY, instantly, directly, currently, presently, forthwith later, after, then

nuisance *(n.)* PEST, BOTHER, annoyance **pain in the neck**

numb *(adj.)* 1. paralyzed, anesthetized *numb from the cold* 2. insensitive, hardened, unemotional, apathetic, dispassionate, unfeeling *numb from the experience of war* feeling, SENSITIVE

number *(n.)* 1. digit, numeral, AMOUNT, FIGURE *Read the number.* 2. TOTAL, COUNT, QUANTITY *What number of guests will attend?*

Oo

obedient *(adj.)* compliant, submissive, respectful, subservient disobedient, NAUGHTY

obey *(v.)* heed, YIELD, KEEP, submit, comply DISOBEY, DEFY, RESIST

object *(n.)* 1. THING, article, FACT *Examine the rare object.* 2. AIM, GOAL, objective, target, PURPOSE *the object of the meeting*

object *(v.)* oppose, REFUSE, protest, DISAPPROVE, spurn AGREE

obnoxious *(adj.)* offensive, repulsive, unpleasant, disagreeable, odious

observe *(v.)* 1. NOTICE, SEE, behold, DETECT, discern, MIND *Observe the parade.* OVERLOOK 2. HONOR, RECOGNIZE, commemorate *Observe the holiday.*

obtain *(v.)* GET, ACQUIRE, procure, GAIN, SECURE LOSE

obvious *(adj.)* evident, CLEAR, visible, definite, observable, distinct, marked **HIDDEN, obscure**

odd *(adj.)* UNUSUAL, abnormal, QUEER, irregular, atypical, WEIRD, UNIQUE, peculiar, eccentric, quirky **USUAL, typical, ORDINARY**

offend *(v.)* UPSET, IRRITATE, vex, ANNOY, trespass, transgress, sin, displease, disgust, outrage *step on the toes of*

offer *(n.)* bid, proposal, suggestion, proposition **refusal, denial**

offer *(v.)* GIVE, bestow, PRESENT, propose, bid, tender, submit, SURRENDER, proffer **REFUSE, DENY**

often *(adv.)* frequently, repeatedly, regularly **never, rarely**

okay *(n.)* approval, authorization

okay *(adj.)* **1.** reasonable, SOUND, sensible, acceptable, JUST, rational *an okay decision* **2.** satisfied, alright, CONTENT *feel okay*

old *(adj.)* **1.** aged, elderly, senior, mature, grown-up, adult *an old person* **YOUNG 2.** STALE *old bread* **FRESH 3.** ANCIENT, antique, obsolete *old relics* **NEW**
(1) over the hill

omit *(v.)* MISS, disregard, neglect, IGNORE **INCLUDE**

open *(v.)* unfasten, undo, untie, unlock, unseal **CLOSE, SHUT**

open *(adj.)* **1.** unlocked, unsealed, uncovered, ajar *an open door* **SHUT, CLOSED 2.** HONEST, SINCERE, frank, candid *an open conversation* **guarded**

operate *(v.)* **1.** MANAGE, WORK, USE, DIRECT, PERFORM *The farmer operated the bulldozer.* **2.** cut, open up *operate on a patient*

opinion *(n.)* VIEW, viewpoint, IDEA, belief, impression, perspective

opponent *(n.)* RIVAL, competitor, adversary, ENEMY, FOE, antagonist **ally, FRIEND, associate, accomplice, protagonist**

opposite *(adj.)* contrary, unlike, adverse, opposed, dissimilar, contradictory **SAME, similar**

order *(n.)* **1.** sequence, arrangement *alphabetical order* **2.** COMMAND, demand, DIRECTION, RULE, regulation *give an order*

order *(v.)* **1.** sequence, ARRANGE, SORT, classify, categorize, file, systematize *order according to last name* **2.** COMMAND, DIRECT, DEMAND, INSIST, prescribe *Order the children to line up.* **3.** REQUEST, commission *order dinner*

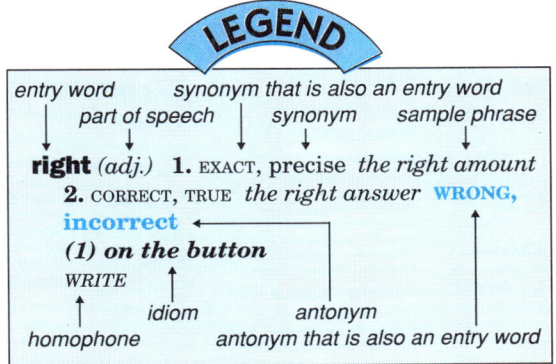

ordinary *(adj.)* COMMON, REGULAR, USUAL, universal **UNIQUE, SPECIAL**

organize *(v.)* ARRANGE, PLAN, ORDER, CONSTRUCT **disorganize**

original *(adj.)* **1.** creative, novel, FRESH, NEW *an original design* **2.** FIRST, primary, initial *the original cast of the play*

outrageous *(adj.)* **1.** FANTASTIC, unconventional *outrageous clothes* **logical, sensible** **2.** excessive, extreme, immodest, immoderate *an outrageous amount of money* **MODEST, conservative**

outstanding *(adj.)* **1.** EXCELLENT, GREAT, SUPERB, TERRIFIC, smashing, sensational *an outstanding performance* **2.** OBVIOUS, CONSPICUOUS, prominent, notable *an outstanding student* **3.** unpaid, DUE, uncollected, payable *an outstanding debt*

overlook *(v.)* **1.** MISS, disregard, IGNORE, neglect *overlook the clue* **2.** EXCUSE, FORGIVE, PARDON *overlook the mistake*

overthrow *(v.)* BEAT, DESTROY, CONQUER, overpower, subdue, overturn, vanquish

own *(v.)* **1.** possess, HOLD, have *own a dog* **2.** ADMIT, CONFESS, acknowledge, avow *own up to a crime* **DENY**

Pp

pack *(n.)* **1.** BAND, GANG, GROUP *a pack of wolves* **2.** package, bundle, parcel *Carry the pack.*

pack *(v.)* load, stuff, STORE, stow, CRAM, compress

pain *(n.)* **1.** ACHE, AGONY, suffering, torture *severe pain* **2.** DISTRESS, MISERY, SORROW, grief, heartache, anguish, torment *the pain of feeling left out*
PANE

pale *(adj.)* DIM, FAINT, wan, pallid, ashen **DARK**
PAIL

panic *(n.)* FRIGHT, ALARM, TERROR, DREAD, dismay, trepidation, hysteria **CALM, tranquil**

paper *(n.)* **1.** document, RECORD, manuscript, composition, certificate *She wrote a paper about dinosaurs.* **2.** stationery, papyrus, letterhead *Write a letter on nice paper.*

pardon *(v.)* FORGIVE, absolve, excuse, CLEAR, acquit, liberate

part *(n.)* **1.** PIECE, portion, SHARE, slice, division, component, FRACTION, fragment, element, feature, DETAIL, SECTION *a part of the puzzle* **WHOLE, sum** **2.** role, character *a part in a play*

party (n.) **1.** affair, EVENT, reception, festivity, spree, fling, celebration, CEREMONY, feast, FESTIVAL *a birthday party* **2.** GROUP, gathering, assemblage *How many are in your party?*

pass (n.) **1.** ROAD, avenue, WAY *take the pass across the mountain* **2.** gorge, ravine *It was a deep mountain pass.* **3.** PERMIT, LICENSE, NOTE *need a hall pass*

pass (v.) **1.** elapse, lapse, CEASE *The time will pass.* **2.** MOVE, proceed, CONTINUE, GO *Pass by the school.* **3.** SEND, DELIVER, hand *Pass the note.* **4.** surpass, EXCEED, excel *The airplane passed the speed of sound.* **5.** DIE, CEASE *When did your uncle pass away?* **6.** APPROVE, enact, LICENSE, PERMIT, ALLOW *Congress passed the bill into law.*

past (adj.) former, previous, prior, earlier **present, future**

paste (v.) glue, STICK, bind, ATTACH, bond, fuse, secure, cement

patch (v.) MEND, REPAIR, FIX, restore

path (n.) **1.** trail, track, ROAD, WAY, COURSE, ROUTE, passage *a path through the woods* **2.** orbit, circuit *Earth's path around the sun*

patience (n.) tolerance, endurance, perseverance, composure, calmness, aplomb **impatience, excitability**
PATIENTS

patient (adj.) understanding, CALM, persevering, PERSISTENT **IMPATIENT, skittish**

pattern (n.) model, SAMPLE, prototype, specimen

pause (n.) DELAY, REST, interval, respite
PAWS

pause (v.) DELAY, REST, HESITATE, WAIT, waver **CONTINUE, proceed, persist**
catch one's breath
PAWS

clue: pause

answer: catch one's breath

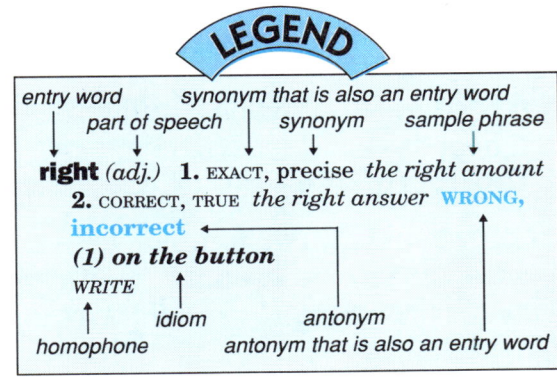

pay *(n.)* payment, salary, wages, allowance, compensation, remittance, stipend

pay *(v.)* SETTLE, square, discharge, reward, compensate, remit **foot the bill**

peace *(n.)* **1.** CALM, QUIET, stillness, respite *peace in the house* **2.** truce, armistice *peace between nations* WAR **3.** EASE, COMFORT, serenity, harmony, concord, solace *peace of mind* **discord, conflict, strife**
PIECE

peaceful *(adj.)* CALM, STILL, settled, tranquil, composed, pacific, placid, serene

peak *(n.)* TOP, summit, apex, acme, pinnacle, zenith **BASE, BOTTOM**
PEEK

peel *(n.)* rind, SKIN
PEAL

people *(n.)* **1.** humans, persons, folk, individuals *A thousand people participated in the parade.* **2.** PUBLIC, population, society, COMMUNITY, masses, populace *a park for the people*

perfect *(v.)* IMPROVE, refine

perfect *(adj.)* flawless, unblemished, PURE, COMPLETE, ACCURATE **faulty, flawed**

perform *(v.)* **1.** DO, ACHIEVE, execute, FULFILL, ACT, enact, commit, EFFECT *perform the work* **2.** ENTERTAIN, function *perform in the play*

perfume *(n.)* aroma, fragrance, SCENT

permanent *(adj.)* **1.** lasting, enduring, perpetual, everlasting, eternal *a permanent home for the puppy* **2.** unchangeable, unalterable, fixed *a permanent tooth*

permission *(n.)* consent, leave, LICENSE, LIBERTY, authorization

permit *(n.)* LICENSE, voucher, warrant, LIBERTY

permit *(v.)* LET, ALLOW, LEAVE, LICENSE, tolerate, grant, APPROVE, sanction, consent, legalize **FORBID, BAN, prohibit**

persistent *(adj.)* CONSTANT, enduring, DETERMINED, STUBBORN, steadfast, relentless

persuade *(v.)* CONVINCE, INFLUENCE, COAX, URGE, entice, induce, **dissuade**
put the pressure on

pest *(n.)* BOTHER, NUISANCE

pick *(v.)* **1.** select, CHOOSE, TAKE, DECIDE, PREFER, cull *pick a movie* **2.** NAME, appoint, designate, nominate, elect *pick a candidate* **3.** GATHER, pluck *pick flowers*
(1) make up one's mind

picture *(n.)* illustration, drawing, diagram, photo, photograph, snapshot, portrait, likeness, IMAGE, PRINT, engraving

piece (n.) BIT, tidbit, SCRAP, PART, crumb, morsel, FRACTION, fragment, SHARE, portion, division, SECTION, remnant
PEACE

pier (n.) dock, jetty, WHARF, landing, quay

pierce (v.) DRILL, puncture, bore, poke, RIDDLE, perforate

pile (n.) heap, mound, mass, store, SUPPLY

pile (v.) COLLECT, GATHER, amass, accumulate, stack

pill (n.) tablet, MEDICINE, capsule, lozenge

pitch (v.) 1. THROW, CAST, FLING, hurl, toss *pitch a ball* 2. erect, RAISE *pitch a tent*

pity (n.) compassion, MERCY, sympathy

pity (v.) sympathize, commiserate, condole

place (n.) 1. location, locality, SPOT, site, POINT, position *a place on the map* 2. AREA, REGION, district, quarter, territory, tract, ENVIRONMENT, surroundings, habitat *a quiet place to live*

plain (adj.) SIMPLE, unadorned, ORDINARY, natural **decorated, FANCY, ornate**
PLANE

plan (n.) DESIGN, scheme, sketch, chart, draft, program, schedule, COURSE, agenda, tactics, program, procedure, proposal, policy, platform, strategy, stratagem

plan (v.) 1. ARRANGE, ORGANIZE, schedule, PROGRAM *Let's plan the day's events.* 2. scheme, anticipate, PLOT, conceive, devise, contrive, concoct, propose, INVENT, IMAGINE *We plan to buy a boat.* 3. DESIGN, chart, SKETCH, draft *a plan for a three-bedroom house*

play (n.) SHOW, drama, performance

play (v.) 1. romp, frolic, frisk, sport, gambol, caper *Play outside.* 2. engage, COMPETE, contend *Next week we play another team.* 3. OPERATE, WORK *play the piano* 4. TOY, trifle *play with someone's feelings* 5. PERFORM, ACT *play a leading role*
(1) horse around

pleasant (adj.) agreeable, delightful, pleasurable, amiable
unpleasant, DISGUSTING

please (v.) SERVE, gratify, pander, PROVIDE, oblige **displease, OFFEND**

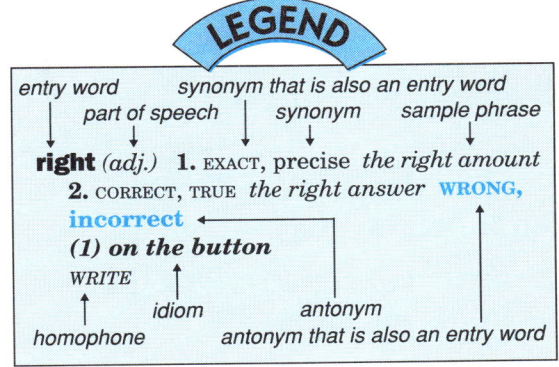

91

pledge *(n.)* PROMISE, VOW, oath, *covenant*

pledge *(v.)* PROMISE, vow, guarantee

plentiful *(adj.)* abundant, numerous, RICH, fruitful, FULL, ample, copious, profuse sparse, SCANT, MEAGER

plenty *(n.)* ENOUGH, abundance, sufficiency scarcity

plot *(n.)* **1.** PLAN, conspiracy, scheme, strategy *a plot to overthrow a government* **2.** theme, ACTION *a plot of a story* **3.** patch, site *a plot of land*

plow *(v.)* WORK, till, cultivate, furrow

poem *(n.)* rhyme, verse, lyric, ballad

point *(n.)* **1.** END, TIP *the point of the pencil* **2.** GOAL, AIM, END, PURPOSE *the point of the discussion*

point *(v.)* SHOW, indicate, gesture, denote, HINT, imply

poison *(n.)* potion, venom, toxin, contaminate, pollutant

poison *(v.)* CONTAMINATE, pollute, INFECT, taint, corrupt

polite *(adj.)* COURTEOUS, KIND, gracious, accommodating, respectful, obliging, refined, civil RUDE, IMPOLITE, discourteous, insulting

pollute *(v.)* CONTAMINATE, defile, taint, foul, sully

ponder *(v.)* THINK, WONDER, reflect, CONSIDER, contemplate, meditate, envisage, ruminate, presume

poor *(adj.)* **1.** penniless, needy, destitute, impoverished, HUMBLE, unpretentious *homeless and poor* RICH, affluent, wealthy **2.** wretched, woeful, pitiable, pathetic, forlorn *a poor neighborhood* GOOD, VALUABLE, FORTUNATE **3.** INFERIOR, unsatisfactory, faulty, sorry *poor telephone service* EXCELLENT, exceptional, FINE
(1) in the red (2) down on one's luck
POUR, PORE

pop *(v.)* BURST, EXPLODE, detonate

popular *(adj.)* **1.** FAVORITE, well-liked, FAMOUS, approved, accepted *a popular singer* unpopular **2.** current, COMMON, prevailing *a popular style of music*

pose *(n.)* posture, POSITION, ATTITUDE, deportment, stance, carriage

pose *(v.)* **1.** model, SIT *pose for a picture* **2.** PRETEND, feign, masquerade *pose as a policeman* **3.** PRESENT, EFFECT, REPRESENT *pose a problem for a debate*

position *(n.)* **1.** PLACE, locality, locale, SPOT *The batter is in position.* **2.** employment, JOB, POST *hired for the position* **3.** STATE, CONDITION, STATION, situation, circumstances *a position of authority* **4.** posture, POSE, ATTITUDE *the position of your body*

positive *(adj.)* **1.** CLEAR, SURE *a positive identification* **negative, doubtful** **2.** CONFIDENT, decided, emphatic, hopeful, optimistic, promising, heartening *a positive feeling about winning the race* **pessimistic, cynical**

possess *(v.)* **1.** OWN, have *possess three cats* **2.** DEMONSTRATE, evidence, manifest *possess great musical talent*

possible *(adj.)* LIKELY, feasible, potential, practicable, achievable IMPOSSIBLE, **inconceivable,** ABSURD
within reach

pour *(v.)* stream, FLOW, RUSH, issue, spout
come down in buckets
POOR

• Guess the Idiom •

clue: pour

answer: come down in buckets

power *(n.)* **1.** force, STRENGTH, MIGHT, ENERGY, vigor, potency *the king's power* **2.** ABILITY, capacity, INFLUENCE *the power to succeed*

powerful *(adj.)* **1.** STRONG, forceful, mighty, potent, commanding *a powerful leader* **powerless, WEAK** **2.** muscular, hale, robust *a powerful runner*
(1) packing a punch

practice *(n.)* drill, training, exercise, EXPERIENCE, rehearsal

practice *(v.)* REHEARSE, PREPARE, REPEAT, recite, reiterate, drill

praise *(n.)* approval, HONOR, applause, tribute, commendation, acclaim

praise *(v.)* APPROVE, HONOR, COMPLIMENT, commend, FLATTER, credit, APPLAUD, CHEER, congratulate CONDEMN, **denounce,** DISAPPROVE, **reprimand**
pat on the back
PRAYS, PREYS

pray *(v.)* ADORE, WORSHIP, supplicate
PREY

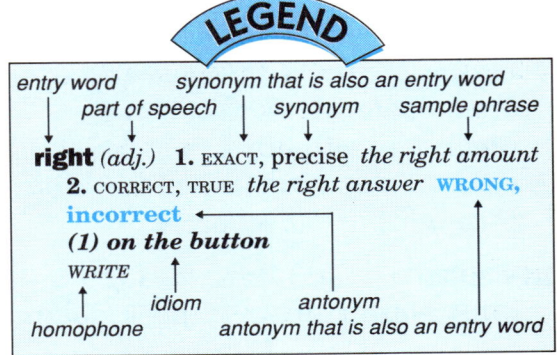

precious (*adj.*) **1.** costly, priceless, VALUABLE *a precious jewel* worthless, USELESS, trashy **2.** beloved, DEAR, DARLING, cherished, prized *a precious child*

predict (*v.*) foresee, foretell, forecast, divine, prophesize

prefer (*v.*) FAVOR, CHOOSE, select, elect

prepare (*v.*) **1.** READY, CONDITION, TRAIN, PRACTICE *prepare for the Olympics* **2.** PROVIDE, FIX, COOK, ARRANGE, ORDER *prepare a meal*

present (*n.*) GIFT, PRIZE, FAVOR, offering, legacy, bequest, gratuity

present (*v.*) **1.** OFFER, GIVE, bestow, SHOW, PRODUCE *present an award* **2.** PERFORM, DISPLAY, EXHIBIT, STAGE *present a play* **3.** INTRODUCE *present a visitor*

preserve (*v.*) PROTECT, KEEP, MAINTAIN, GUARD, SAVE, safeguard, shield, CONSERVE WASTE, squander

press (*v.*) **1.** PUSH, depress, compress, SQUEEZE, flatten *Press the button.* **2.** hasten, HURRY *press to get there on time* **3.** URGE, impel, PERSUADE, provoke, motivate *Let's press the committee to take a vote.* **4.** BEG, implore, plead, appeal *press for forgiveness* **5.** CONTINUE, MOVE *press on through the dense forest*

pretend (*v.*) simulate, pose, AFFECT, DECEIVE, ACT, mock, feign

pretty (*adj.*) BEAUTIFUL, LOVELY, ATTRACTIVE, appealing, bonny, FAIR, HANDSOME UGLY, homely, unsightly, PLAIN

prevent (*v.*) **1.** hinder, impede, thwart, obstruct, INTERRUPT *prevent forest fires* ENCOURAGE, incite, INSPIRE **2.** BLOCK, prohibit, FORBID, disallow *prevent deer hunting* ALLOW, PERMIT, grant *(1) nip in the bud*

• Guess the Idiom •

clue: prevent

answer: nip in the bud

prey (*n.*) VICTIM, sufferer, scapegoat, quarry predator, hunter PRAY

price (*n.*) COST, VALUE, CHARGE, expense, FEE

pride (*n.*) self-respect, self-esteem, conceit, vanity, haughtiness humility, humbleness PRIED

print (*n.*) PICTURE, etching, lithograph, photograph, snapshot

print *(v.)* engrave, MARK, stamp

private *(adj.)* **1.** solitary, secluded *a private location* **2.** personal, individual, SECRET, concealed, CONFIDENTIAL *a private letter* PUBLIC, OPEN

prize *(n.)* FAVOR, GIFT, REWARD, AWARD, trophy, memento, bonus PRIES

probably *(adv.)* LIKELY, possibly, predictably

problem *(n.)* **1.** difficulty, handicap, disability, plight, setback, drawback, obstacle, misfortune, mishap, EMERGENCY, predicament, dilemma, crisis, quandary *a health problem* **2.** RIDDLE, PUZZLE, MYSTERY, enigma, paradox *Solve the problem.* solution, explanation **3.** FAULT, DEFECT, flaw *the problem with the radio* **4.** MATTER, issue *consider your financial problem*
(2) can of worms

produce *(v.)* **1.** CREATE, MAKE, INVENT, MANUFACTURE, CONSTRUCT, fabricate, originate *produce a new product.* **2.** BEAR, beget *produce a healthy baby* **3.** PROVIDE, FURNISH, render, DELIVER *produce a fine performance* **4.** SHOW, EXHIBIT *The attorney produced evidence in court*

product *(n.)* goods, merchandise, commodity, stock

profit *(n.)* gain, RETURN, benefit, advantage loss, expenditure

project *(n.)* **1.** PLAN, scheme, proposal, design *present a project for review* **2.** TASK, ACTIVITY, undertaking, venture *a good project for a rainy day*

promise *(n.)* oath, WORD, assurance, guarantee, pledge, vow

promise *(v.)* PLEDGE, vow, guarantee, ASSURE, AGREE
give one's word

• Guess the Idiom •

clue: promise

answer: give one's word

pronounce *(v.)* **1.** utter, SPEAK, articulate *Pronounce the word correctly.* **2.** DECLARE, affirm *pronounce them husband and wife*

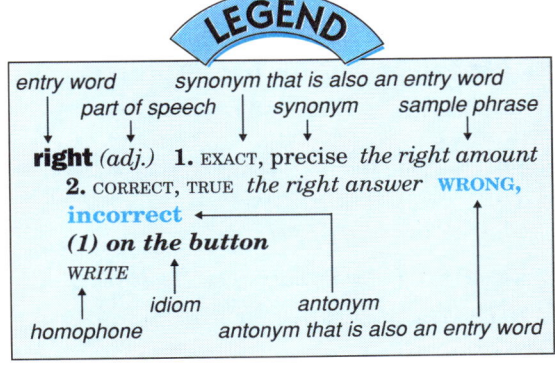

proof *(n.)* evidence, testimony, confirmation

proper *(adj.)* **1.** CORRECT, FIT, fitting, suitable, APPROPRIATE, applicable *the proper clothes* IMPROPER, incorrect **2.** RIGHT, seemly, JUST, decent, respectable, virtuous *the proper thing to do* IMPROPER, indecent

property *(n.)* **1.** land, HOUSE, estate, acreage *buy a piece of property* **2.** belongings, holdings, assets *your personal property* **3.** feature, trait, CHARACTERISTIC, attribute *One property of water is that it is liquid.*

protect *(v.)* DEFEND, GUARD, SHELTER, harbor, PRESERVE, shield, screen ABANDON, DESERT, forsake
take under your wing

proud *(adj.)* NOBLE, stately, dignified, haughty, arrogant, boastful, supercilious HUMBLE, MODEST

prove *(v.)* CONVINCE, SATISFY, PERSUADE, SHOW, ESTABLISH, JUSTIFY, CONFIRM, verify, authenticate, attest disprove

provide *(v.)* GIVE, SUPPLY, furnish, PRODUCE deprive

public *(adj.)* SOCIAL, civil, civic, communal PRIVATE

pull *(v.)* **1.** haul, tug, DRAW, tow, lug, heave, JERK, wrench *Pull the wagon uphill.* PUSH **2.** strain, stretch *He pulled a muscle.*

pun *(n.)* JOKE, RIDDLE, jest, witticism

punch *(v.)* HIT, STRIKE, pound, BEAT, flog, smite, scourge

punish *(v.)* penalize, FINE, SCOLD, discipline, avenge, revenge, admonish, chastise, chasten, persecute, reprove REWARD, PRAISE
throw the book at, send up the river

• Guess the Idiom •

clue: punish

answer: throw the book at

pure *(adj.)* **1.** CLEAN, CLEAR, unpolluted, spotless, stainless, virgin, untouched, FRESH *pure water* impure, polluted, contaminated **2.** INNOCENT, guiltless, virtuous, modest, decent, chaste *live a pure life* IMMORAL, WRONG, CORRUPT **3.** uniform, unmixed *pure silver* **4.** SHEER, absolute, unmitigated *pure happiness*

purpose *(n.)* GOAL, AIM, intent, OBJECT, objective, END, intention, REASON

push (v.) **1.** shove, thrust, press, FORCE, DRIVE, propel *Push him down.* PULL, DRAG **2.** jab, press *Push the button.* **3.** CONVINCE, ENCOURAGE, prod, INFLUENCE, URGE, incite, compel, impel, pressure *Push him to make a decision.*
(3) drive someone up the wall

put (v.) **1.** LAY, PLACE, SET, deposit, ARRANGE, LOCATE, LEAVE *Put the books on the table.* REMOVE, withdraw **2.** thrust, THROW, launch *Put the rocket into space.* **3.** SAY, STATE, EXPRESS *put it mildly* **4.** apply *She put her design sense to good use.*

puzzle (n.) RIDDLE, MYSTERY, enigma, paradox
a hard nut to crack

puzzle (v.) CONFUSE, BAFFLE, bewilder, mix up, mislead, DISTURB, mystify, confound

Qq

quaint (adj.) UNUSUAL, ODD, UNIQUE, STRANGE, peculiar COMMON, ORDINARY, conventional

quake (v.) SHAKE, VIBRATE, tremble, shudder, shiver, quiver

qualified (adj.) FIT, suited, ABLE, skilled, experienced, capable, competent, licensed, certified
unqualified, ill-suited, incompetent

qualify (v.) fit, SUIT, LICENSE, certify

quality (n.) **1.** NATURE, trait, CHARACTERISTIC, PROPERTY *Her sweetness is an appealing quality.* **2.** excellence, CONDITION, stature, caliber *The quality of the photograph was excellent.*

quantity (n.) AMOUNT, SUM, TOTAL, extent

quarrel (n.) argument, disagreement, FIGHT, tiff, tussle, scrape, dispute, fracas
a war of words

quarrel (v.) squabble, bicker, clash, FIGHT, ARGUE, dispute, DISAGREE, tussle, wrangle, oppose, RESIST
have words, fight like cats and dogs

queer (adj.) ODD, STRANGE, WEIRD, UNUSUAL, peculiar, UNIQUE, uncommon, eccentric, quirkish, outlandish, questionable, abnormal, irregular, atypical typical, ORDINARY, USUAL

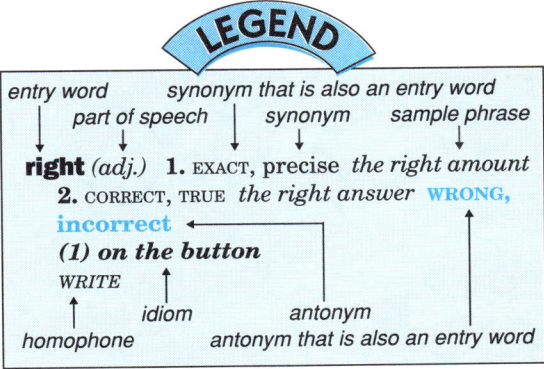

question (n.) REQUEST, appeal, plea, inquiry, entreaty ANSWER, response, retort

question (v.) 1. interrogate, ASK, INQUIRE *question the suspect* ANSWER, RESPOND, retort 2. dispute, DOUBT, debate *question someone's judgment* affirm (1) **give the third degree**

quick (adj.) 1. FAST, RAPID, speedy, swift, HASTY, fleet, nimble, brisk *a quick meal* SLOW, gradual, sluggish 2. SUDDEN, curt, abrupt, blunt *a quick decision* delayed, postponed 3. SMART, BRIGHT, INTELLIGENT, CLEVER, WITTY *a quick mind* DUMB, STUPID, doltish

quiet (n.) CALM, stillness, silence NOISE, din, clamor

quiet (v.) CALM, hush, silence, lull, muffle, stifle, suppress, subdue, quell arouse, provoke

quiet (adj.) 1. SILENT, speechless, hushed, STILL, mute, dumb *a quiet audience* NOISY, LOUD, clamorous 2. CALM, STILL, inactive *quiet water* ACTIVE, bustling 3. CALM, passive, submissive, TAME, subdued, placid *a quiet horse* spirited, lively, frisky 4. SHY, reserved, bashful *a very quiet child* outgoing, bold, confident

quit *(v.)* **1.** STOP, discontinue *Quit talking.* CONTINUE, proceed
2. LEAVE, RESIGN, renounce, retire, relinquish, forsake, ABANDON, DESERT, abdicate *He quit his job.*
(1) call it a day (2) throw in the towel

quiz *(n.)* TEST, exam, examination, PUZZLE

quote *(v.)* **1.** cite, REPEAT, STATE *quote an author's work*
2. NAME, SET, ESTABLISH, MENTION *quote a price*

Rr

race *(n.)* **1.** breed, PEOPLE, tribe, nation *proud of one's color and race* **2.** CONTEST, MATCH, COMPETITION, meet, rivalry *Are you competing in the race?*

race *(v.)* **1.** RUSH, HURRY, HUSTLE, RUN, hasten, speed, DASH *She had to race to get things done.* **2.** COMPETE *race against an opponent*

racket *(n.)* NOISE, hubbub, disturbance, din, uproar, clamor, commotion, tumult
RACQUET

rage *(n.)* **1.** ANGER, madness, frenzy, fury, wrath, fierceness, ferocity *The insult left her in a rage.*
2. fashion, fad, craze *Bell-bottom pants are the rage again.*

ragged *(adj.)* **1.** SHABBY, sloppy, unkempt, untidy, frumpish, scraggly *a ragged appearance*
2. jagged, serrated, barbed, irregular *She cut her finger on the ragged edge.*

raid *(n.)* invasion, ATTACK, assault, foray, onslaught, blitz

raid *(v.)* INVADE, ATTACK, assault, ambush, beset, STORM

rain *(n.)* drizzle, shower, sprinkle, spray, STORM, downpour, gale, flood, torrent, deluge
REIGN, REIN

raise *(v.)* **1.** LIFT, ELEVATE, SUPPORT, hoist *raise a flag* lower, drop
2. INCREASE, promote, heighten, awaken, arouse, spark, invigorate *raise interest in the community* DECREASE, diminish
3. REAR, breed *raise horses*
4. cultivate, GROW *raise tomatoes*
5. COLLECT, GATHER *raise money*
RAYS, RAZE

random *(adj.)* casual, disorganized, haphazard, serendipitous organized, structured, systematic

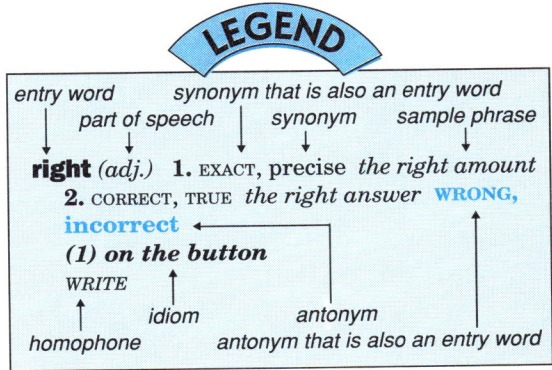

range *(n.)* SCOPE, extent, variance, SPACE, amplitude

rank *(n.)* standing, POSITION, STATION, status, CLASS, GRADE, level

rank *(v.)* ARRANGE, ORDER, classify, SORT

rank *(adj.)* ROTTEN, moldy, stinking, SOUR, FOUL, rancid, putrid

rapid *(adj.)* FAST, QUICK, swift, speedy, HASTY, fleeting, expeditious SLOW, sluggish, gradual, deliberate

rare *(adj.)* uncommon, SCARCE, UNUSUAL, distinctive COMMON, USUAL, ORDINARY, plentiful

rascal *(n.)* rogue, scoundrel, scamp, VILLAIN, knave

rate *(n.)* **1.** COST, CHARGE, PRICE, standard, valuation *pay the hourly rate* **2.** QUANTITY, AMOUNT, DEGREE *the rate of growth* **3.** SPEED, velocity, pace, tempo *The train travels at a rate of 100 miles per hour.*

rate *(v.)* **1.** PRICE, estimate, VALUE, appraise, evaluate, MEASURE, assess *Rate the cost of repairs.* **2.** evaluate, grade, CONSIDER, regard *Rate their skill.* **3.** DESERVE *rate special attention*

raw *(adj.)* **1.** uncooked, green, unripe *raw vegetables* cooked **2.** unfinished, CRUDE, unpolished *raw wood* **3.** inexperienced, unskilled, untrained *a raw recruit* **4.** irritated *a raw sore throat* **5.** COLD, DAMP *a raw day*

raze *(v.)* DESTROY, RUIN, demolish, obliterate BUILD, CREATE
RAYS, RAISE

reach *(v.)* **1.** STRETCH, EXTEND *The rope reaches across the room.* **2.** accomplish, attain, EARN, FULFILL, realize *Strive to reach your goal.*

read *(v.)* STUDY, EXAMINE, peruse **bury oneself in**
REED

• Guess the Idiom •

clue: read

answer: bury oneself in

ready *(adj.)* prepared, fitted, WILLING, disposed unprepared, incomplete
in the saddle

real *(adj.)* **1.** GENUINE, TRUE, CERTAIN, authentic, factual, valid *a real ruby* FAKE, phony, counterfeit, bogus **2.** actual, substantial, tangible, material *Are ghosts real?* IMAGINARY, legendary

realize (v.) COMPREHEND, UNDERSTAND, grasp, conceive, determine, CONCLUDE, fathom *get through one's head, get the picture*

rear (n.) BACK, tail, END, posterior FRONT, face, anterior

rear (v.) RAISE, foster, EDUCATE

reason (n.) 1. CAUSE, motive, AIM, PURPOSE, stimulus *the reason for the meeting* 2. explanation, EXCUSE, justification, rationale *the reason one is late*

reason (v.) THINK, JUDGE, CONSIDER, contemplate, deliberate, REFLECT

recall (v.) 1. REMEMBER, recollect, reminisce, muse *I don't recall the exact number.* FORGET 2. revoke, withdraw, CANCEL, retract, rescind, veto, override *The manufacturer recalled one of its models.* enact, affirm

receive (v.) GET, ACQUIRE, ACCEPT, inherit GIVE, PRESENT, bestow

recess (n.) BREAK, intermission, vacation, respite

recipe (n.) DIRECTIONS, formula, prescription

reckless (adj.) CARELESS, rash, negligent, foolhardy, HASTY, impetuous CAREFUL, CAUTIOUS, prudent

reckon (v.) THINK, CONSIDER, BELIEVE, regard, contemplate, suppose, surmise

recognize (v.) 1. REMEMBER, KNOW, IDENTIFY, distinguish *I recognize the man in the picture.* 2. ADMIT, acknowledge, APPRECIATE *I recognize I am wrong.*

recommend (v.) APPROVE, endorse, commend, sanction, advocate disparage

record (n.) LIST, register, chronicle, catalog, inventory, COPY

record (v.) WRITE, inscribe, register, ENTER

reduce (v.) LESSEN, DECREASE, SUBTRACT, withdraw, deduct, CONTRACT, DROP, dwindle, diminish, subside INCREASE, RAISE *make a dent in*

reflect (v.) 1. mirror, RETURN, REPRODUCE *reflect my image* 2. THINK, CONSIDER, muse, meditate, deliberate *reflect on a disagreement* 3. SHOW, DISPLAY, PRESENT, DEMONSTRATE, manifest *reflect a positive attitude*

refuse (n.) rubbish, GARBAGE, TRASH, WASTE, rubble, debris

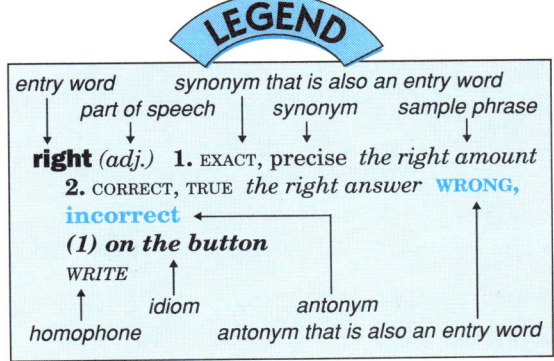

refuse (v.) decline, REJECT, DENY, repel, spurn **accept, admit** *turn down, put one's foot down*

regardless (adv.) notwithstanding, despite, besides

region (n.) AREA, district, quarter, territory, ZONE, sector

regret (n.) remorse, SORROW, CONCERN, grief, heartache, MISERY, DISTRESS, contrition, penitence

regret (v.) lament, repent, rue, bewail, deplore **rejoice** *cry over spilled milk*

◆ Guess the Idiom ◆

clue: regret

answer: cry over spilled milk

regular (adj.) 1. USUAL, ordinary, customary *just a regular day* **UNUSUAL, odd** 2. CONSTANT, STEADY, recurrent, uniform *a regular heartbeat* **irregular, intermittent** 3. symmetrical *a regular shape* **asymmetrical**

rehearse (v.) REPEAT, recite, PRACTICE

reject (v.) 1. decline, snub, REFUSE, DISCARD *reject the invitation* **ACCEPT** 2. DISMISS, spurn, DENY, oust, expel, exile *reject the possibility of surprise* **RECOGNIZE** (1) *give the cold shoulder, leave out in the cold, turn thumbs down*

relax (v.) 1. REST, PAUSE, lounge, loll, EASE, repose *relax with a book* 2. loosen, slacken *relax your hold on the rope*

release (v.) FREE, loose, liberate, extricate **CAPTURE, TRAP** *let off the hook*

relief (n.) 1. HELP, assistance, AID, SUPPORT *send relief to the victims* 2. COMFORT, EASE *a feeling of relief*

religious (adj.) 1. devout, HOLY, pious, reverent *a religious ceremony* **impious** 2. FAITHFUL, CONSISTENT, fervent, devoted *a religious fan* **fickle, changeable**

remain (v.) 1. STAY, WAIT, REST *Remain at work.* **LEAVE, depart** 2. CONTINUE, LAST, abide, prevail *remain a loyal friend* **abandon, discontinue, forsake**

remark (n.) COMMENT, statement, utterance, SAYING, commentary

remark (v.) SAY, EXPRESS, utter

remember (v.) recollect, RECALL, RECOGNIZE, KNOW, MEMORIZE, retain **FORGET** *have on the tip of one's tongue*

remind (v.) prompt, SUGGEST
ring a bell

remove (v.) withdraw, TAKE, RID, eliminate, extract transfer, retain, deposit

repair (v.) FIX, PATCH, remedy, restore, renew, mend, rectify BREAK, dismantle, impair

repeat (v.) **1.** REPRODUCE, DUPLICATE *Repeat the assignment.* **2.** REHEARSE, PRACTICE, ECHO, relate, report, reiterate *Repeat the words to yourself.*
(2) hammer into one's head

• Guess the Idiom •

clue: repeat

answer: hammer into one's head

reply (n.) ANSWER, response, acknowledgment, comeback, reaction, rejoinder

reply (v.) ANSWER, RESPOND, retort QUESTION, ASK

represent (v.) PICTURE, portray, REPRODUCE, depict

reproduce (v.) REPEAT, DUPLICATE, COPY

reputation (n.) CHARACTER, FAME, renown, distinction, INFLUENCE, prestige

request (n.) demand, appeal, inquiry, entreaty

request (v.) ASK, solicit, appeal, beseech DENY

require (v.) **1.** NEED, WANT *We require food and water to live.* **2.** DEMAND, DIRECT, INSIST, ORDER *Require the children to make their own beds.*

rescue (v.) **1.** FREE, SAVE, liberate *rescue the sailors* ABANDON
2. recover, reclaim, restore, IMPROVE *They work to rescue the beaches from erosion.*

research (v.) STUDY, READ, EXAMINE, INVESTIGATE, EXPLORE

resign (v.) QUIT, forsake, LEAVE, relinquish, renounce

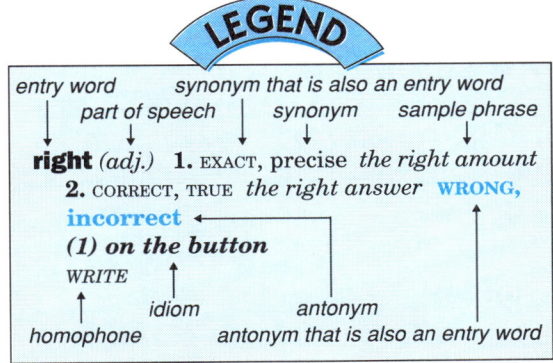

LEGEND

entry word → synonym that is also an entry word
part of speech → synonym → sample phrase

right (adj.) **1.** EXACT, precise *the right amount*
2. CORRECT, TRUE *the right answer* WRONG, incorrect
(1) on the button
WRITE
↑ idiom antonym
homophone antonym that is also an entry word

103

resist *(v.)* **1.** FIGHT, oppose, confront *Resist the enemy.* YIELD, SURRENDER **2.** IGNORE, STAND, withstand, thwart, curb *Resist the temptation.* submit
(1) make a stand, not give an inch

• Guess the Idiom •

clue: resist

answer: make a stand

respect *(n.)* **1.** regard, HONOR, admiration, esteem, homage, deference *Respect your elders.* **2.** DETAIL, particular, feature, point *In one respect, your plan is solid.*

respect *(v.)* regard, esteem, HONOR, ADMIRE, venerate, revere

respond *(v.)* ANSWER, react, REPLY, retort QUESTION

responsible *(adj.)* **1.** liable, accountable, answerable *responsible for equipment and uniforms* **2.** dependable, reliable, trustworthy, capable *a responsible student* irresponsible, unreliable
(1) falling on one's shoulders

rest *(n.)* **1.** CALM, EASE, QUIET, relaxation, PAUSE *a rest in the storm* **2.** NAP, SLEEP, repose *Take a rest on the couch.* **3.** remainder, remnant, residue, surplus *Give the rest of the food to the dog.*

restaurant *(n.)* cafe, bistro, delicatessen, canteen, diner, luncheonette

restless *(adj.)* **1.** moving, unstable, wandering, roving *a restless child* QUIET, sedate **2.** uneasy, NERVOUS, fretful, discontented, jittery, apprehensive, skittish *a restless mood* CALM, relaxed **3.** sleepless, wakeful, insomnious *tired after a restless night's sleep*

result *(n.)* END, EFFECT, outcome, consequence, sequel CAUSE

result *(v.)* arise, FOLLOW, HAPPEN, ensue CAUSE

• Guess the Idiom •

clue: responsible

answer: falling on one's shoulders

return (v.) **1.** reappear *The students return to the classroom.* **2.** restore, renew, revert *return to original condition* **3.** replace *Return the file to the drawer.* **4.** repay *Return the money.*

revenge (n.) retaliation, vengeance, reprisal, vendetta **taste of one's own medicine, get even with**

reverse (v.) TURN, transpose, invert

review (v.) STUDY, reconsider, revise, EXAMINE, reexamine **brush up on**

revolution (n.) **1.** revolt, rebellion, mutiny, uprising *the American Revolution* **2.** rotation, movement, circuit, cycle *one revolution around the sun*

reward (n.) PRIZE, bounty, FAVOR, AWARD, bonus, compensation **punishment, penalty**

rewrite (v.) revise, alter, edit, redraft, revamp

rich (adj.) **1.** wealthy, affluent, prosperous *my rich uncle* **POOR, penniless** **2.** lavish, LUXURIOUS, extravagant, SPLENDID, sumptuous, opulent *a rich home* **modest, humble** **3.** abundant, profuse *a rich harvest* **meager, SPARE**
(1) rolling in dough

rid (v.) **1.** FREE, CLEAR, RELEASE *Rid yourself of all your fears.* **2.** DESTROY, ELIMINATE *She got rid of the mosquitoes.*

◆ Guess the Idiom ◆

clue: rich

answer: rolling in dough

riddle (n.) PUZZLE, MYSTERY, PROBLEM, enigma, quandary **can of worms**

ridicule (v.) INSULT, jeer, mock, TEASE, taunt, deride, satirize **praise, compliment**

ridiculous (adj.) FOOLISH, ABSURD, preposterous, laughable, ludicrous, inept **praiseworthy, sensible, commendable, SOUND**

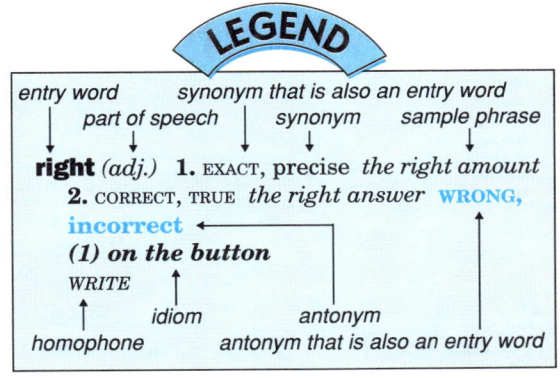

LEGEND

entry word → synonym that is also an entry word
part of speech → synonym sample phrase
right (adj.) **1.** EXACT, precise *the right amount* **2.** CORRECT, TRUE *the right answer* **WRONG, incorrect**
(1) on the button
WRITE ↑ idiom antonym
homophone antonym that is also an entry word

105

right (*n.*) **1.** privilege, due *the right to an attorney* **2.** CLAIM, ownership, title *the right to the property*
WRITE. RITE

right (*adj.*) **1.** EXACT, ACCURATE, precise *the right amount* **2.** CORRECT, TRUE *the right answer* WRONG, **incorrect,** FALSE **3.** FAIR, JUST, HONEST, upright, lawful, APPROPRIATE *the right thing to do*
(1) on the button
WRITE, RITE

rigid (*adj.*) STIFF, inflexible, unbending, STRICT, stern FLEXIBLE, **adaptable, elastic, pliable**

rim (*n.*) BORDER, EDGE, SIDE, brim, margin, skirt, fringe, verge

ring (*n.*) **1.** CIRCLE, hoop, loop *a plastic ring* **2.** GANG, BAND, clan, clique *a car theft ring*
WRING

ring (*v.*) **1.** chime, toll, peal, sound, tinkle *Ring the bell.* **2.** encircle, surround *The police ring the building.*
WRING

riot (*n.*) clash, STRUGGLE, disturbance, tumult, BRAWL, revolt, uproar, fray, fracas

rip (*v.*) slash, slit, SPLIT, rend

ripe (*adj.*) READY, mature, finished, aged RAW, **green, immature**

rise (*v.*) **1.** ELEVATE, arise, ascend *The dough will rise.* FALL, SINK, DESCEND **2.** INCREASE, ADD, CLIMB, mount, AMOUNT, ascend *The population will rise.* DECREASE **3.** arise, WAKE, get up *rise in the morning*

risk (*n.*) CHANCE, jeopardy, DANGER, HAZARD, peril
a long shot

risk (*v.*) BET, GAMBLE, CHANCE, stake, wager, venture, DARE
play with fire, stick your neck out, go out on a limb

rival (*n.*) competitor, OPPONENT, ENEMY, FOE, antagonist, adversary **teammate, partner**

road (*n.*) STREET, lane, avenue, boulevard, passage, alley, WAY, track, ROUTE, COURSE
RODE

roam (*v.*) WANDER, range, rove, ramble, meander, traipse

rob (*v.*) STEAL, loot, sack, rifle, STRIP, RAID, fleece, pilfer, despoil, deprive, divest, ravage

robber (*n.*) bandit, THIEF, outlaw, crook, CRIMINAL, burglar, pickpocket, brigand, pirate

rock (*n.*) **1.** STONE, pebble, boulder *The sailboat was wrecked on the rocks.* **2.** mineral, gem, ore *Diamonds and rubies may be called rocks.*

rock (*v.*) sway, swing, wobble, totter, reel, oscillate

rod (*n.*) pole, STICK, wand, cane, staff, scepter

role *(n.)* **1.** PART, CHARACTER, position *the starring role* **2.** DUTY, TASK, function *your office role*
ROLL

roll *(n.)* **1.** bun, bread, loaf *Butter the roll.* **2.** TURN, SPIN, somersault, flip *Do a forward roll.*
ROLE

roll *(v.)* **1.** TURN, whirl, revolve, rotate *Roll the wheel.* **2.** bind, WRAP, swathe *Roll the rug.*
ROLE

romantic *(adj.)* **1.** fictional, imaginative *a romantic tale* **2.** amorous, passionate, sentimental, lovelorn, TENDER, SENSITIVE *in a romantic mood*

roof *(n.)* COVER, canopy, SHELTER

room *(n.)* **1.** AREA, SPACE, extent, expanse *room for one more* **2.** ward, apartment, chamber *the storage room*

root *(n.)* **1.** tuber, rootlet *the root of a tree* **2.** CAUSE, origin, beginning, SOURCE, basis, REASON, derivation *the root of her anger*

rot *(v.)* SPOIL, DECAY, decompose, putrefy, molder

rotten *(adj.)* **1.** decayed, stinking, FOUL, rancid, RANK, SOUR, moldy, putrid *a rotten piece of meat* FRESH **2.** DISHONEST, CORRUPT, treacherous *He played a rotten trick.*

rough *(adj.)* **1.** uneven, bumpy, rocky, COARSE, bristly *a rough texture* SMOOTH **2.** RUDE, HARSH, uncivil, IMPOLITE, churlish *rough manners* POLITE **3.** stormy, tempestuous *rough weather* CALM **4.** HARD, DIFFICULT, TOUGH *a rough test* EASY
RUFF

round *(adj.)* curved, circular, spherical, globular

route *(n.)* WAY, COURSE, PATH, ROAD
ROOT

royal *(adj.)* NOBLE, MAJESTIC, regal, imperial, kingly

rub *(v.)* **1.** stroke, massage, knead, stimulate *rub someone's back* **2.** WIPE, polish, scour, SCRUB, scrape *Rub off the tarnish.*

rude *(adj.)* blunt, gruff, curt, discourteous, IMPOLITE, churlish, impertinent, insolent, impudent, flippant, boorish POLITE, **courteous, gracious**

rugged *(adj.)* hardy, STURDY, robust, TOUGH, durable, stalwart FRAGILE, **delicate,** WEAK

ruin *(v.)* mar, SPOIL, tarnish, deface, disfigure, DESTROY, demolish, defile, debase, impair

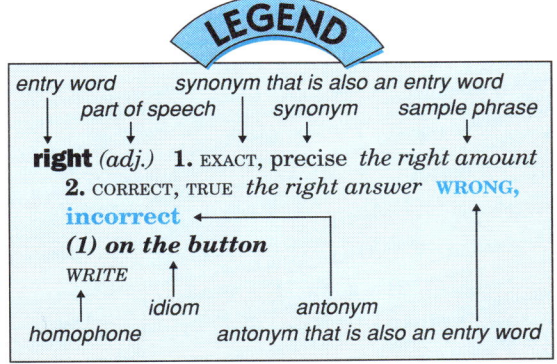

rule (n.) LAW, ORDER, regulation, statute, mandate, principle, standard, doctrine, decree, tenet, precept

rule (v.) GOVERN, reign, CONTROL, COMMAND, MANAGE, dominate **call the tune, hold sway**

ruler (n.) LEADER, CHIEF, head, monarch, KING, emperor, czar, lord, sovereign, president

rumor (n.) GOSSIP, hearsay FACT

run (v.) 1. jog, HURRY, scurry, RUSH, DASH, dart, sprint, RACE, bound, bolt, trot, canter, gallop, lope *run down a street* 2. ESCAPE, flee, abscond *run from the law* REMAIN, STAY 3. OPERATE, WORK, MANAGE *run a machine*

rural (adj.) COUNTRY, rustic, pastoral, agrarian, agricultural urban, citified

rush (v.) HURRY, hasten, speed, DASH, HUSTLE, scurry, scoot, sprint dally, delay **beat the pavement, shake a leg**

rusty (adj.) corroded, WORN

Ss

sad (adj.) 1. sorrowful, UNHAPPY, discouraged, GLOOMY, downcast, dispirited, somber, GLUM, BLUE, melancholy, mournful, dejected, dismal, morose, crestfallen, despondent, doleful, woeful, forlorn, woebegone *sad feelings* HAPPY, joyful, fortunate, contented, GLAD, ecstatic, CHEERFUL 2. POOR, MISERABLE, wretched *a sad state of affairs* GOOD, VALUABLE
(1) down in the dumps

safe (adj.) 1. protected, guarded, SECURE, exempt, invulnerable *a safe place to hide* endangered, unsafe, DANGEROUS, exposed, hazardous 2. SURE, reliable, trustworthy *a safe plan of action* RISKY, uncertain
(1) out of the woods

◆ Guess the Idiom ◆

clue: rush

answer: beat the pavement

safety (n.) security, protection, preservation, invulnerability DANGER, peril

sail (v.) 1. float, cruise, skim, coast, navigate, embark *sail across a lake* 2. pilot, STEER, navigate *sail a boat* SALE

same *(adj.)* ALIKE, similar, matched, EQUAL, equivalent, IDENTICAL, uniform, indistinguishable DIFFERENT, **dissimilar, unalike**

sample *(n.)* example, PATTERN, model, specimen, COPY, prototype

sample *(v.)* TASTE, TRY, EXPERIENCE, TEST

sane *(adj.)* SOUND, lucid, rational, sensible CRAZY, **insane**

satisfactory *(adj.)* **1.** acceptable, pleasing *a satisfactory meal* **2.** sufficient, ADEQUATE, ample, enough *a satisfactory amount*

satisfy *(v.)* **1.** PLEASE, gratify *satisfy a desire* **2.** FILL, sate, satiate *satisfy an appetite*

savage *(adj.)* **1.** BRUTAL, VIOLENT, FEROCIOUS, fierce, cold-blooded *a savage attack* **2.** WILD, uncivilized, barbarous *a savage person*

save *(v.)* **1.** RESCUE, liberate, DELIVER *save the victim* **2.** KEEP, STORE, PRESERVE, secure, accumulate, HOLD, hoard, reserve, amass *save money* SPEND, **squander**
(2) *squirrel away*

say *(v.)* TELL, STATE, CLAIM, DECLARE, MENTION, refer, REMARK, recite, ANNOUNCE, notify, disclose, divulge, assert, proclaim, profess, vouch, attest
put into words

saying *(n.)* motto, phrase, slogan, expression, proverb, catchword, maxim, axiom, adage

scanty *(adj.)* meager, sparing, sparse **abundant, profuse**

scarce *(adj.)* RARE, uncommon, infrequent, wanting, SCANTY, deficient COMMON, **abundant, plentiful**

scare *(v.)* FRIGHTEN, startle, ALARM, SHOCK, daunt, THREATEN, BULLY, terrify, dismay, menace, intimidate ASSURE, CALM, SOOTHE
make one's hair stand on end

• Guess the Idiom •

clue: scare

answer: make one's hair stand on end

scary *(adj.)* frightening, spooky, terrifying, horrifying

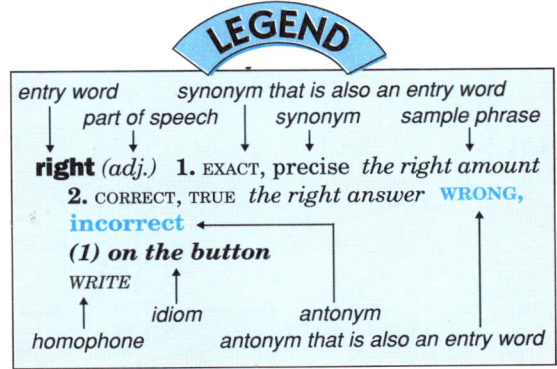

LEGEND

entry word → synonym that is also an entry word
part of speech → synonym → sample phrase

right *(adj.)* **1.** EXACT, precise *the right amount* **2.** CORRECT, TRUE *the right answer* WRONG, **incorrect**
(1) *on the button*
WRITE ↑ ↑ idiom ↑ antonym
homophone   antonym that is also an entry word

scatter *(v.)* **1.** strew, sprinkle, disperse, SPREAD, DISTRIBUTE *Scatter the seeds.* GATHER **2.** disperse, disband, SEPARATE, DISSOLVE *The crowd began to scatter.*

scene *(n.)* VIEW, landscape, survey, vision

scent *(n.)* SMELL, odor, fragrance, aroma, PERFUME, essence, bouquet stench

school *(n.)* institute, academy, COLLEGE, university

scold *(v.)* reprimand, BLAME, chide, reproach, rebuke, reprove, berate
give someone a piece of your mind

clue: scold

answer: give someone a piece of your mind

scope *(n.)* RANGE, extent

scramble *(v.)* **1.** HURRY, RUSH, skedaddle, scurry *He scrambled to get ready for work.* **2.** MIX, BLEND, COMBINE, merge *Scramble the eggs.* **3.** COMPETE, STRUGGLE, vie *The children scramble for first place in line.*

scrap *(n.)* BIT, fragment, morsel, remnant, particle, crumb

scrap *(v.)* DISCARD, ABANDON, forsake, demolish retain

scream *(v.)* CRY, screech, shriek, SHOUT
yell one's head off, blow your stack

clue: scream

answer: yell one's head off

scribble *(v.)* scrawl, jot, doodle, WRITE

scrub *(v.)* scour, clean, swab

seal *(v.)* CLOSE, FASTEN, secure OPEN, RELEASE, unlock

search *(n.)* HUNT, quest, pursuit, CHASE, exploration

search *(v.)* SEEK, EXAMINE, scan, INVESTIGATE, INSPECT, scrutinize, probe, HUNT, EXPLORE, INVESTIGATE, rummage, rifle
go through with a fine-tooth comb, leave no stone unturned

secret *(n.)* MYSTERY, CONFIDENCE

secret *(adj.)* **1.** PRIVATE, personal, individual, SPECIAL *a secret diary* PUBLIC, **disclosed, known** **2.** stealthy, mysterious, unknown, HIDDEN, concealed, clandestine, furtive, surreptitious, obscure *a secret plan* **shared, accessible,** OPEN

(2) keeping something under one's hat

section *(n.)* PART, PIECE, portion, segment, division, FRACTION, component, feature, department

secure *(adj.)* **1.** SAFE, protected, guarded, invulnerable *a secure hiding place* **unsafe,** OPEN, **precarious** **2.** CONFIDENT, self-confident, poised, sanguine *a secure person* INSECURE, **doubtful**

• Guess the Idiom •

clue: secret

answer: keeping something under one's hat

Go CRAZY with WORDS!

scent

STENCH

FRAGRANCE

see *(v.)* **1.** NOTE, NOTICE, OBSERVE, perceive, distinguish, DISCOVER, discern, DETECT, SPOT, behold, regard, picture, IMAGINE *see the bird take off* IGNORE, **disregard** **2.** UNDERSTAND, APPRECIATE, EXPERIENCE *see the truth* **3.** accompany, escort *see her to the door* **(1) lay eyes on**
SEA

seek *(v.)* **1.** SEARCH, LOOK, INVESTIGATE *seek someone in hiding* **2.** ATTEMPT, TRY, strive, endeavor *seek to improve their living conditions*

seem *(v.)* APPEAR, LOOK
SEAM

selfish *(adj.)* CHEAP, miserly, STINGY, inconsiderate, heedless, THOUGHTLESS, CARELESS **selfless, GENEROUS**

sell *(v.)* vend, market, peddle, hawk, retail, exchange, barter **BUY, acquire, purchase**
CELL

send *(v.)* post, mail, ship, dispatch, transmit, forward, CONVEY **RECEIVE**

sense *(n.)* **1.** FEELING, sensation, perception, impression *a sense of fear* **2.** REASON, JUDGMENT, conviction, MIND, understanding, intellect *use common sense*
CENTS

sensitive *(adj.)* **1.** touchy, testy, temperamental, MOODY, peevish *a sensitive talk* **2.** vulnerable, susceptible *sensitive to criticism* **hardened, indifferent** **3.** TENDER, painful *a sensitive bruise*

separate *(v.)* PART, DIVIDE, sever, DETACH, DISCONNECT **ATTACH, JOIN, CONNECT**

separate *(adj.)* apart, isolated, SINGLE, lone, remote **ATTACHED, connected, joined,** UNITED

serious *(adj.)* **1.** solemn, EARNEST, SOBER, GRIM, staid, ardent *a serious movie* **light, playful, funny** **2.** GRAVE, CRITICAL, weighty, severe *a serious medical problem* **unimportant**

serve *(v.)* AID, HELP, ASSIST, oblige, SATISFY, PLEASE

set *(n.)* **1.** setting, scene, backdrop *the set for a play* **2.** COLLECTION, GROUP, BUNCH *a set of dishes*

set *(v.)* **1.** PUT, PLACE, LOCATE, LAY *Set it down on the table.* **2.** FIX, ESTABLISH, SETTLE, determine, regulate, ADJUST *Set the price.*

set *(adj.)* FIRM, unchanging, unyielding, adamant *carved in stone*

settle *(v.)* **1.** LIVE, abide, INHABIT *settle in a new town* **2.** PAY, compensate, remit, square *settle a debt*

several *(adj.)* SOME, various, MANY **few**

sew *(v.)* stitch, mend, darn, PATCH, embroider, suture
SO

shabby *(adj.)* SORRY, WORN, run-down, wretched, threadbare, RAGGED

shake *(v.)* **1.** QUAKE, tremble, shudder, rattle, shiver, twitch, quiver, VIBRATE, jolt, jar, rouse, oscillate *shake with fear* **2.** agitate *Shake the bottle of juice before you drink it.*

shame *(n.)* disgrace, dishonor, ignominy, embarrassment, humiliation, guilt, remorse
PRIDE, HONOR

shape *(n.)* FORM, outline, PATTERN, FIGURE, mold, silhouette

share *(n.)* PART, PIECE, portion, serving, division, dividend
WHOLE

share *(v.)* DIVIDE, DISTRIBUTE, apportion, allot

sharp *(adj.)* **1.** cutting, piercing *a sharp knife* blunt, DULL **2.** keen, SENSITIVE, QUICK, ALERT *A dog has sharp senses.* DULL, SLOW, dense **3.** CLEVER, astute, shrewd *a sharp detective* STUPID, dim-witted **4.** SEVERE, SERIOUS, acute, INTENSE, agonizing, excruciating *a sharp pain*

sheer *(adj.)* **1.** PURE, utter, CLEAR, absolute *sheer delight* **2.** THIN, FINE, CLEAR, transparent, diaphanous *sheer cloth* opaque
SHEAR

shelter *(n.)* SAFETY, haven, retreat, ROOF, asylum, refuge, sanctuary EXPOSE, reveal

shelter *(v.)* HIDE, PROTECT, DEFEND, shield, screen

shine *(n.)* gloss, sheen, glaze, polish, luster

shine *(v.)* **1.** glisten, SPARKLE, shimmer, GLOW, glimmer, dazzle *The moonlight shines on the lake.* **2.** polish, burnish *Shine the car.*

shock *(n.)* **1.** surprise, astonishment, awe, bewilderment *the shock of seeing something disappear* **2.** CRASH, impact, collision *The shock cracked the axle.* **3.** jolt, paralysis *an electric shock*

shock *(v.)* **1.** AMAZE, SURPRISE, ASTONISH, stagger *The magic trick will shock you.* **2.** OFFEND, UPSET, disgust, outrage, appall *The violence in the film may shock you.* **3.** electrify, stun *Don't touch a live wire; it will shock you.*
(1) raise some eyebrows

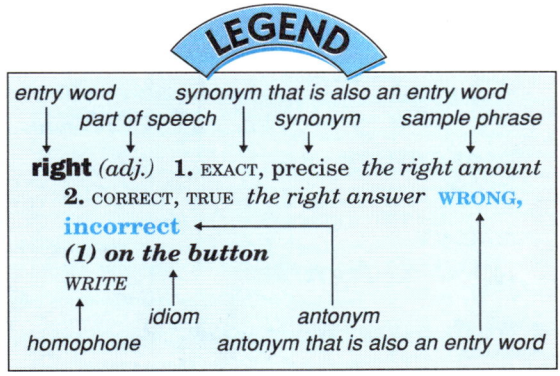

shocked *(adj.)* **1.** amazed, startled, astonished, staggered, appalled, aghast *shocked by her honesty* **2.** alarmed, unnerved, frightened *shocked by the news* **(1) can't believe one's eyes**

short *(adj.)* **1.** BRIEF, concise, condensed, succinct *a short story* LONG, **lengthy 2.** LITTLE, SMALL, puny *a short man* TALL, **towering 3.** RUDE, terse, brusque, pithy *He spoke in a short manner.* POLITE, FRIENDLY

shorten *(v.)* condense, CONCENTRATE, DECREASE, crop, SHRINK, abridge, abbreviate, REDUCE, diminish **lengthen, ENLARGE, SWELL, GROW, INCREASE**

shout *(v.)* YELL, CALL, DECLARE, EXCLAIM, SCREAM, shriek **whisper, murmur** **raise the roof**

show *(n.)* **1.** exhibit, exhibition, DISPLAY, PLAY, performance, production, program *The show begins at 8:00.* **2.** sight, spectacle *The fireworks show was dazzling.*

show *(v.)* **1.** DEMONSTRATE, TEACH *show someone how to draw* **2.** LEAD, reveal, indicate, POINT, PRESENT, GUIDE, usher, EXPOSE, UNCOVER *show the way* **CONCEAL, HIDE, mask 3.** PROVE, manifest, disclose *show that the answer is correct* **(2) shed light on**

shrink *(v.)* LESSEN, REDUCE, dwindle, minimize, SHORTEN, diminish, condense, CONTRACT, CONCENTRATE, abridge, abbreviate **EXPAND, INCREASE, ENLARGE**

shut *(v.)* CLOSE, secure, SEAL, slam, FASTEN, LOCK **OPEN, unfasten**

shy *(adj.)* bashful, TIMID, modest, coy, reserved, shrinking, retiring, demure, diffident, sheepish **BOLD, outgoing, forthright, outspoken, overt, brazen**

sick *(adj.)* ILL, ailing, unwell, diseased, unhealthy, infirm, FEEBLE, indisposed **WELL, HEALTHY** **under the weather**

• Guess the Idiom •

clue: sick

answer: under the weather

sickness *(n.)* illness, DISEASE, ailment, malady, affliction

side *(n.)* **1.** EDGE, BORDER, margin, verge *the side of the paper* **2.** TEAM, faction *Which side are you rooting for?* SIGHED

side *(v.)* SUPPORT, JOIN, advocate, CHAMPION, sanction SIGHED

sign *(n.)* **1.** NOTICE, advertisement, poster, BILL, handbill, placard *Hang up the sign.* **2.** indication, HINT, symptom *a sign of the flu* **3.** MARK, token, SYMBOL *a sign that someone had been there*

sign *(v.)* endorse, initial, inscribe, autograph

silent *(adj.)* **1.** QUIET, soundless, STILL, CALM, sedate, placid, pacific *The house was silent.* LOUD, NOISY **2.** unexpressed, unstated, inferred, understood, implicit, insinuated *a silent agreement* **3.** inactive, passive, dormant, resting, lifeless, inanimate *The volcano was silent.*

silly *(adj.)* FOOLISH, senseless, RIDICULOUS, ABSURD, daft, idiotic, fatuous, frivolous, trifling, imprudent, inept, preposterous, asinine reasonable, sensible

simple *(adj.)* **1.** PLAIN, unadorned, ORDINARY, unaffected *a simple design* ELABORATE **2.** EASY, effortless, CLEAR *a simple recipe* DIFFICULT, COMPLEX **3.** naive, unsophisticated, inexperienced, FOOLISH *a simple child*
(2) a real snap

sincere *(adj.)* HONEST, frank, OPEN, candid, direct, TRUE, REAL, GENUINE INSINCERE, dishonest

sing *(v.)* chant, carol, hum, vocalize, warble, croon

single *(adj.)* **1.** lone, sole, solitary, ALONE *a single cabin in the woods* multiple **2.** unmarried, unwed *a single man*

sink *(v.)* **1.** submerge, submerse, immerse *sink to the bottom of the river* float, emerge, RISE **2.** LESSEN, REDUCE, depress, plummet, plunge *The prices will sink.* INCREASE, grow

sit *(v.)* **1.** REST, PAUSE, REMAIN, repose *Sit for a while.* **2.** perch, settle, roost, squat *Sit on the chair.*

size *(n.)* bulk, volume, mass, extent, AMOUNT, gauge, SCOPE, magnitude, dimension
SIGHS

sketch *(v.)* DRAW, portray, picture, ILLUSTRATE, outline, draft, REPRESENT, trace, depict

skill *(n.)* ABILITY, talent, knack, aptitude, expertise, adroitness

skin *(n.)* **1.** hide, fur, pelt, coat *the skin of a bear* **2.** rind, husk, PEEL, crust *the skin of an orange*

skinny *(adj.)* THIN, LEAN, slender, slight, underweight, lank, spare, gaunt FAT, obese, CHUBBY

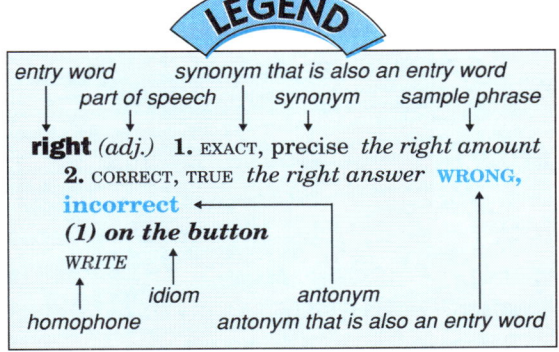

skip *(v.)* **1.** HOP, JUMP, SPRING, LEAP, gambol *skip down the sidewalk* **2.** MISS, OMIT, disregard *skip a word* INCLUDE

slant *(n.)* diagonal, SLOPE, pitch, angle, ramp, gradient

slave *(n.)* vassal, pawn, captive, serf master

sleep *(v.)* slumber, NAP, DOZE, snooze, repose WAKE **hit the sack, hit the hay**

slim *(adj.)* **1.** THIN, SKINNY, slender, gaunt, lank, svelte, lithe *a slim man* FAT, **corpulent, plump,** CHUBBY **2.** SMALL, trifling, insignificant *a slim chance for survival*

slip *(n.)* ERROR, MISTAKE, BLUNDER, oversight, offense, failing

slip *(v.)* slide, glide, skid, stumble

slope *(n.)* SLANT, pitch, angle, incline, tilt, ramp, gradient

slope *(v.)* TIP, LEAN, incline, slant, tilt

sloppy *(adj.)* **1.** MESSY, untidy, disordered, DIRTY, slovenly, unkempt, disheveled *a sloppy room* NEAT, TIDY **2.** CARELESS, THOUGHTLESS, neglectful, rash *Her work was sloppy.* CAREFUL, **painstaking, thoughtful**

slow *(adj.)* **1.** sluggish, leisurely *a slow walk* FAST, **speedy, swift** **2.** DULL, deficient, retarded *a slow learner* QUICK, SHARP, BRIGHT **3.** GRADUAL *a slow improvement* **abrupt**

sly *(adj.)* CUNNING, shrewd, crafty, artful, astute, wily, furtive

small *(adj.)* **1.** LITTLE, TINY, wee, puny, minute, compact, miniature, diminutive *a small animal* BIG, HUGE, **colossal, gigantic** **2.** slight, SCANT *a small amount of money* **3.** modest, MINOR, trivial, UNIMPORTANT *a small effort* IMPORTANT

smart *(adj.)* **1.** INTELLIGENT, BRIGHT, WISE, shrewd, CUNNING, ALERT, SHARP, apt, quick-witted, CLEVER, astute, canny, BRILLIANT, ingenious *a smart child* DUMB, STUPID, DULL, **dimwitted** **2.** stylish, neat, fashionable, trendy, modish, swanky, dapper *a smart dress* **dowdy, old-fashioned**

smash *(v.)* CRUSH, compress, shatter, demolish REPAIR

smell *(n.)* odor, aroma, SCENT, whiff, fragrance, extract, stench, essence, bouquet

smell *(v.)* **1.** sniff, inhale, BREATHE, whiff *Smell the rose.* **2.** STINK, reek, putrefy *Rotten eggs smell.*

smile *(v.)* grin, smirk, beam FROWN, **scowl**

smooth *(adj.)* **1.** EVEN, FLAT, LEVEL *Skate on the smooth sidewalk.* **uneven, bumpy, wrinkled,** ROUGH **2.** polished, slippery, slick, sleek *slip on the smooth surface* ROUGH **3.** creamy *Mix the batter until it is smooth.*

sneak *(v.)* slink, creep, prowl, STEAL, skulk, lurk

Go CRAZY with WORDS!

smell: SNIFF, INHALE, WHIFF

sneaky *(adj.)* shifty, foxy, deceitful, furtive, covert, devious

soak *(v.)* drench, steep, immerse, submerge DRY

sober *(adj.)* **1.** temperate, abstemious *The alcoholic will work hard to stay sober.* intoxicated, DRUNK **2.** SERIOUS, somber *a sober occasion* frivolous

social *(adj.)* **1.** FRIENDLY, gregarious, convivial *a very social person* **2.** PUBLIC *a social setting*

soft *(adj.)* **1.** fleecy, fluffy, limp, FLEXIBLE, pliable, malleable *soft to the touch* HARD, STIFF, RIGID **2.** lenient *a soft attitude toward youthful offenders* STUBBORN, unyielding, HARSH **3.** MILD, GENTLE *a soft detergent*

solve *(v.)* EXPLAIN, decode, unravel, resolve, decipher
get to the bottom of

some *(adj.)* SEVERAL, various
MANY
SUM

song *(n.)* TUNE, jingle, melody, music, refrain, anthem

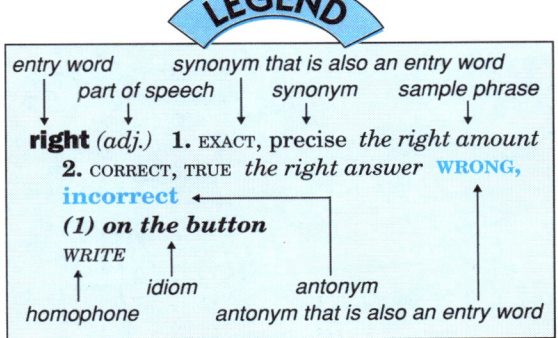

LEGEND — entry word, part of speech, synonym that is also an entry word, synonym, sample phrase
right *(adj.)* **1.** EXACT, precise *the right amount* **2.** CORRECT, TRUE *the right answer* WRONG, incorrect
(1) on the button
WRITE
homophone, idiom, antonym, antonym that is also an entry word

soothe (v.) **1.** EASE, CURE, COMFORT, appease *The medicine soothes the pain.* AGGRAVATE, worsen, intensify **2.** CALM, QUIET, pacify, cajole *soothe someone's temper* rouse, provoke, harass
(2) **take the edge off**

sophisticated (adj.) experienced, suave, civilized, urbane CRUDE, unrefined, INNOCENT, naive

sore (n.) WOUND, CUT, affliction, infection, boil
SOAR

sore (adj.) painful, TENDER, irritated, hurt, infected
SOAR

sorrow (n.) grief, PAIN, REGRET, woe, sadness, heartache, MISERY, DISTRESS, remorse, anguish HAPPINESS, gaiety, joy

sorry (adj.) **1.** remorseful, apologetic, HUMBLE, repentant, penitent, contrite *I feel sorry for the trouble I have caused.* **2.** MISERABLE, SHABBY, wretched *The house was in sorry condition.* EXCELLENT, superior, SPLENDID

sort (n.) TYPE, KIND, CLASS, VARIETY, species

sort (v.) ORDER, classify, ARRANGE, DISTRIBUTE

sound (n.) NOISE, tone, din, racket

sound *(adj.)* **1.** TRUE, CORRECT, reasonable, rational, sensible *a sound argument* faulty **2.** well, HEALTHY, hale *He felt sound enough to compete.* unsound, unhealthy

sour *(v.)* SPOIL, ferment, curdle

sour *(adj.)* **1.** tart, SHARP, BITTER, acidic, pungent *a sour apple* sweet **2.** brooding, crabby, dour, sullen, grumpy *a sour mood*

source *(n.)* ROOT, CAUSE, beginning, origin, derivation

souvenir *(n.)* keepsake, memento, token, relic, vestige

space *(n.)* **1.** ROOM, leeway, AREA, extent, capacity *enough space to fit one more* **2.** heavens, cosmos, universe, firmament *travel into outer space* **3.** opening, gap, cleft, interval, void *Leave a space between the desks.*

spare *(v.)* FORGIVE, PARDON, RELEASE, CLEAR, absolve PUNISH

spare *(adj.)* EXTRA, reserve, surplus, supplemental

sparkle *(v.)* glitter, glisten, twinkle, scintillate

speak *(v.)* **1.** SAY, PRONOUNCE, articulate *Speak your lines.* **2.** TELL, utter, EXPRESS, DECLARE, spout, rant *Speak the truth.* **3.** chat, chatter, converse, GOSSIP, prattle *Speak with a friend.*

spear *(n.)* lance, javelin

special *(adj.)* **1.** distinct, UNUSUAL, RARE, unique *Seeing a fox in the forest is a special experience.* commonplace **2.** significant, memorable, earthshaking, pressing *a special awards ceremony* **3.** EXTRAORDINARY, spectacular, astounding, overwhelming, impressive, breathtaking, WONDERFUL, FANTASTIC *The astronauts' landing on the moon was a special event.* ORDINARY, USUAL

speech *(n.)* **1.** LECTURE, address, TALK, utterance, discourse, oration *give a speech* **2.** LANGUAGE, dialect, articulation, talk *Dogs and cats lack speech.*

speed *(n.)* haste, swiftness, velocity

spell *(n.)* **1.** MAGIC, POWER, charm, incantation *under the wizard's spell* **2.** period, interval, TIME *a rainy spell*

spell *(v.)* WRITE, decipher, encode

spend *(v.)* **1.** expend, disperse, donate, CONTRIBUTE, squander, fritter, EXHAUST *spend money* SAVE, CONSERVE **2.** PASS, USE, consume *spend time on a farm*

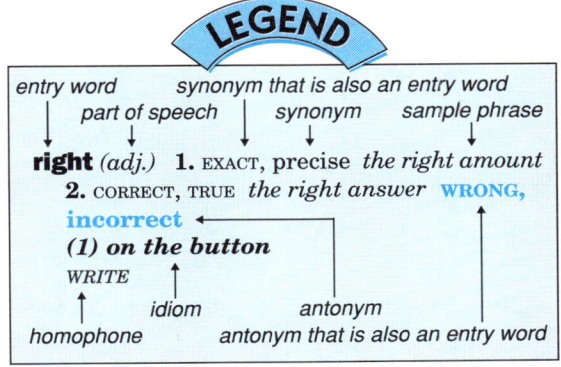

spicy (adj.) HOT, pungent, STRONG, SHARP, piquant MILD, BLAND

spin (v.) TURN, rotate, revolve, whirl, twist, swirl, reel, gyrate

spirit (n.) **1.** COURAGE, ENERGY, vitality *the fighting spirit* **2.** GHOST, vision, spook, specter, phantom, apparition *Can you see the spirit?*

spite (n.) venom, malice, resentment, rancor, pique, enmity, animosity affection, goodwill

splendid (adj.) stately, MAJESTIC, GRAND, MAGNIFICENT, GORGEOUS, sumptuous dreadful

split (n.) CRACK, fissure, breach

split (v.) **1.** cleave, halve, bisect, slice, sever, rend *split a log* CONNECT, JOIN **2.** SHARE, DIVIDE, DISTRIBUTE *split a pizza*

spoil (v.) **1.** BOTCH, fumble, BUNGLE, muff, RUIN, mar, HARM, DESTROY, defile *spoil a game* **2.** DECAY, decompose, putrefy, molder *The milk will spoil.*

spoon (n.) scoop, ladle, dipper

spot (n.) STAIN, blot, blotch, flaw, speck, blemish, pimple, DEFECT, imperfection

spot (v.) SEE, NOTICE, NOTE, OBSERVE, DETECT, discern, RECOGNIZE

spread (v.) **1.** INCREASE, MULTIPLY, STRETCH, EXPAND, REPRODUCE, propagate *The bird spreads its wings.* REDUCE, DECREASE **2.** DISTRIBUTE, PASS, TELL, ANNOUNCE, divulge, circulate *Spread the news.* withhold, CONCEAL **3.** SCATTER, disperse, strew, sprinkle *Spread the seeds.* GATHER, collect **4.** smear, daub *Spread the jelly on the bread.*

spring (v.) **1.** LEAP, bound, JUMP *spring over a rock* **2.** emerge, originate *spring from within*

spy (n.) agent, scout, informer, snoop, investigator

spy (v.) SEE, behold, DETECT, DISCOVER, OBSERVE, INVESTIGATE

squeeze (v.) **1.** PRESS, compress, pinch, CRUSH, squish *squeeze into a small space* **2.** HUG, embrace *squeeze a child*

stab (v.) PIERCE, STICK, spear, gore, lance, hack, puncture, ENTER, penetrate, perforate

stable (n.) stall, barn, shed

stable (adj.) **1.** fixed, steadfast, solid, FIRM *a stable fence* unstable, FLIMSY **2.** enduring, lasting, CONSISTENT, PERMANENT *a stable government* tentative, TEMPORARY **3.** staunch, resolute *a stable outlook* **4.** SANE, rational *a stable personality* irrational, CRAZY

stage (n.) **1.** platform, theater, playhouse *an actor on the stage* **2.** STEP, DEGREE, point, period *a stage in a frog's development*

stage (v.) **1.** PLAN, ARRANGE, PRODUCE *stage a fund-raiser* **2.** PERFORM *stage a play*

stain *(n.)* smudge, MARK, smear, blemish, SPOT

stain *(v.)* soil, sully, begrime, tarnish, blot, blemish

stale *(adj.)* **1.** OLD, DRY, musty, moldy *stale bread* FRESH **2.** uninteresting, trite, COMMON, flat *a stale joke*
(2) old hat

stand *(n.)* **1.** stall, booth, kiosk *a lemonade stand* **2.** dais, lectern, pulpit, rostrum *speak from a stand*

stand *(v.)* **1.** RISE, arise *Stand on a chair.* **2.** BEAR, endure, suffer, stomach, tolerate, sustain *stand the pain* RESIST

• Guess the Idiom •

clue: stale

answer: old hat

stare *(v.)* GAZE, gape, gawk, ogle, peek, SPY
keep an eye on
STAIR

Go CRAZY with WORDS!

stare

start *(n.)* **1.** beginning, threshold, verge, outset *the start of the game* ending **2.** origin, CAUSE, ROOT, SOURCE *the start of Earth Day*

start *(v.)* **1.** BEGIN, commence, initiate, launch, open, INTRODUCE *Start the music.* END, CEASE, discontinue, HALT, CONCLUDE **2.** originate, CAUSE, arise, rouse *start trouble* STOP **3.** startle, JUMP, flinch *start from the loud noise*
(1) hit the road, get one's feet wet, get cracking

• Guess the Idiom •

clue: start

answer: get one's feet wet

state *(n.)* **1.** COUNTRY, commonwealth, LAND, nation *Hawaii was the fiftieth state to join the union.* **2.** CONDITION, situation, plight *a state of confusion*

state *(v.)* TELL, EXPRESS, DECLARE, CLAIM, assert

station *(n.)* **1.** STOP, terminal, depot *a train station* **2.** PLACE, location, situation, STAGE *Each leg of the relay race began at a different station.*

statue *(n.)* monument, sculpture, casting

stay *(n.)* SUPPORT, brace, prop, buttress

stay *(v.)* **1.** WAIT, REMAIN, loiter, LINGER, dawdle, tarry, lag, PAUSE, REST, repose, abide *Stay for a few minutes.* LEAVE, depart **2.** STOP, CHECK, HOLD, restrain *stay the disease* **3.** DELAY, detain, hinder, HOLD *stay the decision* continue
(1) plant oneself, stick around

• Guess the Idiom •

clue: stay

answer: plant oneself

steady *(adj.)* **1.** CONSISTENT, REGULAR, CONSTANT, invariable, uniform, unfluctuating *She had a steady pulse.* **unsteady, erratic, inconsistent** **2.** FIRM, fixed, STABLE, unyielding *a steady base for the marble sculpture* **unstable**

steal *(v.)* **1.** TAKE, ROB, loot, plunder, filch, thieve, fleece, poach, pilfer, despoil, purloin *steal the jewels* **2.** kidnap, abduct *steal the child*
STEEL

steep *(adj.)* SHEER, abrupt, precipitous

steer *(v.)* navigate, pilot, DIRECT, GUIDE, CONDUCT, GOVERN
be in the driver's seat

step *(n.)* **1.** STAGE, POINT, period *a step in the printing process* **2.** stair, rung, tread *He climbed each step of the ladder.*

stick *(n.)* ROD, mace, club, staff, wand, truncheon

stick *(v.)* **1.** glue, PASTE, bind *Stick the pieces together.* **2.** adhere, CLING, ATTACH *stick to a wall*

stiff *(adj.)* **1.** RIGID, unbending, inflexible, FIRM, unyielding *a stiff piece of leather* **limp, SOFT, pliant** **2.** STRICT, severe, stern, austere *a stiff penalty* **lenient, lax**

still *(n.)* silence, QUIET, CALM

still *(v.)* muffle, stifle, CALM, suppress, censor, mute, quell

still *(adj.)* **1.** CALM, motionless, inactive, dormant, stagnant, STABLE, inert, stationary, tranquil, placid, serene *The boat disturbed the still water.* **ACTIVE, mobile** **2.** hushed, mute, QUIET, noiseless *a still audience* **NOISY, LOUD**

still *(adv.)* yet, however, nevertheless

stingy *(adj.)* SELFISH, CHEAP, tight-fisted, frugal, thrifty, miserly, penny-pinching, ungenerous **GENEROUS, giving**

stink *(v.)* SMELL, reek, stench

stir *(v.)* **1.** churn, WHISK, BEAT, MIX, agitate *Stir the mixture.* **2.** MOVE, BUDGE *stir from the tent* **3.** awaken, arouse, ALERT, DISTURB, stimulate, prompt *stir the dogs*

stone *(n.)* ROCK, mineral, gem, jewel, pebble

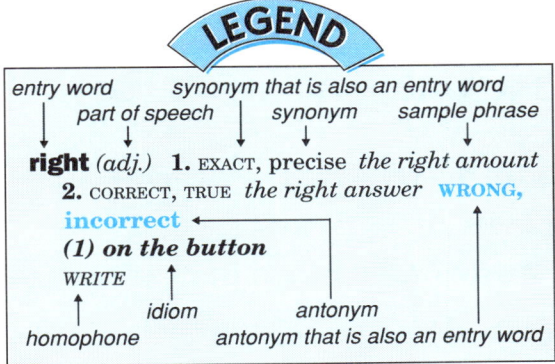

stop (v.) **1.** HESITATE, WAIT, PAUSE *Stop at the gate before you go in.* **proceed, START 2.** HALT, END, FINISH, discontinue, stem, CEASE, QUIT, STAY, SHUT, CLOSE, CHECK, CANCEL, desist, terminate, culminate, suspend, CONCLUDE, abort *Stop the violence.* **BEGIN, COMMENCE, CONTINUE 3.** prohibit, PREVENT, BAN, outlaw, FORBID, oppose, overrule *Stop the hunting.* **ALLOW, PERMIT 4.** arrest, restrain, foil, CHECK, BLOCK, impede *Stop an enemy in its tracks.*
(2) cut short, call it a day, hold your horses

◆ Guess the Idiom ◆

clue: stop

answer: hold your horses

store (n.) shop, market, mart, depot, boutique, stall, booth

store (v.) SAVE, KEEP, stow, stock, hoard, reserve

storm (n.) downpour, hurricane, gale, tornado, cyclone, typhoon, deluge, tempest, squall

storm (v.) ATTACK, assault, RAID, overrun

story (n.) **1.** TALE, fable, novel, LEGEND, myth, fiction, romance, fantasy, parable, narrative, account *Read a story.* **2.** LIE, fib, falsehood *caught telling a story* **3.** level, FLOOR, STAGE, tier *the second story of the building*

straight (adj.) **1.** direct, unswerving, undeviating *a straight path* **TWISTED, CROOKED 2.** FAIR, honorable, HONEST, upright *straight conduct*
(1) as the crow flies
STRAIT

strange (adj.) ODD, WEIRD, QUEER, CURIOUS, peculiar, UNUSUAL, atypical, UNIQUE, abnormal, uncommon, EXTRAORDINARY, quirkish **commonplace, ORDINARY**

stranger (n.) FOREIGNER, outsider, visitor, alien **FRIEND**

stray (v.) WANDER, rove, ROAM, straggle, meander

stray (adj.) LOST, wandering, homeless, unwanted

strength (n.) **1.** POWER, MIGHT, force, vigor, fortitude *the strength of the team* **weakness 2.** sturdiness, soundness, solidity *the strength of the wood*

strengthen (v.) fortify, reinforce, empower **weaken, debilitate**

stress *(n.)* **1.** strain, pressure, tension, anxiety, apprehension *relief from the stress* **2.** emphasis, accent, WEIGHT, EFFORT, exertion, force *place stress on doing a good job*

stress *(v.)* emphasize, underline, accentuate

stretch *(v.)* **1.** tighten, PULL, strain *stretch a rope* CONTRACT **2.** EXTEND, lengthen, INCREASE, elongate *stretch a practice session* **3.** EXAGGERATE *stretch the truth*

strict *(adj.)* **1.** RIGID, demanding, inflexible, unbending, stringent, stern, vigilant *a strict teacher* lenient **2.** severe, STIFF *a strict penalty* lenient, moderate **3.** FORMAL, prim, straitlaced, CORRECT, austere *a strict dress code*

strike *(v.)* **1.** HIT, pound, PUNCH, swat, assault, ram, collide, smite *Strike the punching bag.* **2.** delete, OMIT, ELIMINATE, CANCEL *Strike from the entry list.* ADD, include

string *(n.)* THREAD, cord, rope, line, cable, tie

strip *(n.)* PIECE, length, slip, BAND

strip *(v.)* **1.** undress, disrobe, UNCOVER, doff *strip down to one's underwear* **2.** divest, REMOVE, deprive *strip a leader of power*

stroll *(v.)* saunter, amble, promenade, ramble *stretch your legs*

strong *(adj.)* **1.** powerful, mighty, forceful, commanding *a strong coach* **2.** muscular, athletic, STURDY, SOUND, TOUGH, hardy, hale, robust, stalwart *a strong athlete* WEAK, FEEBLE, frail **3.** potent, extreme, INTENSE *strong coffee* BLAND, tasteless, DILUTED **4.** ENTHUSIASTIC, ardent, zealous *a strong supporter* indifferent, casual

struggle *(n.)* **1.** FIGHT, QUARREL, CONTEST, conflict, skirmish *break up a struggle* **2.** LABOR, EFFORT, exertion *a struggle to survive*

struggle *(v.)* **1.** ATTEMPT, WORK, strive, LABOR, toil *struggle to meet a deadline* **2.** FIGHT, oppose *They struggled with the town council.*

stubborn *(adj.)* **1.** headstrong, willful, DETERMINED, contrary, unyielding, unbending, obstinate *a stubborn attitude* FLEXIBLE, yielding **2.** enduring, PERSISTENT, tenacious, persevering *a stubborn illness* TEMPORARY

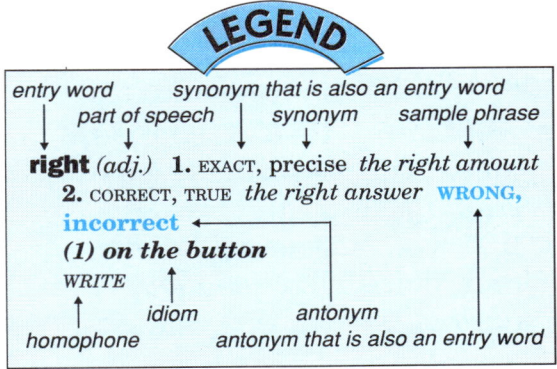

study (n.) **1.** den, office, studio, sanctum *Sit in the study.* **2.** examination, analysis *a study of the wetlands*

study (v.) READ, EXAMINE, INSPECT, INVESTIGATE, RESEARCH, scrutinize, peruse **bone up on, crack a book, hit the books**

♦ Guess the Idiom ♦

clue: study

answer: hit the books

stuff (n.) **1.** belongings, property, assets *Let's move our stuff to the new house.* **2.** EQUIPMENT, trappings, merchandise, wares, goods, paraphernalia *all the stuff in the box* **3.** MATTER, substance, MATERIAL *What is that red stuff?*

stupid (adj.) **1.** SILLY, FOOLISH, RIDICULOUS, ABSURD, fatuous *a stupid joke* **reasonable** **2.** DENSE, DULL, DUMB, idiotic, daft, doltish, stolid *a stupid animal* **SMART, INTELLIGENT** **3.** uneducated, illiterate, IGNORANT, brutish *a stupid response to the question* **educated**

sturdy (adj.) **1.** RUGGED, hardy, robust, stout, stalwart *a sturdy ship captain* **frail** **2.** TOUGH, FIRM, STRONG, durable *a sturdy container* **FLIMSY, FRAGILE**

style (n.) **1.** WAY, METHOD, MANNER, mode, technique, system, approach *style of living* **2.** FASHION, chic *the latest style*

subject (n.) **1.** theme, topic, POINT, MATTER, CONTENT, substance *the subject of the report* **2.** dependent, subordinate, INFERIOR *the king and his subjects*

substitute (n.) replacement, proxy, alternate, backup, standby, surrogate

substitute (v.) CHANGE, REPLACE, exchange, interchange, SWITCH

subtract (v.) REDUCE, withdraw, OMIT, ELIMINATE, REMOVE, EXCLUDE, deduct **ADD, INCREASE**

succeed (v.) **1.** ACHIEVE, accomplish, attain, prosper, flourish, thrive *succeed at school* **FAIL** **2.** FOLLOW, ensue *Who succeeded the last president?* **precede**

success (n.) **1.** achievement, accomplishment *success in a new job* **failure** **2.** FORTUNE, LUCK, welfare, prosperity *success in life* **misfortune, poverty**

sudden *(adj.)* abrupt, RAPID, surprising, unexpected, unanticipated, unforeseen GRADUAL, deliberate

suggest *(v.)* **1.** propose, advise, intimate *He suggested we go for a swim.* **2.** HINT, indicate *Coughing suggests a cold.*

suit *(v.)* fit, QUALIFY, SATISFY, comply

sulk *(v.)* fret, scowl, mope, glower, brood, muse

summary *(n.)* synopsis, outline, abstract, brief, digest

sunrise *(n.)* dawn, dawning, LIGHT, daybreak, MORNING SUNSET

sunset *(n.)* evening, sundown, nightfall, dusk, twilight SUNRISE

superb *(adj.)* FINE, EXCELLENT, SPLENDID, admirable, worthy, distinguished, EXTRAORDINARY, superior, striking, WONDERFUL

supply *(n.)* reserve, STORE, stock, hoard, inventory, stockpile, cache withhold

supply *(v.)* GIVE, PROVIDE, FURNISH, PRODUCE, bestow, confer, allocate, replenish withhold

support *(n.)* AID, HELP, assistance hindrance

support *(v.)* **1.** MAINTAIN, HELP, ASSIST, BACK, patronize, abet *support the family* oppose **2.** CONFIRM, reinforce, substantiate, corroborate *The evidence supports the decision.* **3.** BEAR, CARRY, uphold, BRACE, buttress, prop, STAY *support the weight* **(1) bring home the bacon**

sure *(adj.)* **1.** CERTAIN, definite, CONFIDENT, positive, proven, unfailing *a sure success* doubtful, uncertain **2.** CONFIDENT, decided, settled, convinced *a sure feeling about the decision* **3.** SAFE, SECURE *a sure place to hide* unprotected, DANGEROUS, UNSAFE **4.** dependable, reliable, FAITHFUL, tested, trustworthy *a sure friend* untrustworthy **in the bag**

surprise *(v.)* ASTONISH, AMAZE, astound, bewilder, dumbfound, THRILL, startle, awe, DAZE

surrender *(v.)* YIELD, ABANDON, renounce, relinquish HOLD, KEEP, retain

suspect *(v.)* **1.** distrust, mistrust, DOUBT *suspect his honesty* **2.** THINK, BELIEVE, IMAGINE, GUESS, conjecture, ASSUME, presume *suspect that something will happen* **(1) smell a rat**

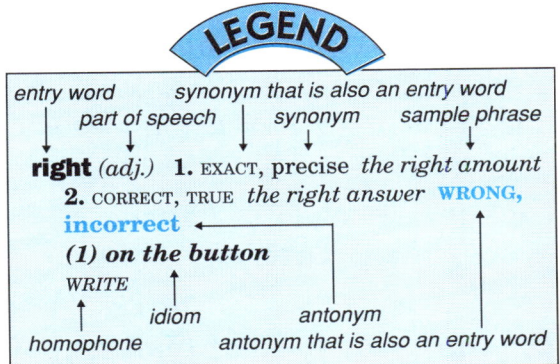

swamp *(n.)* bog, marsh, moor, morass, quagmire

swear *(v.)* **1.** CURSE, blaspheme *swear out loud* **2.** vow, affirm, assert *swear to continue*

swell *(v.)* INCREASE, ENLARGE, dilate, EXPAND, distend SHRINK, DECREASE, contract

swim *(v.)* wade, dip, paddle, plunge, float, glide

switch *(v.)* CHANGE, TURN, shift, replace, swap

sword *(n.)* blade, saber, cutlass, rapier, foil

symbol *(n.)* **1.** emblem, insignia, badge, totem, trademark, SIGN, token, FIGURE *The flag is a symbol of the school.* **2.** simile, metaphor, imagery *The eagle in the story is a symbol for freedom.*

Tt

take *(v.)* **1.** CHOOSE, select, PICK *Take a card from the deck.* replace **2.** RECEIVE, ACCEPT *take a gift from one's friend* GIVE **3.** GRAB, STEAL, ROB, seize, CAPTURE, deprive *take what does not belong to you* free, RETURN

tale *(n.)* STORY, fable, LEGEND, fiction, myth, parable TAIL

talent *(n.)* GIFT, SKILL, ABILITY, aptitude, knack, expertise, dexterity, adroitness

talk *(v.)* SPEAK, SAY, TELL, chat, chatter, COMMENT, GOSSIP, lecture, DECLARE, CLAIM, prattle, converse, assert, divulge

tall *(adj.)* **1.** HIGH, lofty, elevated, towering *the tall, 20-story building* SHORT **2.** BIG, LARGE *A giraffe is a tall animal.* SMALL, TINY

tame *(adj.)* OBEDIENT, domesticated, WILLING, meek, MILD, docile, housebroken WILD, untamed *under one's thumb*

◆ Guess the Idiom ◆

clue: tame

answer: under one's thumb

task *(n.)* DUTY, WORK, JOB, LABOR, undertaking, chore, assignment

taste *(n.)* **1.** FLAVOR, zest *the taste of the food* **2.** JUDGMENT, discernment, liking, preference *good taste in clothes*

taste *(v.)* SAMPLE, partake, TRY, EXPERIENCE, savor, relish

Go CRAZY with WORDS!

taste

teach *(v.)* EDUCATE, TRAIN, drill, INSTRUCT, enlighten, INFORM, DIRECT LEARN, discover

teacher *(n.)* instructor, educator, tutor

team *(n.)* SIDE, faction, GROUP, crew, BAND, COMPANY, PARTY, GANG

tear *(n.)* HOLE, slit, rent, fissure

tear *(v.)* RIP, slash, slit, pull, SPLIT, rend mend

tease *(v.)* mock, pester, BOTHER, RIDICULE, taunt, INSULT, jeer, badger, torment, harass, provoke, vex, tantalize, gibe, deride *drive someone nuts*

tell *(v.)* **1.** notify, INFORM, advise, recite *Tell someone about the election.* **2.** CONFESS, STATE, MENTION, proclaim, relate, ANNOUNCE, divulge, recount, disclose, reveal, profess *Tell the truth.*
(1) break the news

temper *(n.)* **1.** disposition, MOOD, humor, NATURE, CHARACTER *looking for a dog with a sweet temper* **2.** ANGER, irritation, animosity, hostility *Control your temper.*

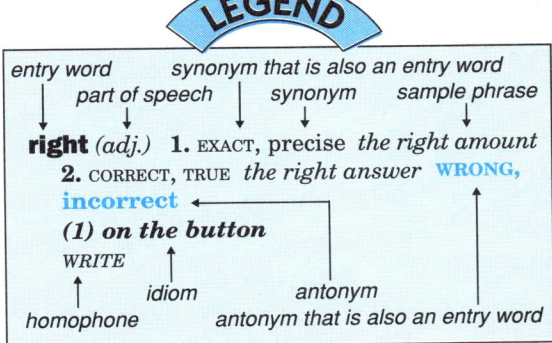

LEGEND

entry word — synonym that is also an entry word
part of speech — synonym — sample phrase

right *(adj.)* **1.** EXACT, precise *the right amount* **2.** CORRECT, TRUE *the right answer* WRONG, incorrect
(1) on the button
WRITE
↑ idiom   antonym
homophone   antonym that is also an entry word

temper *(v.)* **1.** soften, reduce, moderate *temper his anger* **2.** harden *temper steel*

temporary *(adj.)* passing, BRIEF, fleeting, short-lived, momentary, transient **PERMANENT**

tempt *(v.)* LURE, ATTRACT, seduce, LEAD, PERSUADE, entice, induce

tender *(adj.)* **1.** SOFT, DELICATE, FRAGILE *tender skin* **2.** compassionate, KIND, GENTLE, loving *tender loving care* **HARSH, unkind,** MEAN **3.** SENSITIVE, painful *a tender wound*

tense *(adj.)* **1.** uneasy, ANXIOUS, worried, concerned, stressed, apprehensive *a tense person* **relaxed,** CALM **2.** TIGHT, stretched, strained, RIGID, taut *a tense rope*
(1) all wound up
TENTS

terrible *(adj.)* HORRIBLE, AWFUL, frightful, dreadful, GHASTLY, HORRID, dire, hideous, grisly **WONDERFUL, MARVELOUS, terrific**

test *(n.)* QUIZ, examination, trial

test *(v.)* EXAMINE, evaluate, QUESTION, TRY
bounce something off someone

• Guess the Idiom •

clue: test

answer: bounce something off someone

thankful *(adj.)* GRATEFUL, obliged, indebted, beholden **ungrateful**

therefore *(adv.)* consequently, accordingly, thus, then

thick *(adj.)* **1.** WIDE, DEEP, bulky, solid, squat, stodgy *thick stone walls* **THIN, NARROW, SKINNY** **2.** gooey, gummy, DENSE, viscous *a thick liquid* **runny, watery**

thief *(n.)* ROBBER, bandit, brigand, pirate, plunderer, burglar, swindler, pickpocket, looter

• Guess the Idiom •

clue: tense

answer: all wound up

thin *(adj.)* **1.** SLIM, SKINNY, LEAN, spare, slender, underweight, drawn, lank *a thin person* FAT **2.** NARROW *thin ice* WIDE **3.** SHEER, FINE, diaphanous *thin fabric* THICK

thing *(n.)* **1.** OBJECT, ITEM, entity, contraption, article, DEVICE, GADGET *Pack your things.* **2.** act, deed, EVENT *Peculiar things have happened.*

think *(v.)* **1.** ponder, WONDER, meditate, REFLECT, CONSIDER, contemplate, IMAGINE, envisage, ruminate *Think about recycling.* **2.** BELIEVE, suppose, IMAGINE, presume, ASSUME, conceive, suppose, surmise *He thinks we should pay lower taxes.* **3.** STUDY, EXAMINE, JUDGE, deliberate *Think about the clues.*
(3) use your head

thought *(n.)* IDEA, notion, fancy, reflection, CONCEPT, perception, impression, supposition

thoughtful *(adj.)* **1.** CONSIDERATE, KIND, attentive *thoughtful enough to send flowers* **inconsiderate, RUDE** **2.** reflective, pensive, studious, wistful, nostalgic *thoughtful about the past* **3.** mindful, prudent, heedful *always thoughtful of others* **IGNORANT, rash**

thoughtless *(adj.)* CARELESS, inconsiderate, neglectful, heedless, negligent **CAREFUL, CONSIDERATE**

thread *(n.)* fiber, cord, filament

threaten *(v.)* **1.** menace, intimidate, torment, terrorize *Threaten the dog.* **2.** loom, impend, forebode *A storm threatens to engulf the town.*

thrill *(v.)* PLEASE, EXCITE, arouse, stimulate
tickled pink

throw *(v.)* toss, sling, FLING, hurl, PITCH, CAST, chuck, pelt, project, shoot, PASS

tickle *(v.)* **1.** TOUCH, stroke, titillate *tickle one on the arm* **2.** PLEASE, AMUSE, DELIGHT *She was tickled by the gift.*

tie *(n.)* necktie, cravat

tie *(v.)* **1.** knot, snag *Tie a bow.* **2.** fasten, hitch, JOIN, ATTACH, link, fetter, hobble *Tie the boat to the dock.* **3.** WRAP, bind, bundle, secure, truss *Tie up the package.*

tidy *(adj.)* CLEAN, NEAT, orderly, organized, IMMACULATE **MESSY, SLOPPY, disheveled**

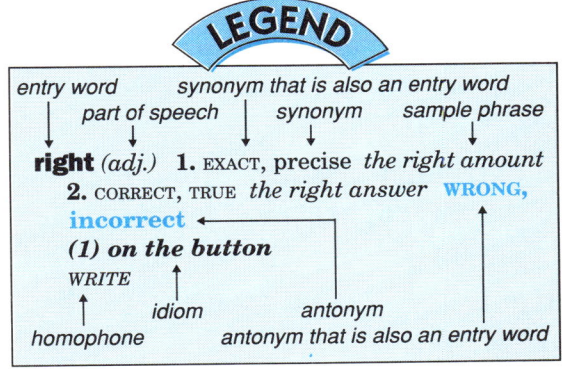

tight *(adj.)* **1.** close-fitting, taut, FIRM, SECURE, clingy *a tight diving suit* LOOSE **2.** STINGY, close-fisted *a tight budget* GENEROUS, giving

time *(n.)* period, term, interval, PAUSE, gap, season, SPELL, age, interlude
THYME

timid *(adj.)* SHY, bashful, modest, retiring, reserved, demure *afraid of one's own shadow*

• Guess the Idiom •

clue: timid

answer: afraid of one's own shadow

tiny *(adj.)* LITTLE, SMALL, wee, puny, miniature, dwarf HUGE, massive, LARGE, IMMENSE

tip *(n.)* **1.** END, POINT, PEAK, extremity *the tip of the pencil* **2.** REWARD, gratuity *a tip for the waiter*

tip *(v.)* LEAN, incline, tilt

tired *(adj.)* sleepy, drowsy, WEARY, fatigued, sluggish, jaded rested, invigorated, refreshed

together *(adv.)* joint, UNITED, concerted ALONE, SEPARATE

tool *(n.)* GADGET, appliance, utensil, contraption, DEVICE, INSTRUMENT, apparatus, implement

top *(n.)* **1.** lid, COVER, stopper, cap *the top of the jar* **2.** apex, acme, pinnacle, zenith *the top of her class* BOTTOM **3.** PEAK, crest, summit, TIP, crown *the top of the mountain* BASE

total *(n.)* SUM, TOTAL, WHOLE, AMOUNT, QUANTITY portion, PART

total *(adj.)* COMPLETE, FULL, ENTIRE partial, incomplete

touch *(v.)* FEEL, HANDLE, grope, finger, fondle, EXPERIENCE

tough *(adj.)* **1.** STRONG, FIRM, RUGGED, hardy, stalwart *a tough acrobat* TENDER, delicate **2.** lasting, durable *made of tough plastic*

toy *(n.)* trinket, plaything

toy *(v.)* trifle, PLAY, dally, jest, dabble

trade *(v.)* swap, EXCHANGE, barter

train *(v.)* EDUCATE, INSTRUCT, TEACH, tutor, school, drill, COACH, discipline

traitor *(n.)* renegade, deserter, rebel, turncoat, dissident, heretic

translate • trick

Go CRAZY with WORDS!

touch

translate *(v.)* EXPLAIN, interpret, decode, clarify, SOLVE, unravel, decipher code, encode

transport *(v.)* CARRY, BEAR, haul, DELIVER, CONVEY

trap *(v.)* CATCH, GRAB, CAPTURE, seize, arrest, snare, ensnare, entrap RELEASE, FREE
bait the hook

trash *(n.)* rubbish, GARBAGE, WASTE, JUNK, REFUSE

travel *(v.)* MOVE, journey, ramble, VOYAGE, PASS, traverse

treat *(v.)* **1.** USE, HANDLE, wield, MANAGE *Treat the tools with care.* **2.** ENTERTAIN, AMUSE, CHEER *treat my friends to a great show* **3.** nurse, doctor, minister, remedy *Treat the wound.* **4.** finance, spend, fund *Treat the children to pizza.*

trick *(n.)* **1.** JOKE, gag, hoax, fraud, jest, antic, prank, caper, ILLUSION, deception, delusion *He played a trick on his friend.* **2.** LURE, wile, stratagem *They used a trick to catch the thief.*

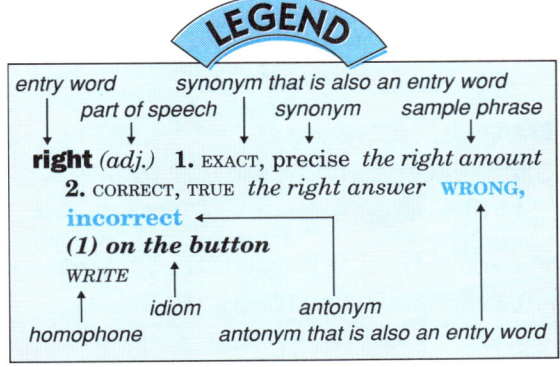

LEGEND
entry word   synonym that is also an entry word
    part of speech   synonym   sample phrase
right *(adj.)* **1.** EXACT, precise *the right amount* **2.** CORRECT, TRUE *the right answer* WRONG, incorrect
(1) on the button
WRITE
    idiom   antonym
homophone   antonym that is also an entry word

133

trick (v.) FOOL, bluff, DECEIVE, outwit, CHEAT, delude, dupe, defraud *pull the wool over one's eyes*

trip (n.) JOURNEY, outing, VOYAGE, flight, expedition, passage, VISIT, tour, excursion, pilgrimage

trip (v.) FALL, stumble, falter, flounder, stagger

troop (n.) troop, COMPANY, squad TROUPE

trouble (n.) **1.** difficulty, hardship, inconvenience, toil *car trouble* **2.** DISTRESS, suffering, adversity *He made trouble in the family.*
(2) a real pickle

◆ Guess the Idiom ◆

clue: trouble

answer: a real pickle

trouble (v.) BOTHER, DISTURB, inconvenience, ANNOY, vex, DISTRESS APPEASE

true (adj.) **1.** REAL, actual, valid, GENUINE *a true ruby* FAKE, phony **2.** CORRECT, ACCURATE, confirmable *a true statement* FALSE, untrue, bogus **3.** HONEST, upright, FAITHFUL, sincere, GENUINE, LOYAL, steadfast, SOUND, reliable, dependable, trustworthy *a true love* unfaithful

trust (n.) FAITH, CONFIDENCE, belief, reliance, assurance distrust, suspicion

trust (v.) BELIEVE, DEPEND, rely *count on*

truth (n.) FACT, reality, certainty, actuality, veracity, verity, verisimilitude LIE, falsehood

try (v.) **1.** ATTEMPT, SEEK, STRUGGLE, AIM, strive, aspire, endeavor, venture *Try to reach the top of the mountain.* **2.** SAMPLE, TASTE, EXPERIENCE *Try eating an oyster.* **3.** undertake, tackle *Try scuba diving.*
(1) bend over backward

◆ Guess the Idiom ◆

clue: try

answer: bend over backward

tumble *(v.)* FALL, stumble, topple

tune *(n.)* jingle, SONG, melody

turn *(n.)* CHANCE, period, stint, shift, stretch

turn *(v.)* **1.** SPIN, revolve, rotate, screw *Turn the knob.* **2.** REVERSE, swivel, hinge, BEND, TWIST, pivot, invert *Turn around.* **3.** CURVE, swerve, maneuver, jockey, veer *Turn to the left.* **4.** DIVERT, AIM, DIRECT, point *He turned his attention away from the problem.*

twist *(v.)* **1.** wring *Twist the towel.* **2.** writhe, contort *twist and turn while dancing* **3.** wind, encircle *Twist the cord around the bag.*

type *(n.)* KIND, SORT, CLASS, GROUP

Uu

ugly *(adj.)* unattractive, unsightly, homely, GHASTLY, hideous PRETTY, HANDSOME, GORGEOUS

uncover *(v.)* disclose, reveal, EXPOSE, divulge, BARE, unwrap, DISCOVER COVER, CONCEAL

understand *(v.)* COMPREHEND, SEE, GET, DRAW, grasp, perceive, CONCLUDE, deduce, fathom, resolve *get the picture, get it through your head, put two and two together*

unfriendly *(adj.)* aloof, distant, COLD, HOSTILE, malevolent FRIENDLY, cordial, WARM, hospitable

unhappy *(adj.)* SAD, cheerless, GLOOMY, BLUE, sorrowful, tragic, downcast, dispirited, depressed, pessimistic, morose, crestfallen, despondent, doleful, woeful, mournful, melancholy, wretched, hapless, forlorn HAPPY, GLAD, joyous, cheerful, spirited, gleeful, jubilant

unique *(adj.)* RARE, UNUSUAL, exceptional, distinctive, SPECIAL, matchless COMMON, USUAL

unimportant *(adj.)* petty, slight, paltry, trivial, trifling, insignificant IMPORTANT, significant *nothing to sneeze at*

united *(adj.)* **1.** joined, TOGETHER, combined *the United States* SEPARATE, INDEPENDENT **2.** agreeing, harmonious, unanimous *united in their opinions* divided, combative, contentious

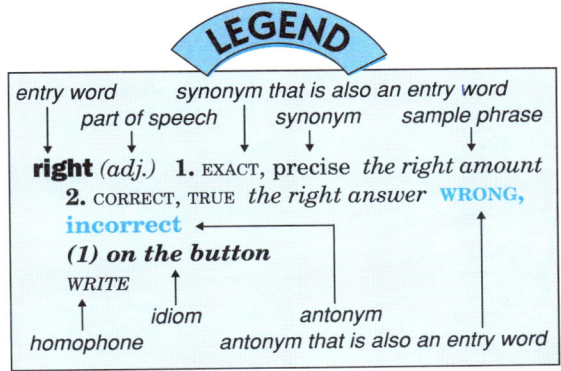

unnecessary *(adj.)* NEEDLESS, USELESS, dispensable, expendable, irrelevant, superfluous NECESSARY, ESSENTIAL

untrue *(adj.)* **1.** FALSE, WRONG, incorrect, INACCURATE, erroneous *an untrue statement* TRUE, CORRECT **2.** unfaithful, disloyal, treasonous, traitorous, deceitful, dishonorable *an untrue friend* FAITHFUL, dependable, reliable

unusual *(adj.)* UNIQUE, DIFFERENT, STRANGE, ODD, CURIOUS, uncommon, unconventional, unprecedented, exceptional USUAL, commonplace, ORDINARY, standard, everyday

unwilling *(adj.)* opposed, averse, loathe, reluctant, disinclined WILLING, compliant, READY

upset *(v.)* **1.** BOTHER, DISTURB, perturb, ANNOY, IRRITATE, rattle, OFFEND, disgust, outrage, disconcert *upset one's mother* appease, pacify **2.** overturn, capsize, invert *upset the canoe* **3.** BEAT, OVERTHROW *upset the competition*
(1) make waves, tie in knots

urge *(v.)* **1.** BEG, plead, beseech *urge one to continue* **2.** PUSH, PRESS, DRIVE, FORCE, impel *The jockey urged his horse on.*

use *(n.)* utility, benefit, application, usage

use *(v.)* **1.** utilize, apply, EMPLOY, avail, wield, HANDLE, brandish *use all my skills to do the job* **2.** expend, consume, EXHAUST *use up the gas*

useful *(adj.)* **1.** HELPFUL, HANDY, practical, efficient, beneficial *a useful tool* USELESS **2.** SOUND, QUALIFIED, serviceable, applicable *a useful suggestion*

useless *(adj.)* **1.** pointless, valueless, worthless *a useless vehicle* USEFUL, NECESSARY, practical **2.** fruitless, futile, vain, frivolous *a useless attempt* beneficial, effective

♦ Guess the Idiom ♦

clue: upset

answer: tie in knots

usual *(adj.)* NORMAL, COMMON, REGULAR, FAMILIAR, customary, FREQUENT, habitual UNUSUAL, irregular, uncommon

Vv

vague *(adj.)* uncertain, doubtful, obscure, indefinite CLEAR, OBVIOUS, specific, distinct
on the fence

• Guess the Idiom •

clue: vague

answer: on the fence

valiant *(adj.)* BRAVE, DARING, courageous, intrepid, GALLANT, heroic, valorous, chivalrous COWARDLY, fearful

valley *(n.)* glen, ravine, gorge, gulch, crater, chasm, abyss, vale

valuable *(adj.)* 1. PRECIOUS, costly, priceless, EXPENSIVE *a valuable piece of jewelry* worthless 2. IMPORTANT, USEFUL, HELPFUL, beneficial *a valuable lesson*

value *(n.)* 1. WORTH, importance, merit, stature *the value of a good education* 2. PRICE, COST, fare, RATE *The value of baseball cards has increased.*

vanish *(v.)* DISAPPEAR, DISSOLVE, FADE, evaporate APPEAR, materialize
go down the drain

• Guess the Idiom •

clue: vanish

answer: go down the drain

variety *(n.)* 1. KIND, TYPE, SORT, CLASS *a rare variety of day lily* 2. assortment, diversity *a variety of colors*

vary *(v.)* CHANGE, alter, deviate, differ CONTINUE

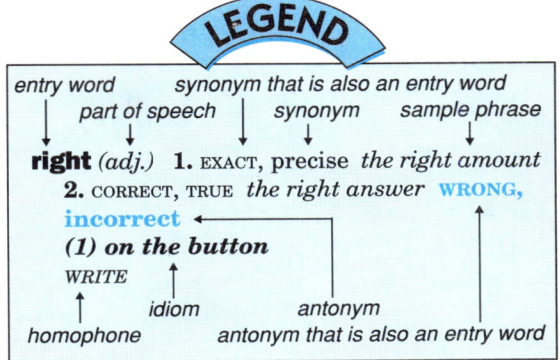

LEGEND

entry word — synonym that is also an entry word
part of speech — synonym — sample phrase

right *(adj.)* 1. EXACT, precise *the right amount* 2. CORRECT, TRUE *the right answer* WRONG, incorrect
(1) on the button
WRITE
homophone — idiom — antonym
antonym that is also an entry word

137

vast *(adj.)* HUGE, ENORMOUS, IMMENSE, colossal **cramped, minute**

vehicle *(n.)* carriage, carrier, conveyance, transport

verbal *(adj.)* oral, spoken, stated, unwritten, told **non-verbal**

verdict *(n.)* JUDGMENT, decision, finding, OPINION, sentence

vertical *(adj.)* upright, plumb, erect, perpendicular **HORIZONTAL**

vessel *(n.)* **1.** container, receptacle *a clay vessel* **2.** ship, boat, craft *a sailing vessel*

vibrate *(v.)* SHAKE, QUAKE, tremble, quiver, oscillate, twitch

vicious *(adj.)* WICKED, CRUEL, ruthless, BRUTAL, SAVAGE **KIND, docile, gentle, virtuous**

victim *(n.)* PREY, loser, scapegoat, sufferer, quarry **assailant**

victory *(n.)* triumph, conquest, SUCCESS, mastery **DEFEAT**

view *(n.)* **1.** SCENE, vista, survey, sight, vision, spectacle *a beautiful ocean view* **2.** OPINION, JUDGMENT, belief, hunch, impression, perspective *one's view on after-school sports*

view *(v.)* survey, scan, behold, WITNESS

villain *(n.)* CRIMINAL, scoundrel, rogue, knave, outlaw, hoodlum, culprit, felon, miscreant **HERO**

violent *(adj.)* raging, WILD, unruly, riotous, disorderly, FURIOUS, turbulent, wrathful **peaceful, GENTLE, MILD**

visit *(v.)* **1.** CALL, STOP, sojourn *visit a neighbor* **2.** TALK, chat, converse *visit on the phone*

voice *(n.)* articulation, words, tone, SPEECH, utterance, LANGUAGE

voyage *(n.)* JOURNEY, TRIP, expedition, cruise

Ww

wages *(n.)* salary, PAY, earnings, compensation

wage *(v.)* **1.** undertake, CONDUCT, pursue *wage war against an enemy* **2.** BET, stake, GAMBLE *wage a dollar*

wait *(v.)* **1.** STAY, PAUSE, REMAIN, LINGER, lag, dawdle *Wait a moment.* **CONTINUE, proceed, resume 2.** HESITATE, waver, tarry, loiter, DELAY, postpone, falter *He waited to make the decision.*
(1) hold your horses, keep your shirt on
WEIGHT

wake *(v.)* rouse, arouse, awaken, stimulate, STIR **SLEEP**

Go CRAZY with WORDS!

walk

walk (v.) STEP, hike, STROLL, trek, stride, trudge, shuffle, tramp, tread, MARCH, tiptoe, amble, saunter, promenade **jog, RUN, RACE**

wall (n.) barricade, fence, obstacle

wander (v.) **1.** ramble, rove, range, ROAM, STRAY *The cows wander over the field.* **2.** swerve, deviate *The car wandered all over the road.*

want (v.) HOPE, DESIRE, hunger, crave, yearn, WISH, LONG, hanker, REQUIRE, aspire

war (n.) conflict, battle, COMBAT, warfare **PEACE**

warm (adj.) **1.** tepid, heated, sunny *warm water* **COOL, CHILLY 2.** cordial, FRIENDLY, open, welcoming *a warm welcome* **RUDE, brusque, distant**

warn (v.) **1.** ALERT, CAUTION *warn the villagers* **2.** INFORM, notify, advise, admonish, CRITICIZE *warn someone not to do it again*

wash (v.) cleanse, SCRUB, launder, swab

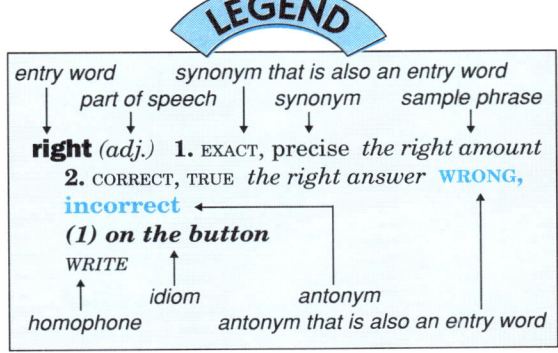

waste (n.) **1.** GARBAGE, TRASH, REFUSE, rubbish *dispose of waste* **2.** excrement, sewage *human waste* **3.** loss, misuse *a waste of time*
WAIST

waste (v.) **1.** dwindle, wither, perish, pine, wane *slowly waste away* **2.** fritter, squander, SCRAP, lavish, dissipate *waste money* SAVE **3.** dally, trifle, dawdle *waste time doing nothing*
WAIST

watch (v.) MIND, ATTEND, OBSERVE, regard, spectate, behold, VIEW, WITNESS

water (n.) **1.** river, stream, brook, creek, rivulet, brook, bourn, spring, fountain, ocean, sea, billows *Throw the pebble in the water.* **2.** tide, current, ebb, flow, torrent *The water came up to the sand dunes.*

water (v.) irrigate, moisten, sprinkle, dampen

wave (n.) ripple, swell, breaker, billow, surge, undulation
WAIVE

wave (v.) flutter, flap, swing, sway, VIBRATE
WAIVE

way (n.) **1.** MANNER, METHOD, mode, means, FASHION, system, STYLE, process, structure, technique, operation, arrangement, procedure *the way to do something* **2.** COURSE, PATH, ROUTE, track *on the way to school*
WEIGH

weak (adj.) **1.** frail, FRAGILE, FLIMSY, unsound, DELICATE *a weak chair* STURDY, STRONG, potent **2.** FEEBLE, infirm, sickly, debilitated, sluggish, decrepit, languid *a weak child* HEALTHY, STRONG **3.** powerless *a weak army* invincible, forceful **4.** thin, watery, diluted, impotent *weak tea* STRONG **5.** DIM *a weak light* bright
(2) on your last legs
WEEK

wealth (n.) riches, treasure, FORTUNE, abundance, affluence poverty

wear (v.) **1.** clothe, invest, don *Wear your new belt.* **2.** IRRITATE, fray *wear on one's nerves* **3.** PRODUCE, CREATE *wear a hole in a rug*
WARE

weary (adj.) TIRED, fatigued, exhausted, sleepy, drowsy, sluggish, jaded rested, ALERT

weave (v.) plait, braid, interlace

weep (v.) CRY, sob, lament, wail, whimper, blubber, mourn

weight (n.) **1.** heaviness, burden, LOAD, gravity *the weight of the logs* **2.** importance, import, INFLUENCE, SCOPE *the weight of public opinion*
WAIT

weird (*adj.*) 1. ODD, STRANGE, UNUSUAL, CURIOUS, UNIQUE, peculiar *a weird sound* natural 2. QUEER, mysterious, bizarre, eerie, uncanny *a weird set of circumstances* ORDINARY, COMMON

welcome (*n.*) greetings, salutation, reception

welcome (*v.*) GREET, receive, salute, hail, host

well (*n.*) spring, fountain, SOURCE

well (*adv.*) 1. HEALTHY, sound, hearty, hale *feeling well* 2. satisfactorily, correctly *do well on the test*
(2) with flying colors

• Guess the Idiom •

clue: well

answer: with flying colors

wet (*adj.*) 1. DAMP, moist, soggy, soaked, saturated, drenched, flooded *a wet towel* DRY, parched, brittle 2. rainy, humid *a wet day* DRY, arid

wharf (*n.*) PIER, jetty, landing, quay

whine (*v.*) CRY, whimper, moan, groan, grumble, snivel
WINE

whip (*v.*) lash, scourge, PUNISH, BEAT, flog

whole (*adj.*) COMPLETE, undivided, ENTIRE, intact, unbroken, SOUND partial, INCOMPLETE, PART
HOLE

wicked (*adj.*) BAD, EVIL, unprincipled, IMMORAL, VICIOUS, sinful, sinister, CORRUPT, villainous, unscrupulous, depraved KIND, GOOD, virtuous

wide (*adj.*) LARGE, BROAD, VAST, extensive, roomy, spacious NARROW, THIN

wild (*adj.*) 1. untamed, SAVAGE, barbarous, uncivilized *a wild animal* 2. FEROCIOUS, raving, frenzied, HYSTERICAL, VIOLENT, delirious, turbulent *a wild attack*

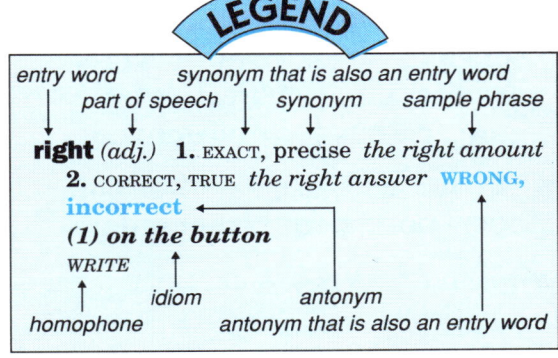

willing *(adj.)* READY, agreeable, inclined, disposed UNWILLING, averse

win *(v.)* **1.** SUCCEED, triumph, BEAT, overcome, OVERTHROW, vanquish *win at tennis* LOSE, forfeit **2.** ACQUIRE, EARN, GAIN, procure *win a prize* LOSE, squander
(1) take the cake

clue: win

answer: take the cake

wipe *(v.)* RUB, polish, CLEAN, swab, mop

wisdom *(n.)* SENSE, sensibility, intelligence, insight

wise *(adj.)* INTELLIGENT, learned, sensible, sage, shrewd, acute, erudite, philosophical ignorant, FOOLISH, uneducated

wish *(n.)* will, DESIRE, intention, GOAL, HOPE, REQUEST, mandate

wish *(v.)* WANT, DESIRE, HOPE, hanker, crave
set your heart on

witness *(n.)* spectator, bystander, onlooker

witness *(v.)* **1.** SEE, behold, OBSERVE, WATCH, NOTE *witness a crime* **2.** attest, testify *witness before a judge*

witty *(adj.)* FUNNY, amusing, SHARP, droll

wizard *(n.)* **1.** magician, sorcerer, conjurer *The wizard concocted a magic potion.* **2.** EXPERT, authority, master, whiz, virtuoso *She was a wizard with computers.*

wonder *(n.)* awe, amazement, astonishment

wonder *(v.)* THINK, ponder, meditate, speculate, peruse, marvel

wonderful *(adj.)* MARVELOUS, SPLENDID, INCREDIBLE, amazing, astonishing, miraculous, stupendous, EXTRAORDINARY, spectacular TERRIBLE, AWFUL, HORRIBLE

clue: wish

answer: set your heart on

wood *(n.)* timber, log, lumber, plank, BOARD
WOULD

woods *(n.)* forest, woodland, grove, thicket, bush

word *(n.)* **1.** term, phrase, label *Spell the word.* **2.** statement, report *a word from our sponsor* **3.** PROMISE, pledge *Keep your word.*

work *(n.)* **1.** JOB, employment, profession, calling, DUTY, function *the work of a teacher* **play, sport, recreation** **2.** EFFORT, drudge, drudgery, grind, exertion, travail *a lot of work* **3.** RESULT, EFFECT *good work*

work *(v.)* **1.** toil, LABOR, grind, function, exert *work at the office* **PLAY, frolic, dally** **2.** OPERATE, HANDLE, CONDUCT, manipulate, MANAGE *work the machine* **3.** function, PERFORM *The radio does not work.* **4.** SHAPE, FORM *work the clay*

workers *(n.)* employees, crew, staff, faculty, personnel, labor, laborers

worn *(adj.)* SHABBY, faded, RAGGED, threadbare, SORRY

worry *(n.)* CONCERN, CARE, anxiety, DISTRESS, agitation

worry *(v.)* **1.** fret, CARE, FUSS, fidget, grieve *worry about one's grades* **2.** BOTHER, DISTURB *worry your parents* **3.** TEASE, pester, harass, torment, tantalize, harry, plague *worry the dog*
(1) be tied up in knots

worship *(v.)* ADORE, RESPECT, idolize, venerate, revere

worth *(n.)* **1.** VALUE, COST, valuation, appraisal, assessment, evaluation, CHARGE, expense *the worth of a house* **2.** merit, QUALITY, virtue, integrity *the worth of a person*

wound *(n.)* CUT, injury, ulcer, laceration, abrasion, trauma

wrap *(v.)* ENCLOSE, envelop, surround, encircle, COVER, muffle, bundle, truss, shroud, enshroud **unwrap, OPEN, reveal, uncover**
RAP

wreck *(v.)* DESTROY, RUIN, RAZE, demolish, sack, annihilate, decimate

wrinkle *(n.)* crease, furrow, pucker

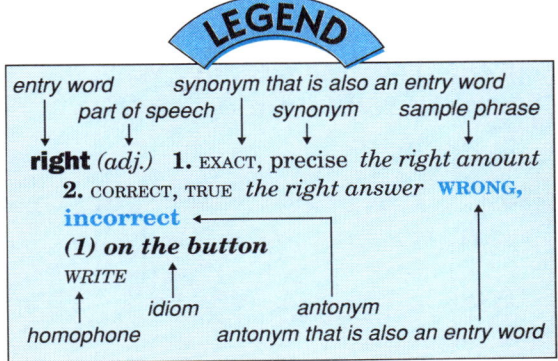

143

write *(v.)* **1.** jot, SCRIBBLE, scrawl, pen, PRINT, NOTE, imprint, inscribe, engrave *Write your name on the paper.* **2.** COMPOSE, author, draft *write a story* **3.** document, RECORD *Write down the results of the experiment.* **4.** correspond, COMMUNICATE, ANSWER *Write your grandparents soon.* RIGHT

wrong *(adj.)* **1.** FALSE, UNTRUE, incorrect, mistaken, INACCURATE, erroneous *the wrong answer* CORRECT, RIGHT **2.** BAD, WICKED, IMMORAL, IMPROPER, unjust, CORRUPT *on the wrong side of the law* JUST, GOOD
(1) out in left field

Yy

yard *(n.)* grounds, garden, court, enclosure, compound

yell *(v.)* SHOUT, CALL, SCREAM, screech, shriek

yield *(n.)* **1.** crop, harvest, PRODUCT *a good yield of corn* **2.** REWARD, recompense, interest *the annual yield on your savings account*

yield *(v.)* **1.** BEAR, PRODUCE, impart, confer *yield a good harvest* **2.** SURRENDER, relent, submit, defer, relinquish, succumb *yield to the enemy*

young *(n.)* CHILDREN, offspring, litter, brood

young *(adj.)* youthful, childish, immature, infantile, juvenile, junior, puerile OLD, senior, adult *wet behind the ears*

youth *(n.)* **1.** child, youngster, MINOR, dependent, juvenile *an after-school recreation program for youths* adult **2.** adolescence, childhood *in one's youth* adulthood, maturity

Zz

zany *(adj.)* FOOLISH, SILLY, wacky, goofy, nonsensical sensible, logical

zeal *(n.)* ENTHUSIASM, passion, fervor, ardor

zero *(n.)* nothing, none, nil, naught, null

zone *(n.)* REGION, AREA, district, quarter, territory, locality, tract

CLASSIC StoryTellers

Frances Harper Junior High School
4000 East Covell Blvd.
Davis, CA 95618

MILDRED TAYLOR

Mitchell Lane PUBLISHERS

P.O. Box 196
Hockessin, Delaware 19707

Titles in the Series

Judy Blume

Stephen Crane

F. Scott Fitzgerald

Ernest Hemingway

Jack London

Katherine Paterson

Edgar Allan Poe

John Steinbeck

Harriett Beecher Stowe

Mildred Taylor

Mark Twain

E.B. White

CLASSIC StoryTellers

MILDRED TAYLOR

by Mélina Mangal

Copyright © 2005 by Mitchell Lane Publishers, Inc. All rights reserved. No part of this book may be reproduced without written permission from the publisher. Printed and bound in the United States of America.

Printing 1 2 3 4 5 6 7 8
Library of Congress Cataloging-in-Publication Data

Mangal, Mélina.
   Mildred Taylor / Mélina Mangal.
      p. cm. (Classic storytellers)
   Includes bibliographical references and index.
      ISBN 1-58415-311-3 (library bound)
   1. Taylor, Mildred D. —Juvenile literature. 2. Authors—America—20th century—Biography—Juvenile literature. 3. African American authors—Biography—Juvenile literature. 4. Americans—Ethiopia—Juvenile literature. 5. Ohio—Biography—Juvenile literature. I. Title. II. Series
PS3570.A9463Z77 2005
813'.54—dc22
                                      2004002047

ABOUT THE AUTHOR: Mélina Mengal received her Master's of Science degree in Library Science from the University of North Carolina at Chapel Hill, and holds Bachelor's degrees in Business Administration and French. She has published three biographies and her works of fiction and non-fiction appear in various anthologies. She also works as a school media specialist in Minnesota, where she lives with her husband.

PHOTO CREDITS: Cover, pp. 1, 3, 6 Penguin Group Inc.; pp. 13, 20 Corbis; p. 29 Getty Images; p. 35 Barbara Marvis

PUBLISHER'S NOTE: This story is based on the author's extensive research, which she believes to be accurate. Documentation of such research is contained on page 44. While every possible effort has been made to ensure accuracy, the publisher will not assume liability for damages caused by inaccuracies in the data, and makes no warranty on the accuracy of the information contained herein. This story has not been authorized nor endorsed by Mildred Taylor.

The internet sites referenced herein were active as of the publication date. Due to the fleeting nature of some web sites, we cannot guarantee they will all be active when you are reading this book.

Contents

MILDRED TAYLOR
by Mélina Mangal

Chapter 1	Born into Stories	7
	FYInfo: The African American Storytelling Tradition	11
Chapter 2	Growing up During Segregation	13
	FYInfo: Segregation in the United States	19
Chapter 3	Dreams of Writing and Travel ...	21
	FYInfo: The Peace Corps	27
Chapter 4	To Africa and Beyond	29
	FYInfo: Ethiopia	33
Chapter 5	The Writing Life	35
	FYInfo: Coretta Scott King Awards	40

Chronology 41
Timeline in History 42
Glossary 43
Further Reading 44
    For Young Adults 44
    Works Consulted 44
    On The Internet 45
Chapter Notes 46
Index 48

*For Your Information

From the time she was a young girl, Mildred knew she wanted to be a writer. The family stories she heard sparked her imagination. The more Mildred learned about her family history, the more she wanted to share it with the rest of the world.

Chapter 1

BORN INTO STORIES

When she was ten years old, Mildred Taylor shared some of the stories of her family with her classmates at school. Mildred was an African American whose great-grandparents had been slaves. Her family had a long tradition of storytelling, and Mildred loved to listen to tales told by her father. She looked forward to family gatherings when her uncles and aunts would share details of their own stories.

"I was always engrossed by them," she remembered. "Many of the stories were humorous, some were tragic, but all told of the dignity and survival of a people living in a society that allowed them few rights as citizens and treated them as inferior. Much history was in those stories, and I never tired of hearing them. There were stories about slavery and the days following slavery. There were stories about family and friends."[1]

Despite facing hardships and prejudice, people in her family had been courageous. They had accom-

Chapter 1 BORN INTO STORIES

plished many things. Mildred thought her classmates would enjoy hearing these inspiring stories.

She was wrong.

"The children laughed at me and wouldn't believe the stories that I was telling,"[2] she said.

The children were wrong. Mildred WAS telling the truth about her family's history. At that time, few history books included the accomplishments of African Americans. Mildred's white classmates

> Roll of Thunder, Hear My Cry *was published in 1977. It has received many awards in the U.S. and abroad. It has even been made into a television miniseries.*

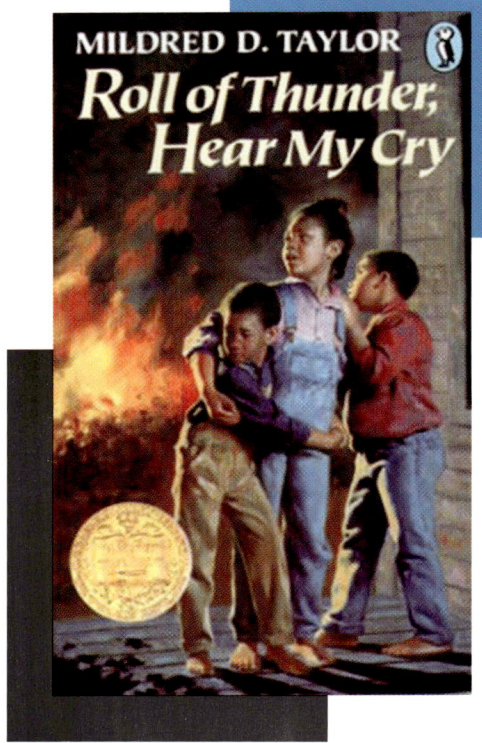

had never heard of black people owning large amounts of land, or of black people saving a forest, or of black people saving an entire community with water from their well. Mildred's classmates assumed she made all these things up.

"It was at this point that I realized that I wanted to convey how I saw black people and what black history was about,"[3] Mildred said. She made up her mind to become a writer. "I was thinking it would be nice to have an impact on people and to be well known and especially to walk into a bookstore or library and see my books. I thought that would be the greatest thing in the world,"[4] she explained.

Mildred made her dream come true. She has become an important writer for young people, bringing history to life. She has even received international recognition with her books being translated into many languages.

By the end of 2004, Mildred had written nine books and won many awards. In 1977, Mildred received the highest children's literature award in the United States, the Newbery Award, for *Roll of Thunder, Hear My Cry*. In 1985, she received a prestigious European award, the Buxtehude Bulle Award.

In 2003, Mildred became the first winner of a new award for children's and young adult literature, the NSK Neustadt Prize for Children's Literature. This award, given by the University of Oklahoma and *World Literature Today*, an international publication, was established to honor writers who have made significant contributions to children's literature. It is recognized by many as the "American Nobel Prize" and intends to honor writers of the same quality.

Although Mildred Taylor is a highly successful writer, getting her stories published was difficult. Mildred received many rejections before her first story was published. Even now, she faces struggles. Some people want to ban her books. These people believe that Mildred's books are too harsh for children, or that her use of historically accurate words is damaging to young readers.

Chapter 1 BORN INTO STORIES

Mildred refuses to let those critics stop her from telling the truth in her stories. As Mildred said when she won the ALAN Award in 1997, "Just as I have had to be honest with myself in the telling of all my stories, I realize I must be true to the feelings of the people about whom I write and true to the stories told. My stories might not be 'politically correct' so there will be those who will be offended, but as we all know, racism is offensive. It is not polite, and it is full of pain."[5]

Mildred's stories are sometimes painful, sometimes brutal, but always filled with warm and loving support from family and friends. Mildred's books are realistic, showing how life really was in the past. Her strong characters always find a way to find hope for the future, just as Mildred has in her own life.

FYInfo

The African American Storytelling Tradition

Africa

Storytelling has always been an important element in African American culture. The art of storytelling first came to African Americans through slaves from Africa. In Africa, there were different kinds of stories and storytellers. Some storytellers told tales for amusement. Others were traveling storytellers who dramatized their tales. Parents would tell stories to their children as lessons in morality. But the most prominent storytellers were, and still are in many parts of West Africa, the *griots*.

Griots are the historians of the people, who recount the history of families and the community. They inherit their position. In West Africa, some families have been *griots* for generations. *Griots* are revered for their faultless memory. They use music and singing when recounting the historic stories of a village and are considered to be more accurate than history books.

Many slaves who were forced to come to America told stories of their homeland and their capture to their children and other slaves on the plantations. Those that were born into slavery recounted stories they'd heard and experienced. Some of the stories were variations of old African tales. Others were personal accounts or eyewitness stories, which became family histories when passed on to the next generation.

Communities in Africa had shared stories openly. In America, stories were shared more secretly, among families or in churches. Slaves would be punished for speaking their own languages or drumming or practicing any other African traditions. So slaves would tell stories in code. Since that time, some stories have remained closely guarded by families, as a treasure. African American storytelling moved onto the printed page as literacy grew and people began writing their stories so the world could know about slavery and the history of African Americans. But traditional storytelling remains. New storytellers with memory, music, and speech skills are bringing the art of storytelling back into popularity.

Segregation, or laws separating people of different races, began with slavery in 1641 when black people were forced to work on cotton plantations. Black people were not allowed the same freedoms as whites. They were forced to live and work under harsh and brutal conditions for over 300 years.

Chapter 2

GROWING UP DURING SEGREGATION

Mildred Taylor's own story starts with her great-grandfather, who was born into slavery in Alabama. His mother was an African-Indian slave and his father was a white plantation owner. Although many people were born into similar situations, few slave-owning fathers acknowledged their children.

When he was fourteen, Mildred's great-grandfather rode a dangerous horse in a race, against his father's commands. Because his father had threatened to whip him if he disobeyed, the boy ran away, caught a train, and fled to Mississippi.

There he worked hard to earn land. He cleared trees, farmed, and did whatever he could to buy his own property. He eventually owned around 1,000 acres of land and built a house there in the 1870s. Mildred's great-grandmother gave away many acres of land after her husband died, but the Taylor family still owns portions of the original land.

This land offered the family shelter, food, independence, and stories. Mildred's great-grandmother

Chapter 2   GROWING UP DURING SEGREGATION

passed on stories about her life and her husband's childhood as a slave. Although one of her children worked the land, he had to get a job working for the railroad in order to earn enough money to keep it. He met and married a woman who was a teacher. Her income helped the family keep their land.

Their son, Wilbert Lee Taylor, grew up hearing the stories of his ancestors. He also had many experiences of his own, especially when his father went away for months to work on the railroad. As a young man, Wilbert became a trucker. He married Deletha Marie Davis, whose family also owned land in Mississippi. When their first daughter, Wilma, was born, Wilbert Taylor could pass on many of the stories he'd heard as a child. Several years later came another daughter, Mildred.

Mildred Delois Taylor was born on September 13, 1943 in Jackson, the capital of Mississippi. Mildred was just three weeks old when her father came home from work angry and packed his bags. He had almost fought a white man at work. Realizing how dangerous the situation could have been for him and his family, Wilbert decided it was best to leave Mississippi right away. As Mildred recounted, "He said he was leaving the South. He said he was going north because he couldn't stand it a moment longer, living under segregation. That same day, he got on a train and left the South."[1]

Although Wilbert Taylor was very attached to his family and lands, he moved away from the South because of segregation and the lack of opportunities for African Americans. He ended up in Toledo, Ohio, where he quickly found a job in a factory. He worked hard and saved money. In three months his wife and daughters joined him. At first, the family lived with friends from Mississippi. Deletha got a job to help her husband earn money for their own house. Within a year, the Taylors bought a duplex on busy Dorr Street.

Mildred loved the large, white house. She could easily walk to the grocery store, drug store, or beauty parlor. Her school and church were nearby. Just a block away was the Dixie Theater. Mildred and Wilma enjoyed seeing movies there on weekends.

Mildred's parents also liked the house on Dorr Street because of its size. They were able to invite other family members and friends from the South to live with them until they found their own homes.

After the end of World War II, two of Mildred's uncles and their wives moved in. They had recently returned to the United States after serving overseas. People in other parts of the world had treated Mildred's uncles better than they were treated in this country. They had experienced even more segregation by American whites in the armed forces. Like Mildred's father, they refused to live in the segregated South again.

These uncles were just the first of a stream of relatives and friends to come live with the Taylors. Aunts, uncles, and distant cousins would settle in with Mildred's family until they found jobs and housing of their own. Every spare space was used. Even the old basement coal room was turned into living quarters.

Mildred and Wilma loved having so many cousins to play with. They didn't even mind if they sometimes had to give up their bedroom for guests. The girls also enjoyed the company of their aunts and uncles, who would give them the attention they needed if their parents were working or busy. As Mildred said in her Newbery acceptance speech, "During my childhood a family that offered aunts and uncles who were second parents, and cousins who were like brothers and sisters, was as natural to me as a mother and father are to most children." [2]

Mildred walked to school every day. The school, like her neighborhood, was mostly black. The mix of businesses, churches, restaurants, hotel, entertainment, and housing made the neighborhood a small community within a community, where most people knew each other. This setting made Mildred's school comfortable for her.

Mildred loved to read. She would read whenever and wherever she could. "I got into trouble at night when I would sit in the closet

Chapter 2 GROWING UP DURING SEGREGATION

when I was supposed to have been long asleep. I got into trouble during the daytime, too, when I would be sitting somewhere hidden, when I was supposed to have been doing my chores,"[3] Mildred remembered in a speech to the American Booksellers Convention.

Mildred's parents were proud of her reading ability, but they didn't want her reading just anything. When she was eight years old, she became infected with chicken pox. She looked for something to do.

As she said, "I decided to read. Now I read all of my own books several times over, so I went to the bookshelves in the living room. This was a magical place to me because here were stacked all the adult books. Well, I went rummaging through this bookcase, and I found a hardcover volume, and it was really terrific because it had photos in it. The photos were from a movie because the book had been made into a movie. I thought, 'Oh, this is going to be great.' I took the book and I sat down in my father's favorite chair in the living room, and I pulled the blanket around me and began to read."[4]

At first, no one noticed what Mildred was reading. When her aunt saw the cover several days later, she was shocked and told Mildred's mother. "Well, I'm sure she doesn't understand it,"[5] Deletha said. But Mildred answered right away, "Yes, I do, too."[6] Mildred recounted the details of the book. It was about a man who had a love affair and plotted murder. Mildred's mother was shocked. She took the book away, along with all the others in the bookcase. Mildred had to go back to reading children's books!

In 1953, when Mildred was nine years old, her family bought a house on a quiet street in a neighborhood that had been predominately white. The big brick house with three fireplaces, second-floor bedrooms, and a recreation room awed Mildred. This house even had a bathtub with a shower, which was new for her.

With the move came a new school, and a completely different environment. Mildred's new school was integrated with black and white students attending together. The year was 1954. The U.S. Supreme Court had just ruled in the landmark *Brown vs. the Board of Education* case that all schools must be integrated and therefore open to all students, regardless of race.

Because Mildred was the only black student in the sixth grade, she felt the need to do better than her classmates, for fear of being looked down upon because she was black. She feared failure and ridicule more than anything else. She studied hard to become the best student she could be.

There was still time to have fun. The Taylor family went on many excursions and trips. As Mildred wrote in her book *The Gold Cadillac*, "Because my father, my uncles, and my older male cousins all loved cars, we often rode in a caravan out to the park where the men would park their cars in a long, impressive row and shine them in the shade of the trees while the women spread a picnic and chatted, and my sister, younger cousins, and I ran and played. Sometimes we traveled to nearby cities to see other family members or to watch a baseball game. And sometimes we took even longer trips, down country highways into that land called the South."[7]

The family trips to Mississippi were exciting for Mildred. "I remember during our trips south, speeding down winding red roads toward my grandparents' house, with rocks hitting the underbelly of the car," she said. "As a small child, I loved the South. In my early years, the trip was a marvelous adventure, a twenty-hour picnic that took us into another time and another world."[8]

Her mother made wonderful food especially for the journey: cake, sweet potato pie, and fried chicken, with jugs of lemonade and ice-cold water. Eventually, Mildred realized why her mother packed so much food. No restaurants or motels along the way would serve black people.

Mildred started noticing other things about the South as she grew older. Her parents became more cautious as they got closer to Mississippi. She saw "WHITES ONLY" signs in many of the public

Chapter 2 GROWING UP DURING SEGREGATION

places they passed. One summer, Mildred felt almost sick to her stomach with fear as the family crossed the Ohio River into Kentucky. Her parents warned her to remain quiet if white people spoke to her. Mildred said in an interview, "I remember how it was. I remember being told that we couldn't use the restroom. I remember store clerks saying, 'Oh, you can't try those clothes on.' I remember some very racist statements—just like those of some of the characters in *Roll of Thunder* and *The Land*—I remember being terrified as a child when I came across people like that."[9]

But actually being in Mississippi with her relatives was a wonderful, magical time for young Mildred. With her many cousins, Mildred chased butterflies during the day and lightning bugs at night. She would ride a mare named Lady and a mule named Jack. And she heard stories.

"I remember my grandparents' house, the house my great-grandfather had built at the turn of the century, and I remember the adults talking about the past," she said. "As they talked I began to visualize all the family who had once known the land, and I felt as if I knew them, too."[10]

These stories filled Mildred with pride and resolve. Some day she would tell her own stories, in her own way.

FYInfo

Segregation in the United States

The Supreme Court

In the United States, segregation was a legal system that kept people of different racial groups separate. The practice started with slavery before the U.S. was even a country, and it continued after the Civil War. Many white people in Southern states were unhappy with the Emancipation Proclamation, which freed all former slaves, and with the abolition of slavery under the Thirteenth Amendment of 1865.

Although more freedoms were granted to black people, and people of all races, under the Fourteenth Amendment of 1868 and the Fifteenth Amendment in 1870, Southern states made their own laws to limit or contradict these rulings. When black people tried to obtain their rights to work in different areas, to own land, or to get paid adequately, they were often beaten and their families terrorized. Many black men were beaten, burned, tortured, and lynched for supposedly looking at a white woman, talking back to a white man, or simply being caught alone after dark.

In 1896, the Supreme Court's ruling in the case of Plessy vs. Ferguson approved the separation of races, the doctrine of "separate but equal." White people made and enforced laws that schools, buses, trains, public restrooms, drinking fountains, and more should be separate. But they were not equal. Nearly everything permitted to blacks was inferior.

Schools for African American children were often dilapidated, leaky buildings without heat or indoor plumbing. Black students received worn and rejected textbooks from white schools. Black students could not ride a school bus even though many of them lived miles away. In the 1930s in Mississippi, the average amount of education money spent on white children was $147. The average amount spent on black students was $11.

Despite the brutal and difficult living conditions forced on black people by segregation, African Americans never stopped challenging the system. Change came through court cases like Brown vs. the Board of Education in 1954, which struck down "separate but equal" policies, and the Civil Rights Act of 1964.

Segregation of public schools became illegal in 1954. When nine black students tried to attend Central High School in Little Rock, Arkansas in 1957, whites reacted violently and even threatened their lives. The "Little Rock Nine" formed their own study group while waiting to attend. Eventually, they were permitted to go to school after President Eisenhower ordered federal troops to safely escort them past protesters.

Chapter 3

DREAMS OF WRITING AND TRAVEL

Mildred entered Scott High School in 1957, the same year that nine African American students integrated Central High School in Little Rock, Arkansas. Although the anger and violence of Little Rock seemed far away from the integrated city of Toledo, Mildred quickly learned that racism was never too far away.

During her freshman year, a controversy erupted over the election of an African American student as Homecoming Queen. Violence seemed inevitable as rumors spread. Some said the football team would boycott the Homecoming game. Others said that the girl who was elected might not be crowned queen after all. Still others said there would be a rumble, a huge fight between black and white students. Some students actually burned an effigy, or replica, of the black Homecoming Queen in protest. After the local television station highlighted the controversy and a group of religious leaders requested a peaceful resolution,

Chapter 3   DREAMS OF WRITING AND TRAVEL

the controversy died down. The African American girl became Homecoming Queen and school life continued.

But life for Mildred had changed. She had experienced and heard about the violently harsh racism in the South. Now she knew that racism was everywhere in America, even in a northern city like Toledo.

Despite the controversy, Mildred did well in her classes, especially English. Her drive to succeed was fueled by her fear of failure. She was often the only African American student in her classes. Even though Scott High School was integrated—half of the students were black, half were white—the distribution of students within classes was uneven. Higher-level college preparatory classes, such as the ones that Mildred took, tended to have mostly white students. Many black students had come from black schools with fewer resources and opportunities. Few of those students were prepared for advanced classes.

Of those days, Mildred said, "So often, I felt like the token black. I became accustomed to it, but I never felt comfortable with it...I was always aware that all black people would be reflected in what I did, good or bad."[1] Mildred kept working hard. She was the only African American student from Scott High School selected for the National Honor Society.

Mildred didn't let the turbulence of racism stop her from being involved in many activities. "I'm afraid I was one of those students who was a class officer, an editor of the school newspaper, and a member of the honor society, when what I really wanted to be was a cheerleader. I remember how disappointed I was when I failed to make the cheerleading squad and my father telling me that I had greater things cut out for me,"[2] Mildred reflected on her high school years. One of those things was writing.

She didn't have any trouble coming up with things to write about. The Taylor family stories sparked many creative ideas. As she said years later, "[My father's] colorful vignettes stirred the romantic in me. I was fascinated by the stories, not only because of what they said or because they were about my family, but because of the manner in which my father told them. I began to imagine myself as a storyteller, making people laugh at their own human foibles or nod their heads with pride about some stunning feat of heroism. But I was a shy and quiet child, so I turned to creating stories for myself instead, carving elaborate daydreams in my mind.

"I do not know how old I was when the daydreams became more than that, and I decided to write them down, but by the time I entered high school, I was confident that I would one day be a writer."[3]

Other students shared that confidence. In their senior yearbook, Mildred's classmates predicted, "The well-known journalist Mildred Taylor is displaying her Nobel Prize winning novel."[4]

Some people didn't think so highly of Mildred's writing. One day a teacher read Mildred's paper to the class as an example of bad writing. Although Mildred questioned her own abilities, she didn't stop writing. She just worked harder.

Encouraged by another teacher and her father, she submitted one of her stories to a citywide fiction contest. Mildred didn't win the contest, but she discovered something that would be far more valuable. She learned more about her own writing style, which helped her focus her writing. In that style, the leading character tells the story. Readers see the events through his or her eyes.

When Mildred graduated in 1961, she decided to enroll at the University of Toledo. She wanted to major in journalism or creative writing, but her parents wanted her to be an education major. They believed it was a more practical choice that would allow her to get a teaching job. Mildred still wrote stories, and took creative writing classes whenever she could.

In 1962, when Mildred was nineteen, she wrote her first novel, *Dark People, Dark World*. The main character was an unhappy blind white man who runs away to the ghettos of Chicago. Mildred sent it to a publisher. She received an encouraging letter from an editor, who suggested that she shorten her story. Because Mildred didn't

Chapter 3   DREAMS OF WRITING AND TRAVEL

know much about the editing and publishing process, she refused to make any changes to her story. She hid it away in a drawer and it was never published. "That was probably the wisest thing I could have done. I had a lot to learn,"[5] Mildred said of the experience.

Mildred kept writing and studying. She read writers like Charles Dickens, Jane Austen, John Steinbeck, and Ernest Hemingway. Mildred tried to write like them, forgetting the storytelling form of first-person narration she'd grown up hearing. She continued trying to win prizes in contests and having her stories published.

"When I was in high school, I began to send my stories off to contests and never won anything. My manuscripts were rejected over and over again. And sometimes the rejection would be so overwhelming, after submitting a story I thought was really good, that I would say 'I'm not going to write again, ever,'"[6] she said.

Because Mildred had not learned much about revision, she never revised her stories before sending them out. Looking back years later, she believed that was the reason she didn't win any contests.

In 1965, Mildred graduated from the University of Toledo with a degree in education and a minor in history. Mildred was now ready for the world, and she wanted to see it. She had decided during high school that she would travel. In 1960, Mildred's classmates elected her to write a report about Senator John F. Kennedy's visit to Toledo while he was running for president. He spoke about his plans for a new government organization called the Peace Corps. Mildred was hooked. She had learned how she could travel.

Mildred applied to the Peace Corps during her junior year in college. She filled out the application forms, went through interviews, wrote essays, and took a number of tests. As part of the application, Mildred had to take a daylong written examination during her senior year. Mildred was worried that she hadn't done well. She was wrong.

Mildred was overjoyed when she received her acceptance letter from the Peace Corps. Her dream would soon come true. Since she was a girl she had dreamed of traveling to exciting faraway lands. Mildred had been especially interested in travel to Africa because of her African American heritage. Ethiopia held special interest for Mildred because of its history and culture. She was very happy when the Peace Corps assigned her to go there. With her Peace Corps invitation letter, Mildred's voyage to Ethiopia was all she could think about.

Mildred's family had different thoughts. For years, they had thought she was simply talking about Africa. They didn't believe she truly intended to go so far away. But when the Peace Corps accepted Mildred, they finally realized that she was serious. They didn't want her to go. Her sister Wilma was the only one excited about Mildred's future in the Peace Corps.

Mildred's uncles didn't believe that she should go abroad to serve America. They had done their duty overseas during World War II and had experienced how unfairly America treated its African American citizens. They feared that Mildred could experience similar conditions. Mildred's mother also didn't want her to go so far away for so long, especially since no woman in the family had ever traveled abroad. She prayed for Mildred and her father to come to an agreement because Wilbert refused to let her go.

"No. No way are you going,"[7] he told her at the Christmas break during her senior year.

Mildred was insistent. Nothing could make her change her mind. "I'm twenty-one now; I can go,"[8] she responded.

Mildred's father had other plans. He took her down to Mississippi, hoping her grandparents could persuade her not to join the Peace Corps. It didn't work. Mildred's grandmother said it was a wonderful opportunity for her. Wilbert was not pleased.

He tried even harder to prevent Mildred from leaving. He would not loan her a car to drive to a required Peace Corps physical exam in Michigan. He refused to drive her there himself. Mildred

Chapter 3   DREAMS OF WRITING AND TRAVEL

did not let that stop her. She ended up being able to take the physical in Toledo.

Wilbert changed his approach. "If you don't go, if you stay, I'll buy you a brand new car. It'll be your graduation present,"[9] he promised her.

But Mildred would not change her mind. Her father would not change his mind either, until the night he met a man from Africa. Then one night, everything changed.

Mildred's father was a deacon in their church. "Something like a miracle happened in church tonight,"[10] he said when he returned home from an evening service. A young African visitor had told his story to the congregation. American missionaries had helped the young man receive an education and come to the United States. He was on his way to becoming a doctor.

Hearing the young African's story changed Wilbert's mind. He now saw the possibilities for Mildred in the Peace Corps. She would have the chance to do important work and make a difference in the lives of many people. After that night, Mildred's father supported her completely as she prepared to enter the Peace Corps.

"God meant for you to do this,"[11] he told her.

Her preparation began the week after she graduated from the University of Toledo in June, 1965. At the University of Utah, she participated in the Peace Corps training camp. Then she spent three weeks teaching English and history at a Navajo Indian Reservation in Arizona. In September, Mildred was on her way to Africa.

FYInfo

The Peace Corps

The Peace Corps is an agency of the federal government. Its three main goals are to help people in many countries through trained volunteers, help others around the world to know and understand Americans, and help Americans get to know and understand other people in different countries.

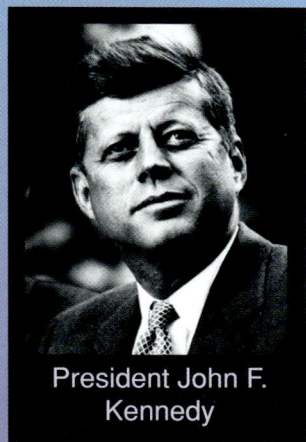

President John F. Kennedy

It was created in 1961. The newly elected President John F. Kennedy wanted a way for college students and other people to serve their country peacefully. Kennedy challenged them to contribute to peace by working and living in developing countries.

Ever since then, the Peace Corps has trained and sent volunteers all around the world with the goal of promoting peace and friendship. Usually volunteers stay for two years. Many of them already speak the language of their host country, or learn it during their stay.

Some volunteers teach English. Others help establish or reconstruct schools or libraries in areas that need them. They might assist a community with farming techniques or medical practices. Others help citizens create or improve sanitation or transportation systems. AIDS education, environmental preservation, and information technology are other issues that volunteers might be involved with.

Since the Peace Corps was founded, over 170,000 volunteers have worked in countries around the globe. In the beginning, volunteers were sent to only six countries. Today, they could be sent to any one of 136 countries, including newly independent or democratic nations in Central Asia or Eastern Europe such as Turkmenistan, Uzbekistan, or Albania.

Countries in which volunteers are placed generally have living conditions very different from the United States, making the job a challenging one. But they learn valuable life lessons and experience that broaden their perspective on life. Mildred Taylor learned so much about Ethiopia during her two-year stay there. In addition, her Peace Corps experience brought her a deeper sense of pride in her heritage.

The rugged landscape of Ethiopia has made it an isolated country with strong cultural traditions. When Mildred Taylor was sent there with the Peace Corps, she fell in love with the country and its proud people.

Chapter 4

TO AFRICA AND BEYOND

Mildred arrived in the mountain village of Yirgalem, Ethiopia. She was twenty-two years old. Her job was to be an English and history teacher. At that time, the adult literacy rate was very low. Schools often lacked basic supplies like paper, pens, pencils and books. They were often located in small huts with only mud benches for seating, just as they are today. Under these conditions, Mildred did her best.

Mildred was the first black American many of the Ethiopians in her village had met. As a descendant of slaves from Africa, she was accepted as one of them. When villagers called her "mother," "sister," or "daughter," she felt even more accepted.

Mildred loved her stay there. The best times of her life as an adult were in Ethiopia, she said years later. Mildred loved the geography of the land. She loved hearing singing in the fields, which reminded her of Mississippi and the South. She loved the strong families, the culture and the rich history of the people. And she loved the storytelling.

Chapter 4   TO AFRICA AND BEYOND

Mildred loved Ethiopia so much that she thought about living there instead of in the United States. She even had nightmares about leaving after her two years were almost over. She would wake up happy when she realized she was still there. In Ethiopia, Mildred was far away from the racism of the United States. Living with the Ethiopians was a positive influence on her. She absorbed the attitude of this culturally strong and confident group of people who were proud of their identity. She felt good about who she was.

In the summer of 1967, Mildred came back to the United States. She remained with the Peace Corps, working as a recruiter and then a training camp instructor. In 1968, Mildred began graduate school at the University of Colorado in Boulder. Another phase of her life was about to begin.

The year 1968 was a tumultuous year in America. Civil rights leader Martin Luther King, Jr. was assassinated. So was presidential candidate Robert F. Kennedy, who believed in many of Dr. King's ideals. Shirley Chisholm became the first black woman to be elected to Congress. Riots erupted all over the country. Students took over campus buildings to demand more African American students and more African American history classes.

Soon after arriving at the University of Colorado, Mildred joined the Black Student Alliance. She teamed up with other African Americans to increase opportunities as well as black pride among black students. Mildred significantly contributed to restructuring the Black Studies Program.

Mildred received her graduate degree in journalism in 1969. Then she created a tutorial and study skills program for the Black Studies Program. After that, Mildred became a study skills coordinator for the University of Colorado. She worked in this job until 1971, and kept writing as well.

An article Mildred wrote about Black Studies caught the attention of a *Life* magazine editor who was visiting the university. That led to an offer to write an article for the magazine. Mildred was thrilled at the opportunity. *Life* was very popular, read by many people across the country.

Mildred asked Black Student Alliance members to critique her first draft. Mildred then revised her article to reflect the changes they suggested. When her article was rejected by *Life* magazine, Mildred was dejected. The editor thought her first draft had been much better and truer.

Mildred questioned why she had let others change her work. The rejection of something that had seemed such a great opportunity caused her to pull back and re-evaluate the direction her life was taking. She headed back to Ethiopia for the summer to figure out what her goals were and how she wanted to accomplish them.

Mildred returned from Ethiopia with a resolve to pursue her writing dream. She finished working for the University of Colorado that school year, then headed for Los Angeles, California. She began writing full time. When she had used up most of her savings account, Mildred found a job as a proofreader and editor for a tax company. She still wrote during her spare time and mailed many of her stories to publishers. But all she received in return were rejection letters. Mildred became frustrated and let down about her writing career. She wondered if she should switch to something else entirely.

One thing was looking up in Mildred's life. Soon after arriving in Los Angeles, she met a man named Errol Zea-Daly. They were married in August, 1972.

In 1973, CBS offered Mildred a job as a television reporter. As exciting as the offer seemed, she did not accept it. She was still determined to write her own stories. As she said later, "Despite the despair from all the rejections from all the publishing houses I had sent my work, somehow I knew that my future as a writer lay not in journalism, but in books."[1]

Mildred quit her proofreading and editing job, and focused on her own writing again. She worked small jobs to get out of the house and to be social. When a friend told her about a contest sponsored

Chapter 4   TO AFRICA AND BEYOND

by the Council on Interracial Books for Children, Mildred decided to enter it.

As Mildred explained in a video interview, "I went home and I looked through all these stories which had been rejected and I found a story that my father had told me that I had written concerning the cutting of trees on the family land. I looked at that story and I thought, this is definitely the story I should submit. But I also didn't know how at first to retell it so that it had that spark that I knew the story needed. The inspiration was the character Cassie Logan."[2]

Mildred had originally thought about retelling the story through her grandmother's eyes. Instead, she rewrote her story in the first person, using the voice of eight-year-old Cassie. Mildred had only four days before the deadline. As she said, "I didn't have a really good typewriter at home, so my friends at work covered for me while I sat in a little back room and typed up the manuscript."[3] Mildred's colleagues also proofread the manuscript before she sent it in. That night, Mildred mailed her story. She barely made the deadline.

Three months later, Mildred received a telegram. She had won the contest! Her story, *Song of the Trees*, was selected as the African American fiction winner.

Mildred flew to New York for her award. There, she discovered that the Council on Interracial Books for Children had sent her manuscript to several publishers. Mildred met with a number of editors who were interested in turning her prize-winning manuscript into a book. Mildred was now in the enviable position of choosing the publisher she wanted to work with. When she met editors Phyllis Fogelman and Regina Hayes at Dial Books, Mildred made her decision. They were the women she wanted to work with. In 1975, Dial published Mildred's story. *Song of the Trees* became her first book. Mildred was now the author she had dreamed of becoming.

FYInfo

Ethiopia

Blue Nile Falls

Ethiopia is in eastern Africa, just north of the Equator. About the same size as California, Arizona, Nevada and Utah combined, it shares borders with Sudan, Eritrea, Somalia, and Kenya. Ethiopia is made up of mountain ranges and plateaus while surrounded mostly by desert. It is home to the Great Rift Valley and the Danakil Depression, the lowest point on the earth's land surface at 381 feet below sea level. The oldest known human skull was found there. The Blue Nile River flows through the western part of the country. At the Blue Nile Falls, one of the world's most breathtaking waterfalls sends its mists into the air, giving it the nickname "Smoke of the Nile."

Unlike most other African nations, Ethiopia was never colonized by Europeans. Its rugged geography kept it isolated throughout the years, helping Ethiopians retain strong languages and traditions. Its fifty-five million people belong to several different ethnic groups. Ethiopia developed its own forms of Christianity and Judaism. In addition, nearly half of the people are Muslim.

Ethiopia's literature, art, music, and ancient architecture highlight a strong and unique culture. Its rich history includes leaders like Emperor Menelik I, who was said to be the son of the Queen of Sheba and King Solomon. When Mildred Taylor was there, Emperor Haile Selassie ruled the country. Although he created a constitution, he remained a monarch for over 40 years, not believing in handing over power to the people.

Life in Ethiopia is often difficult for many of its fifty-five million citizens. In rural areas outside of cities, entire families work to grow food. Water must be carried so the *teff* can grow and be harvested. *Teff* is a protein-rich grain that is used to make *injera*, a staple food in Ethiopia. Mildred probably ate a spicy stew called *wat*, scooped up by the spongy, pancake-like *injera* bread.

When Mildred Taylor first saw a flower-filled meadow in Colorado, she fell in love with it. Just like her great-grandfather, she knew she had to own it and live on it. Since then, Mildred enjoys the mountainous beauty of Colorado daily as she lives and writes.

Chapter 5

THE WRITING LIFE

Although Mildred and Errol divorced in 1975, her writing career took off. As Mildred said about winning the Council for Interracial Books for Children contest, "The amazing thing about having won that contest was that...everything began to go right, finally, as far as the writing was concerned."[1] *Song of the Trees* was named an Honor Book in 1976 by the Coretta Scott King Award committee and won the Jane Addams Children's Book Award.

Visiting her parents in Toledo, Mildred heard a new story from her father and her Uncle James Taylor. It was a story from their childhood about an African America teen who hung out with a couple of white youths. A shopkeeper was killed after the three young men broke into his store. The black teen was accused of murder. The two white teens he'd considered friends were among the mob that set out to lynch him. This story became the foundation of Mildred's most famous book, *Roll of Thunder, Hear My Cry*. Mildred moved back to Toledo and into her family's home to

Chapter 5 THE WRITING LIFE

help care for her parents, who were experiencing medical problems. She kept writing and listening to her father's stories.

Four months before Mildred's *Roll of Thunder, Hear My Cry* was published, Wilbert Taylor died. He was only fifty-six years old. Mildred dedicated the book to his memory. Several months later, the book won the prestigious Newbery Award. It also became an American Library Association Notable Book, and was named one of the best books of the decade in the *New York Times Book Review Best of Children's Books, 1970-1980*. *Roll of Thunder, Hear My Cry* was even nominated for a National Book Award and made into an ABC-TV miniseries.

Mildred moved back to Colorado, bought her own land, and continued writing. Seven more books followed, continuing the saga of the Logan family from Mildred's first two books. Like her first two books, all of Mildred's inspiration and characters came from family members.

Cassie Logan, the central character in several of Mildred's books, is based on characteristics of Mildred's sister Wilma and her Aunt Sadie. Mildred said they were both "feisty and outspoken."[2] But, Mildred added, "Cassie's feelings were definitely my own."[3]

Cassie Logan's parents David and Mary are patterned after Mildred's grandparents. Uncle Hammer is a combination of two of her uncles, James E. Taylor and Eugene Taylor. The character of Mrs. Lee Annie Lees was named after Mildred's grandmother, Mrs. Lee Annie Bryant. The character of young David in the book *The Well: David's Story* was patterned after Mildred's father. In the Logan family books, the elder brother Stacey was also patterned after Mildred's father.

Not only do the characters come from Mildred's family's lives, so do the situations. *The Well: David's Story* is the tale of how young David and his brother cope as his family provides clean water to everyone, even brutal racists, when their county suffers through a drought. Mildred's father had recounted the details of this story to her as another example of family history.

MILDRED TAYLOR

The Road to Memphis combines family history and community history. In this story, Cassie Logan is seventeen and confronting head-on some of the injustices of institutional racism. Mildred did extensive research to present an accurate framework for her characters in the story. By doing this, she allows readers to experience what segregation actually felt like by weaving historic details into the story.

The Gold Cadillac recounts details of a family trip that Mildred remembers from her own childhood. The main character is very much like Mildred. Even her name, Lois, is taken from Mildred's middle name, Delois.

In *The Land*, Mildred presents the history of her great-grandmother and her great-grandfather, who were both born into slavery and bought the acres of land her family still owns in Mississippi. Mildred drew on her own experiences as well. As she wrote in the Author's Note, "Like my great-grandfather, for many years I attempted to obtain land that many said was unattainable, and I have woven many aspects of my struggle into Paul-Edward's story."[4]

Mildred's struggle to buy land started back in the 1970s. She had fallen in love with a meadow filled with flowers in the Rocky Mountains of Colorado. The difficulties of purchasing undeveloped land, along with Mildred's financial limitations, made the purchase almost impossible. With her usual determination, she was able to buy it years later. In 1989, Mildred's daughter came into her life, but so did financial troubles. Mildred almost lost the land because she couldn't get another loan. She prayed that she would be able to keep the land. Shortly afterward she received a phone call from the bank. In what she believed was a miracle, she got the loan she needed. Her family loaned Mildred more money to save another section of land that was in danger of foreclosure. To Mildred, this was a second miracle.

With Mildred's land troubles behind her, she now concentrates on being a mother and on her writing. She writes every day if she can, sometimes for up to seven or eight hours. If she has difficulty

Chapter 5 THE WRITING LIFE

with her story, she may do other things, like researching historical information or reading a book.

When Mildred starts a new book, she first works out the general story in her head. Then she creates an overall outline. She writes an outline for each chapter and imagines scenes that would fit. She may even map out the entire chapter. Later, she revises the manuscript until she gets it where she wants it.

"What I like about being a writer is that I have freedom of choice, basically. I can write whatever I want," she explained. "Also it allows me the freedom of being my own boss, basically. I enjoy that. I enjoy the fact that I can work at night if I want to. If I want to write in the middle of the night from 2:00 till 6 in the morning, I can do that. Or if I want to just sleep late and do nothing that next day, sometimes I'll do that and just take it easy after I've had a long writing session. And so that's one of the really great pleasures of being a writer as a profession."[5]

Mildred has brought history to life for readers all around the globe. Her books have been translated into more than eighteen languages. She has already realized her dream of making an impact on people, and her desire to write true stories continues. She believes it is just as important today to be aware of history. As she said in an interview, "I think each of us needs to know where America was in the past, where we came from–not just African Americans, but Hispanics and Asians and Native Americans. It's about all of us."[6]

She added, "In my books, I have always wanted children of all colors to be able to walk in the shoes of this Logan family. And to understand the value system in the family; the strong family units, the strong black men, the strong black women, the mothers, the fathers, and the grandparents and how they love the children. And I think that children of today should also be able to see how they persevered and how they, even though things were tough for them, they always retained hope, and that they fought for what they believed in."[7]

Mildred's stories are an essential collection of historical fiction. Mildred has contributed an amazing body of literature that has opened the eyes of many readers. As Dianne Johnson, one of the NSK Neustadt Prize jurors, said, "They are modern classics. Mildred D. Taylor's books will remain significant because they are well written, accessible to many audiences, informative, moving–simply, exceptional literature."[8]

FYInfo

Coretta Scott King Awards

Coretta Scott King

The Coretta Scott King Award was created in 1969 by Glyndon Greer, a school librarian. She believed that an award should be given each year to African Americn authors. The award was named after Coretta Scott King because of her ongoing efforts in support of peace and brotherhood. As a civil rights activist and the widow of the Nobel Peace Prize-winning Civil Rights leader Dr. Martin Luther King, Jr., Coretta Scott King continues to be involved in promoting this annual award.

With the initial help and support of Greer, Mabel McKissack, John Carroll and later, Effie Lee Morris and E.J. Josey, it has grown into a prestigious award. Some of the past winners include writers Sharon Bell Mathis, Virginia Hamilton, Nikki Grimes, and illustrators Jerry Pinkney, Tom Feelings, and Pat Cummings.

Coretta Scott King Award books are selected to promote an appreciation and understanding of the "American Dream" as envisioned by Dr. Martin Luther King, Jr. Winners receive a framed citation, an honorarium, and a set of either the *Encyclopaedia Britannica* or *World Book* Encyclopedias. The winners are announced each year during the mid-winter convention of the American Library Association.

Mildred Taylor's first book, *Song of the Trees*, was selected as an Honor Book in 1976. She won the award in 1982 for *Let the Circle Be Unbroken*. She also won awards for *The Friendship* in 1988, *The Road to Memphis* in 1991, and *The Land* in 2002. Only Walter Dean Myers, with five awards, has won more often than Mildred.

As Mildred keeps writing, she continues to explore how people living under such brutal conditions can rise above their circumstances and thrive. No one will be surprised if she wins the Coretta Scott King Award again.

CHRONOLOGY

1943   Born in Jackson, Mississippi on September 13; moves with family to Toledo, Ohio

1953   Moves with family to house in integrated neighborhood in Toledo

1957   Enrolls at Scott High School in Toledo

1961   Graduates from Scott High School; begins college at University of Toledo

1962   Writes novel *Dark People, Dark World*, but it is never published

1965   Receives bachelor's degree in education from University of Toledo; travels to Ethiopia as a Peace Corps volunteer

1967   Returns from Ethiopia; becomes Peace Corps recruiter and trainer

1968   Begins graduate school at University of Colorado in Boulder

1969   Receives Master's degree in journalism from University of Colorado; helps create Black Studies Program at the University of Colorado

1970   Works as Study Skills Coordinator at University of Colorado; returns to Ethiopia for the summer

1971   Moves to Los Angeles, California; works as proofreader and editor

1972   Marries Errol Zea-Daly

1974   Wins Council on Interracial Books for Children Award for *Song of the Trees*

1975   Publishes *Song of the Trees*; divorces Errol Zea-Daly; returns to Toledo

1976   Wilbert Taylor, Mildred's father, dies; publishes *Roll of Thunder, Hear My Cry*

1977   Wins the Newbery Medal for *Roll of Thunder, Hear My Cry*

1978   *Roll of Thunder, Hear My Cry* made into television miniseries

1981   Publishes *Let the Circle Be Unbroken*

1985   From Germany, receives the Buxtehude Bulle Award for *Roll of Thunder, Hear My Cry*

1987   Publishes *The Gold Cadillac* and *The Friendship*

1989   Daughter arrives

1990   Publishes *The Road to Memphis* and *Mississippi Bridge*

1995   Publishes *The Well: David's Story*

1996   Receives the ALAN Award for major contribution to young adult literature

2001   Publishes *The Land*

2003   Receives first annual NSK Neustadt Prize for Children's Literature

2004   Penguin Group U.S.A. reprints *Roll of Thunder, Hear My Cry* as part of their Puffin Modern Classics series

TIMELINE IN HISTORY

1900 One hundred and six black people are lynched during the year.

1901 Theodore Roosevelt becomes president after President William McKinley is assassinated; Alabama ratifies new constitution to prevent blacks from voting through the "grandfather clause."

1903 W.E.B. DuBois publishes *The Souls of Black Folk*.

1908 A race riot in Illinois leads to creation of the National Association for the Advancement of Colored People (NAACP) the following year.

1913 Harriet Tubman, a former slave who became active in the anti-slavery movement, dies.

1917 The United States enters World War I, which began in 1914.

1918 World War I ends.

1920 Women win the right to vote under the Nineteenth Amendment.

1921 The Harlem Renaissance, a period of exceptional creativity by African American artists, writers, and musicians, begins.

1929 The stock market crashes and the Great Depression begins.

1941 The United States enters World War II after the Japanese bomb Pearl Harbor.

1945 World War II ends.

1947 The Cold War between the United States and the Soviet Union begins.

1954 School integration required by *Brown vs. Board of Education* ruling by Supreme Court.

1955 Rosa Parks refuses to move on a bus in Montgomery, Alabama, which begins a bus boycott.

1957 Central High School in Little Rock, Arkansas, becomes integrated by a group of nine black students.

1959 Alaska and Hawaii enter the union.

1963 Dr. Martin Luther King, Jr. leads a civil rights march on Washington, D.C., where he delivers his famous "I have a dream" speech from the steps of the Lincoln Memorial; Congress passes the Gulf of Tonkin Resolution, leading to much greater U.S. involvement in the Vietnam War.

1964 Congress passes the Civil Rights Act.

1968 Dr. Martin Luther King, Jr. and presidential candidate Robert F. Kennedy are assassinated; Shirley Chisholm becomes the first black woman elected to Congress.

1975 U.S. troops leave Vietnam.

TIMELINE IN HISTORY (CONT'D)

1983 U.S. troops invade the Caribbean island of Grenada and win a quick victory.
1989 The Berlin Wall, which symbolizes the division of Germany into West Germany and East Germany, is torn down.
1991 The Soviet Union collapses; the United States leads a coalition of armed forces that forces Iraq out of Kuwait after Iraqi troops under the command of Saddam Hussein invade it.
2001 Terrorists use hijacked airliners to attack New York City and Washington, D.C. on September 11.
2004 The United States invades Iraq and overthrows Saddam Hussein.

GLOSSARY

acknowledge (ack-NAH-lej)
admit something to be true

drought (DROWT)
long period without rainfall

foibles (FOY-bulls)
minor weaknesses of character

integration (in-ta-GRAY-shun)
to allow different racial groups to be together by prohibiting segregation

lynching (LINCH)
killing by hanging without a trial

major (MAY-jer)
to specialize in one area of study.

prejudice (PREH-ja-diss)
having a negative opinion about an individual or group of people based on race or ethnicity.

racism (RAY-siz-um)
practice of intentionally discriminating against people or groups based on their race.

token (TOE-ken)
something serving as a representation of a larger idea or group

vignettes (vin-YETTS)
brief literary sketches

FURTHER READING

For Young Adults

Mildred Taylor Teacher Resource File. Internet School Library. http://falcon.jmu.edu/~ramseyil/taylor.htm

Mildred D. Taylor. The Mississippi Writers and Musicians Project at Starkville High School. http://www.shs.starkville.k12.ms.us/mswm/MSWritersAndMusicians/writers/Taylor.html

Taylor, Mildred. *The Friendship*. New York: Puffin Books, 1998.

Taylor, Mildred. *The Gold Cadillac*. New York: Dial Books for Young Readers, 1987.

Taylor, Mildred. *The Land*. New York: Phyllis Fogelman Books, 2001.

Taylor, Mildred. *Let the Circle Be Unbroken*. New York: Dial Books for Young Readers, 1981.

Taylor, Mildred. *Mississippi Bridge*. New York: Dial Books for Young Readers, 1990.

Taylor, Mildred. *The Road to Memphis*. New York: Puffin Books, 1992.

Taylor, Mildred. *Roll of Thunder, Hear My Cry*. New York: Dial Books for Young Readers, 1976.

Taylor, Mildred. *Song of the Trees*. New York: Bantam Doubleday Dell Books for Young Readers, 1996.

Taylor, Mildred. *The Well: David's Story*. New York: Dial Books for Young Readers, 1995.

Walter, Mildred Pitts. *Mississippi Challenge*. New York: Aladdin, 1992.

Works Consulted

Bennett, Lerone, Jr. *Before the Mayflower: A History of Black America*, Fifth Revised Edition. New York: Penguin, 1982.

Taylor, Mildred D. Contemporary Authors New Revision Series, Volume 115. Detroit: Gale, 2003.

Corona, Laura. *Ethiopia: Modern Nations of the World*. San Diego: Lucent Books, 2001.

Crowe, Chris. *Presenting Mildred D. Taylor*. Twayne's United States Author Series: Young Adult Authors. New York: Twayne Publishers, 1999.

Goss, Linda and Marian E. Barnes. *Talk That Talk: An Anthology of African-American Storytelling*. New York: Simon and Schuster, 1989.

McElmeel, Sharron L. "Mildred D. Taylor." *100 Most Popular Children's Authors: Biographical Sketches and Bibliographies*. Englewood, Colorado: Libraries Unlimited, 1999.

FURTHER READING (CONT'D)

Meet the Author: Mildred D. Taylor. Videotape. Meet the Newbery Author Series. New York: McGraw-Hill, 1992.

Smith, Henrietta. The Coretta Scott King Awards: 1970-1999. Chicago: ALA, 1999.

Taylor, Mildred. "Author's Note." *Gold Cadillac*. New York: Dial Books for Young Readers, 1987.

Taylor, Mildred. "Author's Note." *The Land*. New York: Phyllis Fogelman Books, 2001.

Taylor, Mildred. "Author's Note." *The Well: David's Story*. New York: Dial Books for Young Readers, 1995.

Taylor, Mildred. "Author's Note." *The Friendship*. New York: Dial Books for Young Readers, 1987.

On the Internet

ALAN Acceptance Speech 1997.
http://scholar.lib.vt.edu/ejournals/ALAN/spring98/taylor.html

History of Segregation. CNNfyi.com: Learning Adventures
http://www.cnn.com/fyi/interactive/specials/bhm/backgrounder/segregation.html

Mildred D. Taylor. Gale Group. Biography Resource Center
http://www.africanpubs.com/Apps/bios/1198TaylorMildred.asp?pic=none

Mildred Taylor Teacher Resource File. Internet School Library
http://falcon.jmu.edu/~ramseyil/taylor.htm

Mildred D. Taylor: The Mississippi Writers and Musicians Project at Starkville High School
http://www.shs.starkville.k12.ms.us/mswMSWritersAndMusicians/writers/Taylor.html

"Mildred Taylor." *Voices From the Gaps: Women Writers of Color*. University of Minnesota
http://voices.cla.umn.edu/newsite/authors/TAYLORmildred.htm

NSK Neustadt Prize for Children's Literature. World Literature Today
http://www.ou.edu/worldlit/NSK/NSK.htm

Peace Corps: About the Peace Corps
http://www.peacecorps.gov/index.cfm?shell=learn.whatispc

Rochman, Hazel. "The Booklist Interview: Mildred Taylor." Booklist Youth v. 98. 19
http://archive.ala.org/booklist/v98/se2/69interview.html

CHAPTER NOTES

Chapter 1
Born into Stories

1. Chris Crowe, *Presenting Mildred D. Taylor.* Twayne's United States Author Series: Young Adult Authors. (New York: Twayne Publishers, 1999), p. 8.

2. *Meet the Author: Mildred D. Taylor.* Videotape. Meet the Author Newbery Author Series. (New York: McGraw-Hill, 1992.)

3. Ibid.

4. Ibid.

5. ALAN Acceptance Speech 1997. http://scholar.lib.vt.edu/ejournals/ALAN/spring98/taylor.html

Chapter 2
Growing up During Segregation

1. *Meet the Author: Mildred D. Taylor.* Videotape. Meet the Author Newbery Author Series. (New York: McGraw-Hill, 1992.)

2. Chris Crowe, *Presenting Mildred D. Taylor.* Twayne's United States Author Series: Young Adult Authors. (New York: Twayne Publishers, 1999), p. 6.

3. Ibid., p. 12.

4. Ibid., p. 13.

5. Ibid., p. 14.

6. Ibid., p. 14.

7. Taylor, Mildred, *The Gold Cadillac.* (New York: Dial Books for Young Readers, 1987), "Author's Note."

8. Chris Crowe, *Presenting Mildred D. Taylor.* Twayne's United States Author Series: Young Adult Authors. (New York: Twayne Publishers, 1999), p. 7.

9. Hazel Rochman. *The Booklist Interview: Mildred Taylor.* Booklist Youth v.98. http://archive.ala.org/booklist/v98/se2/69interview.html

10. Chris Crowe, *Presenting Mildred D. Taylor.* Twayne's United States Author Series: Young Adult Authors. (New York: Twayne Publishers, 1999), p. 8.

Chapter 3
Dreams of Writing and Travel

1. Chris Crowe, *Presenting Mildred D. Taylor.* Twayne's United States Author Series: Young Adult Authors. (New York: Twayne Publishers, 1999), p. 17.

2. Ibid, p. 18.

3. Ibid, p. 9.

4. Ibid, p. 17.

5. Ibid, p. 32.

CHAPTER NOTES (CONT'D)

6. *Meet the Author: Mildred D. Taylor.* Videotape. Meet the Author Newbery Author Series. (New York: McGraw-Hill, 1992.)

7. Chris Crowe, *Presenting Mildred D. Taylor.* Twayne's United States Author Series: Young Adult Authors. (New York: Twayne Publishers, 1999), p. 20.

8. Ibid.

9. Ibid.

10. Ibid.

11. Ibid.

Chapter 4
To Africa and Beyond

1. Chris Crowe, *Presenting Mildred D. Taylor.* Twayne's United States Author Series: Young Adult Authors. (New York: Twayne Publishers, 1999), p. 23.

2. *Meet the Author: Mildred D. Taylor.* Videotape. Meet the Author Newbery Author Series. (New York: McGraw-Hill, 1992.)

3. Sharon McElmeel L. *Mildred D. Taylor*, 100 Most Popular Children's Authors: Biographical Sketches and Bibliographies. (Englewood, Colorado: Libraries Unlimited), p. 426.

Chapter 5
The Writing Life

1. *Meet the Author: Mildred D. Taylor.* Videotape. Meet the Author Newbery Author Series. (New York: McGraw-Hill, 1992.) Meet the Author video.

2. Ibid

3. Ibid

4. *The Land*, p. 373

5. *Meet the Author: Mildred D. Taylor.* Videotape. Meet the Author Newbery Author Series. (New York: McGraw-Hill, 1992.)

6. Hazel Rochman. *The Booklist Interview: Mildred Taylor.* Booklist Youth v.98. http://archive.ala.org/booklist/v98/se2/69interview.html

7. *Meet the Author: Mildred D. Taylor.* Videotape. Meet the Author Newbery Author Series. (New York: McGraw-Hill, 1992.)

8. Neustadt Prize for Children's Literature. World Literature Today. http://ou.edu/worldlit/NSK/NSK.htm

INDEX

Africa 11, 25, 26, 27, 29, 33
Arizona 26
Awards 9, 35, 36, 40
Brown vs. The Board of Education ..
.... 17, 19
Bryant, Lee Annie 36
California 31
Coretta Scott King Award ....
.... 9, 35, 40
Davis, Deletha Marie 16
Ethiopia 29, 30, 31, 33
Friendship, The 40
Gold Cadillac, The 17, 37, 41
Griots 11
Integration 16, 21
Kennedy, John F. 24, 26, 27
King, Coretta Scott 9, 35, 40
King, Martin Luther, Jr. 30, 40
Land, The 18, 37, 40, 41
Let the Circle Be Unbroken 40, 41
Mississippi 13, 14, 17, 18
Mississippi Bridge 41
Navajo Indian Reservation 26
Peace Corps 24, 25, 26, 27, 30
Road to Memphis, The 37, 41
Roll of Thunder, Hear My Cry ....
.... 8, 9, 18, 35, 36, 40, 41

Segregation 14, 19
Slavery 7, 11, 13, 19
Song of the Trees 32, 35, 40, 41
Storytelling 7, 8, 11, 29
TV Miniseries 36
Taylor, Eugene 36
Taylor, James 35, 36
Taylor, Mildred
    ALAN Award 10
    Birth 14
    Buxtehude Bulle Award 9
    College 23, 24, 26
    Divorce 35
    Jane Addams Award 35
    High School 21, 22
    Marriage 31
    Newbery Award 9, 15
    NSK Neustadt Prize 9
    School 15, 16
    Travel to Mississippi 17, 18
Taylor, Wilbert Lee 14, 25, 36
Taylor, Wilma 14, 15, 25, 36
Toledo 14, 22, 24, 35
Well: David's Story, The 36, 41
World War II 15, 39
Zea-Daly, Errol 31, 35

Frances Harper Junior High School
4000 East Covell Blvd.
Davis, CA 95618